In the
Absence
Of a
Mother's Love

A Survivor's Story

A Memoir by Anna Lee Barrett

Cover design by Mary B.

I am a daughter, sister, mother,
caretaker, friend, and lover.
I am a survivor.

I am a student and teacher,
an artist and creator,
a wounded soul and healer.

I am strengthened by
those who came before me,
those who journey with me,
and those who have yet begun.

I have faith in the human spirit.
I have dreams for myself,
my loved ones, and all mankind.

I want to leave this world a better place.
I share for these reasons...

Contents

ACKNOWLEDGMENTS

The information in this book regarding Attachment was compiled from personal experience; treatment with Drs. Anthea Coster, Michael Orlans, and Terry Levy at the Evergreen Psychotherapy Center and the Attachment Treatment and Training Institute; *Healing Parents, Helping Wounded Children Learn to Trust and Love*, Orlans and Levy, 2006, Child Welfare League of America; and www.attachmentexperts.com. It is not intended to be all inclusive and should not be used for clinical or diagnostic purposes.

Anthea Coster has a doctorate in psychology with a master of arts degree in marriage and family therapy and school counseling, and is a Licensed Professional Counselor in Colorado. Michael Orlans and Terry Levy are foremost experts on Attachment. Internationally renowned authors and trainers who have taught throughout the world, they have more than sixty years of combined experience providing therapy, teaching, consulting, and research related to children, families, and society in public mental health, the criminal justice system, and private practice. Both are Licensed Clinical Psychologists and Certified Master Therapists, co-founders and Lifetime Achievement Award co-recipients of the Association for Treatment and Training in the Attachment of Children (ATTACh), and co-directors of the Evergreen Psychotherapy Center and the Attachment Treatment and Training Institute in Colorado.

AUTHOR'S NOTE

I began journaling thoughts and documenting behaviors in hopes of making sense of emotions beyond my understanding and control. As I wrote of the heartbreak and unexpected ending of an intense but short-lived romance, I noticed a connection between past and present feelings and responses. Familiar though distant, the current ones were similar to those I'd experienced in childhood.

Compelled to research emotional health for insight into my present state of mind, I learned the bond between caregiver and child within the first three years of life, Attachment, affects the emotional and physical development of every human being regardless of color, creed, disability, national origin, race, religion, sex, sexual orientation, or socioeconomic status. Early interactions between caregiver and child form the foundation of human emotions, stored in the limbic brain. This emotional center responds instinctively based on past experiences, not rational thoughts, and cannot be controlled by the thinking brain, the frontal lobe. Thus, there is no direct correlation between intellectual thought and emotional intelligence.

Because intimate relationships draw on experiences rooted in early childhood, if secure interactions between the primary caregiver and child are established, healthy partners and connections follow. If not, unhealthy partners are attracted and dysfunctional relationships form.

As I reflected on the relationship I had with my primary caregiver, I could see that the insecure feelings and unhealthy behaviors I'd experienced in my youth were the same ones I replicated in adult intimate relationships. This awareness inspired me to seek knowledge and understanding of Attachment, how bonds are formed and their effect on emotional development.

My research led me to the Evergreen Psychotherapy Center and the Attachment Treatment and Training Institute in Evergreen, Colorado, where Drs. Anthea Coster, Michael Orlans, and Terry Levy specialize in the research and treatment of children, adults, and families affected by compromised Attachments. Through their Web site, www.attachmentexperts.com, and *Healing Parents, Helping Wounded Children Learn to Trust and Love* (Dr. Michael Orlans and Dr. Terry Levy, 2006, Child Welfare League of America), I compiled facts to provide a fundamental explanation of Attachment:

Attachment, a basic human need, is the deep and enduring biological, emotional, and social connection caregivers and children establish early in life. The Attachment relationship is the core of a child's world and the foundation on which life is built. Children learn the basics of how to think, feel, relate, and communicate from the quality of their early Attachments.

Babies are born to connect instinctively. They look to their caregivers to provide sensitive, nurturing care by responding to their needs, providing human touch, and mirroring emotion through facial expression and eye contact. When caregivers fulfill these needs, a secure Attachment can be formed.

With a nine-month history before birth, the bond between mother and child has the potential to have the most significant influence on a child's development. These two have a symbiotic relationship as the mother's body responds to the needs of the fetus and it depends on her solely for survival. Though the two are connected as one, there are reasons secure Attachments between mother and child, or any caregiver and child, are not properly formed. They include, but are not limited to, sickness of mother or child, separation or death, abuse or neglect, addiction, medical condition, genetics, difficult temperament, stressful environment, marital conflict, and poverty. NOTE: An insecure Attachment indicates a disturbance in care, not an absence of love or intent to harm on the caregiver's part.

Psychiatrist Rene Spitz performed a study in the 1940s proving that children need love to survive (Spitz 1945). Orphaned infants raised in foundling homes were fed and clothed as necessary but otherwise left without human touch or communication to prevent the children from being sickened by human contact and germs. These children became withdrawn, depressed, thin, and sickly. Between 75 percent and 100 percent of the infants died due to the lack of human interaction, a higher death rate than most any disease would have produced. Spitz discovered what is now called "failure to thrive syndrome." Lack of human contact and interaction is gravely damaging and, in fact, lethal to babies and young children.

Many of the brightest and most well-respected individuals from the fields of psychology, medicine, education, and sociology have described the basic ingredients of early childhood development (Institute for American Values 2003; National Research Council 2000). These ingredients are necessary for building a healthy foundation to prevent and solve significant problems in development:

1. *Nurturing and dependable relationships are the building blocks of healthy childhood development. Secure Attachments for children form when caregivers are dependable, available, and sensitive to their needs, enabling the child to rely on the caregiver for continued protection, needs-fulfillment, and guidance. This bond leads to healthy development in all important areas: emotions, relationships, self-esteem, core beliefs, self-control, brain growth, and morality.*

2. *Human beings are hardwired to connect. All babies are born with the capacity to attach, a "prewired" instinct. Healthy Attachment occurs within a close, cooperative, reciprocal relationship. When secure Attachment is not*

triggered by sensitive nurturing care, such as in cases of neglect, abuse, or repeated disruptions in care, an insecure Attachment is formed which often leads to anger, depression, defiance, impulsive behavior, and hopelessness in children.

3. *Attachment changes the brain. The presence or absence of sensitive, nurturing, and loving care during life's early stages not only determines emotional and social development, but it also affects the way the brain develops, profoundly influencing long-term health. The early Attachment relationship alters the brain's structure, chemistry, and genetic expression. Children with insecure Attachments often have altered levels of brain chemicals, resulting in aggression, lack of impulse control, depression, attention deficits, anxiety, and a high risk for substance abuse. The nature of the child's Attachment to the caregiver determines if the brain connections will grow to full potential or waste away.*

4. *Child development is shaped by the interplay of nature and nurture; biology and experience. Biology, including genetic tendencies and vulnerabilities, may provide the starting point, but it's the child's relationships with caregivers that shape the course of growth and development. A safe, positive, and loving environment can overcome depression, anxiety,*

or other tendencies, and even transform these vulnerabilities into strengths. For example, this fact can be observed in fostered and adopted children who have nurturing and protective caregivers but come from an unhealthy genetic background or maltreatment.

5. *Learning self-regulation is essential for child development and lifelong health. Babies are born helpless and totally dependent upon their caregivers for survival and develop the capacity for self-regulation and self-control. This process begins in the womb when the mother's body responds to the fetus and continues into early Attachment when the responsive caregiver attends to the child's needs. Children must have supportive and attuned caregivers to develop the ability to regulate their emotions, impulses, and attention. The inability to self-regulate contributes to the development of conduct disorders, attention deficit disorders, anxiety, and depression, among other serious problems in childhood and adult life.*

6. *The balance between risk factors and protective factors has a powerful effect on development. Risk factors such as difficult-to-soothe infant temperament, neglectful or abusive parenting, poverty, and family violence increase the likelihood of serious problems in childhood and throughout life. The fewer the risk factors, the*

healthier the development. Protective factors including easy temperament, mature and supportive caregivers, and social support buffer children from undue stress and result in resilience, the ability to bounce back from adversity. Children do better when protective factors are increased.

Secure Attachment directly affects learning, brain development, self-control, trust and reciprocity, core beliefs, morality, and resilience. However, children with disrupted Attachments do not properly develop these vital functions because they are more focused on self-preservation and survival, lack self-control, and have elevated stress hormones. There are three risk factors for developing serious Attachment problems:

1. *Parent/caregiver—abuse or neglect, severe psychological problems, alcohol and drug addiction, adolescent parenting, prolonged absence, and family history of maltreatment or compromised Attachment.*

2. *Child—failure to thrive, in-utero drug exposure, difficult temperament, poor "fit" between parent and child, medical conditions, and genetics.*

3. *Environmental—high stress, out-of-home placements, lack of support, and poverty.*

Attachment patterns, which are developed in early childhood and continue throughout life, fall into four categories: secure, avoidant, resistant/ ambivalent, and disorganized/disoriented.

1. *Secure Attachments are formed when children can depend on their caregivers to be available in loving, reassuring ways, especially in times of stress.*

2. *Avoidant Attachments are formed when children have emotionally unavailable and rejecting caregivers. They learn to dismiss their caregivers just as they were dismissed.*

3. *Resistant/Ambivalent Attachments are formed when children have caregivers who are inconsistent, sometimes meeting their needs and sometimes unavailable. They never know what to expect, creating tremendous anxiety.*

4. *Disorganized/Disoriented Attachments are formed when caregivers are physically, emotionally, or sexually abusive; or they neglect their children's basic needs for love, security, protection, or food. This situation is the most dangerous of these patterns.*

There are common traits, patterns, and problems related to compromised Attachment including fear of closeness, defenses, negative core beliefs, biochemical dysregulation, defiance, anxious Attachment patterns, projection, lying, and shame. Concurrent conditions include oppositional defiance disorder (ODD), conduct disorder, anxiety disorder, attention deficit hyperactivity disorder (ADHD), major depression and dysthymic disorder depression, bipolar disorder, and post traumatic stress disorder (PTSD).

Attachment security is the most powerful predictor of life success. Insecure Attachments lead to unhealthy development varying in characteristic and degree of instability. These children often become angry, anxious, depressed, defiant, destructive, impulsive, needy, or hopeless. Common threads are the meaningless of life and deep feelings of unworthiness.

Besides factual information, imagery can provide a powerful depiction of Attachment. Visualize a walking path made from bricks, carefully and meticulously laid by hand one at a time. The ground underneath is solid and leveled with each addition, the spacing between them is measured for precise accuracy, the borders are lined for clarity, and the crevices are filled with cement. Every brick symbolizes a healthy caregiver-child interaction. The boundaries represent guidance, and the cement, unconditional love.

The walk provides a secure and sturdy foundation for future growth. A child may stumble and fall learning to walk and run, but the path will never be the cause of that fall. It will stand firm and support the child, allowing her to pick herself up and continue onward. This scenario represents the emotional foundation of a child with a secure caregiver-child Attachment.

Now imagine a walking path made with natural stones randomly tossed in sand. The loosely-formed foundation holds each stone in an unbalanced, skewed fashion, leaving gaping holes between them. The crevices are filled with a substance that erodes and is in need of constant replacement, and the borders shift with the sand's movement. There is no underlying support or glue holding the walk together.

This route is unsteady and unpredictable, lacking structure. It has obstacles—loose stones with sharp raised edges, pitfalls, and unidentifiable, shifting boundaries. A child will have to watch each step carefully, balance incessantly, and repair damage frequently to avoid injury. The path will most certainly cause the child to stumble and fall. It represents the emotional foundation of a child with a compromised caregiver-child Attachment.

In another scenario, imagine a tightrope walker standing on a platform fifty feet high in the air. Preparing to cross a thin wire, he assesses his surroundings, the conditions, and the path taking him to the other side. He makes judgments based on his findings, knowing body control and balance are the keys to his safe arrival.

Approaching the wire, he tests its tension and his stability by allowing one foot to leave the platform. He can return as many times as he'd like until he's ready to make the leap. Once he leaves the stand, he must remain calm and in control, relying on his calculations, concentration, and steadiness to get him safely to the other side.

Peering down at the unforgiving ground below, he feels secure knowing there's a safety net in place to catch him if he falls. Comfortable taking the risk, he might be nervous, even a little scared, but his mind can relax, knowing he will survive. Regulating his emotions and controlling impulses, this walker's confidence and poise give him the advantage needed for success. Holding his head high, he faces the wire and takes his first step, trusting the support in place. This walker has a healthy caregiver-child Attachment.

Envision the same scenario without a safety net. Realizing there is no reinforcement to keep him out of harm's way, the tightrope walker would be instinctively terrified of leaving the platform. If he makes the slightest mistake, death is imminent. His heart rate would race, his body would shake uncontrollably, and his mind would be unable to think clearly. Incapable of managing the fear, he'd become overly concerned with his safety and panic would inadvertently jeopardize the very thing he was trying to protect, survival. Practically assuring a tragic ending, these circumstances represent an unhealthy caregiver-child bond.

Secure Attachment is vital to survival. This is true throughout the animal kingdom, where babies historically wither and die when separated from their mothers, as was proven in Dr. Spitz's study. Often, replacement caregivers and round-the-clock care are not enough to save them.

In my case, my primary caretaker, my mother, was emotionally incompetent and incapable of responding to my needs. Suffering a compromised Attachment, the primal wound, I lacked the foundation required to develop into an emotionally and physically healthy adult and was instead left to fight for mere survival. I was incapable of comforting myself, controlling obsessive thoughts and impulses, and valuing my own existence, attributes innate in securely attached children. While there were times I wasn't sure how I'd overcome the ensuing despair, giving up was never an option.

Though I'd been completely unaware of its effects previously, a basic knowledge of Attachment allowed me to see the profound impact the relationship I had with my mother had on my emotional development, intimate relationships, and health throughout my life. It colored my feelings and experiences and influenced my every thought. Much like a victim of child abuse, I harbored feelings of guilt, shame, and unworthiness, which left me angry and full of anxiety.

The implications of a compromised Attachment were overwhelming at first, leaving me to question my identity and the integrity of my character. "Was I living an authentic life, or were my personality traits manufactured for survival and therefore less than genuine?" I wondered.

At forty-four years of age, I discovered I didn't know who I was. I searched for an account of a compromised life with which to identify, but what I found was clinical in nature. Published by psychologists, psychotherapists, and doctors, it was intended for diagnostic or teaching purposes, not personal use.

It is well documented by mental health professionals that the best predictor of future behavior is past behavior, and sadly, for some, it's the reason unhealthy and unwanted behaviors are repeated, including those as painful as physical and emotional abuse. I followed that pattern of familiarity by carrying defensive childhood behaviors into my adult life and intimate relationships.

Someone once told me we spend our entire lives recovering from our childhoods. If that were true, wouldn't we be fortunate to spend time building on healthy childhoods, not repairing troubled ones? Unfortunately, that was not the case for me.

Attachment disorder is unlike other psychological afflictions because it involves a malformation of the brain, which results in atypical functioning. While traditional psychotherapy can be successful in addressing behavioral disorders resulting from an insecure Attachment, it's virtually impossible to alter feelings of unworthiness deeply embedded in the limbic brain through behavior modification or intellectual thought. Thus, proven parenting techniques and traditional psychotherapy do not produce expected results for individuals who suffer from compromised Attachments, as evidenced by many orphaned children.

Seeking understanding, support, and healing for my newly discovered condition, I attended a two-week intensive treatment program at the Evergreen Psychotherapy Center and the Attachment Treatment and Training Institute, in Evergreen, Colorado in January 2009. While there, I explored my compromised Attachment, learned of its effects on my emotional development and behavior, and repaired lifelong wounds. By replacing disrupted past experiences with new, healthy ones, I created a secure foundation from which to build a successful future.

The purpose of this writing is healing, mine and others' who may be in a similar situation, may be affected by it, or know someone who is. Written in retrospect from an adult's point of view, at times from the voice of the child within, I speak only of my individual circumstances, feelings, and beliefs as experienced through living, therapy, and treatment. I do not pretend to be an expert on Attachment, not even my own. As I continue to uncover my personal truth, I find healing in understanding and sharing with others, not in judgment or blame.

United by our humanness, we all have challenges in behaviors, relationships, and families. So why is it that some of us can manage them in a healthy manner and others cannot? The answer lies in our experiences in early childhood, the foundation of emotional development and behavior.

Individuals with Attachment disorders struggle with intimacy because they lack the experience and tools to succeed. Many do not have the capacity to navigate the ordinary course of life. Nonetheless, some achieve professional and financial success, as these accolades typically do not require emotional fortitude.

While it's not necessary to know why a compromised Attachment exists, it's crucial to recognize its presence for healing. I was privileged to have my father and his account of the past to help me identify mine, but there are other ways to uncover its existence without knowledge of the first three years of life. Professional therapy or treatment may reveal manifested disorders in a developing child or matured adult indicative of a disruption in Attachment, including those previously mentioned.

If you suspect you or a loved one has experienced a compromised Attachment for any reason, I encourage you to seek the truth. Investigate the circumstances of birth and early childhood by identifying the primary caregiver and assessing the child and caregiver's physical, emotional, and environmental states during that time. Document past and present insecure feelings and inappropriate behaviors, especially those relating to caregivers and intimate partners. Most importantly, consult with a mental health professional specializing in Attachment for the most accurate information and diagnosis.

THE AWAKENING

MATTERS OF THE HEART ARE EMOTIONAL,
NOT RELATED TO RATIONAL THINKING...

<u>Wednesday, October 1</u>

His sudden and unexplained absence following our first romantic night together makes me wonder if our love really existed. Searching for proof, I returned to the scene of the crime, hoping that reconnecting with the past would affirm the truth, or at the very least provide comfort, but it was not to be. Instead, it made me sick!

I was certain TIM was *"The Ideal Man"* for me. Why did he abandon me? What's wrong with me?

Sex and love are not one and the same. Sex is an act and love, an emotion. Because I don't have sex outside of intimate relationships, I don't know how to have one without the other. If he simply wanted physical pleasure, surely he could have found it quicker and easier someplace else.

My therapist Marilyn tells me I need to honor my feelings of disappointment, but I don't know how. While I'm angered by his disappearance and disregard for my feelings, I'd prefer to make excuses for his poor behavior and blame myself for our failed relationship.

I want to learn to validate my anger, so I can experience the full range of my emotions, but getting angry is difficult for me. It's much easier to empathize with others because it allows me to escape unwanted feelings.

To help me see things differently, Marilyn told me to put myself in a friend's shoes. What if someone treated my dear friend Cate the way he treated me? How would I feel? That's easy, I'd be mad as hell.

Thursday, October 2

I went to see a movie with Cate, a love story with two of my favorite actors, Richard Gere and Diane Lane. Feeling tremendous sadness in my own unfulfilled longing for romantic love, I was certain I'd cry through the whole movie and warned her of it.

I've felt that kind of love in the past but didn't experience it with my husband, something I had to come to terms with in my divorce. I loved him, but was not *in love* with him. Believing he'd make a good husband and father, I thought that was enough to make me happy. It wasn't. Sad, but true.

I have different feelings for TIM, feelings of wild, crazy love from the moment we met on that fateful August day in the San Juan Islands. Overwhelmed by his shameless pursuit and my intense emotions, which quickly left me feeling euphoric, vulnerable, and emotionally out of control, I immediately felt safe and scared to death in his presence. These powerful, uncontrollable feelings made no logical sense to me, but I was falling for him just the same.

I'm hurt by the thought of losing him but there's some satisfaction in knowing I'm capable of experiencing passion again. Do I really love him or am I simply idealizing him to fit a dream? If love, how could I have gotten there in such a short period of time and not in twelve years of marriage?

Friday October 3
Today, I'm experiencing pain and anger. I'm infuriated he didn't contact me for nine days afterwards. He could have communicated a need for space if that's what he wanted. Would he have ever made contact again if I hadn't? How was I supposed to feel, like a one-night stand? I don't deserve that!

Though I'm hurt by the way TIM treated me, I'm worried about him. He's trying to be the anchor for everyone in his world, at his own expense. He's the nice guy in the divorce, the perfect dad to his kids in their mother's absence, the strength for his family during his mom's grave illness, the supportive friend for his buddy also going through divorce, and the caretaker of the family business in an economic downturn. I wish I could be there to support him, but it's not my place. I hope he's OK, wherever he is.

A few of my close friends and I went to dinner tonight at Firenze and shared great company, food, and drink. The owner joined us and we exchanged woes over a bottle of champagne. My friends are trying to support me through my sadness and I appreciate the thought, but I don't want to acknowledge my sorrow. I want to pretend it doesn't exist, pretend I'm happy.

Anxiety is plentiful as worrisome thoughts whirl in my head. Where did I go wrong? How can I get him back? What can I do to make him believe in us? How will I survive this loss? I just want these feelings and the spinning in my head to stop, and everything to be as it was before the unfortunate incident.

Saturday, October 4

Two friends and partners, Eric and Kris, had a birthday party for their darling son Isaac. His birth mother was there amongst family and friends, a loving and accepting bunch. They feel like extended family to me.

Eric's mother, Mary, is a confidant and surrogate mother. Knowing what happened with TIM, she tried to comfort me discreetly, but I couldn't control my emotions. I sobbed just looking into her eyes. After an extended stay in the bathroom, I excused myself out the back door and returned home.

Sunday, October 5

I wish Mary had been my mother, to guide me through childhood, friendships, dating and marriage, and the raising of my own children. Conversely, mine offered criticism instead of guidance and unavailability in place of support. She burdened me with adult responsibilities at a young age, overlooked my feelings, and abused me emotionally.

No matter how hard I tried, I couldn't find a way to connect with my mother. She wasn't interested or invested in me. I worked tirelessly to change that but nothing I did ever made a difference. I don't know whose fault it was but she was the adult and I was the child. A mother myself, I can't imagine being disconnected from my own children in that way.

Our relationship caused me constant frustration and great disappointment. I would like to believe her harm was unintentional but I'm incapable of understanding her. Is that hurt, anger, or hate? I'm not sure, maybe all three.

Whatever the case, I've despised her my entire life but have never been able to admit the hatred I feel because it doesn't seem right. How can any decent human being detest his or her own mother? The thought feels unbearable, leading to tremendous guilt and self-loathing.

I suspect the suppression of these feelings is the reason for my inability to experience my own emotions, especially anger, and express them to others. Instead, I discount my feelings and pretend everything is nice. I believe this admission is the first step in my healing process.

Monday, October 6
I went with Bryan, my neighbor and friend, to Purple Café for dinner last night. Had a nice time. Didn't feel like getting ready so no shower. Went in my UGG boots and head-to-toe fleece. He's a good sport!

I didn't sleep at all. Wrote until 11:30 p.m., awoke at 1:15 a.m., and was awake the rest of the night replaying things over and over in my mind. I can hear TIM's words..."don't want to hurt or mislead you," and "you're a good friend." They're degrading because I don't have sex with my friends. One day I won't have these voices in my head, but the pain is too fresh for now.

As I was lying in bed this morning, I realized the heartbreak I feel for TIM is intensified by the void left by my mother. My feelings for the two are different than those I experience with other loved ones, including my children, father, and friends. While I also hold them near and dear in my heart, I feel satisfied with my love for them and theirs for me, and I'm comfortable being human in their presence.

However, intimate relationships are different. I feel a continual need to please and to be perfect and am therefore not able to find peace. I can see that my inability to be at rest in these relationships is a repeat of the one I had with my mother, the most intimate of all.

I want to learn how to settle my mind so my body can rest, but I can't stop the thoughts from spinning. Why did TIM leave? What did I do wrong? If I had reacted differently would he have stayed? Will he come back?

I can't live another day in this lonely place!

Tuesday, October 7
When I began journaling, I imagined I'd write about TIM and my heartbreak over the ending of our relationship and the feelings that resulted. I'd make daily entries in an effort to recognize and understand them and learn from the experience.

I was completely wrong. Buried emotions are surfacing every day, and suddenly I have feelings to experience and stories to share. None of them are new, but putting them on paper is validating them and enabling me to relate them to one another.

I don't know who I am anymore. Am I the person I was born to be or am I someone else because I had to be? In a daily fight for survival, I never had the opportunity to discover myself. My identity feels like a lie now.

I'm not longing for TIM today, though he's woven into my every thought. I still wonder how I feel. "All good things in time," that's what we used to say.

Wednesday, October 8

I had a great time with the kids last night—Thomas (thirteen), Rachel (eleven), and Johnny (nine). We made waffles inside instead of grilling burgers in the rain as planned. Rachel and I listened to loud music and sang together for more than an hour...good for my soul.

I'm working at home, cleaning and organizing. I'm blue, maybe because Wednesday is my day with Marilyn and she's out of town. I'm also reflective, the way she would want me to be.

While I tried endlessly to please my husband Rob, he didn't need or want my efforts. And, he was incapable of expressing love. Overlooking the emptiness in our marriage was how I survived successfully in it. Maybe there was comfort in that kind of love initially, or lack thereof, because I knew how to manage it, but now I want the passion I felt with TIM.

I'm not a patient person. The silence is difficult for me. My feelings are making me sick, literally. I'm mad at myself for being this way.

Outwardly, I always have a smile on my face. While I'm genuinely happy most of the time, maintaining this façade

8

means not being true to myself. I bury unwanted feelings to avoid hurt and disappointment, which allows me to keep smiling. This suppression has prevented me from healing wounds on the deepest level, where they reside.

I bring this unhealthy behavior into my romantic relationships. It means they are continuous work and don't offer the joy and comfort they could or should. I can see it clearly in my past and don't want to repeat this detrimental behavior in the future.

Thursday, October 9

I know that no one can fill the hole in my heart, but I dream of sharing my soul with someone special. That was the hope I had for TIM, maybe because of him or maybe because I'm finally ready to take that risk. Was it realistic for me to expect that under the circumstances? I'm sure not.

I assumed there would be challenges to our relationship and wasn't certain we'd succeed, but I was willing to try. He was not. I thought I was prepared for any outcome. The truth is, I wasn't prepared for his abrupt, inexplicable departure from our short, intense romance.

Will we develop a deeper relationship in time or will our personal journeys continue separately from here? Only time will tell. In the meantime, I want the endless tears and intrusive thoughts to stop.

Friday, October 10

Thomas's birthday. Rachel, Johnny, and I cleaned up debris left from the wind storm while he went to martial arts. I can't believe I have a fourteen-year-old son. Happy Birthday Thomas! Love who you are becoming.

TIM sent a text message two days ago. I cried when I saw it, a welcome release of emotion. Thought I might never hear from him again. He's busy with his mom, the girls, divorce, and work in a declining economy. The stock market is falling, falling, falling...

Don't know how I feel. I miss him terribly but he's starting to feel like a distant memory. It's been three weeks since I've seen him, kissed him. I'm not initiating contact so will wait and see if I hear from him. I wonder if he thinks of me? I hope he and his mother are OK.

Saturday, October 11

Rachel and Johnny had soccer games this morning, thirty-five degrees outside. Rob took Johnny to his and I took Rachel to hers while Thomas stayed home. She had two shots on goal and I was thrilled to have seen them. I visited with old friends, families from our elementary school. It was great seeing everyone!

I cleaned out my voicemail and listened to a message from TIM. It was comforting to hear his voice. I wish we could talk. I miss him. He's not in a good place with the divorce and is not ready to share his life with me. I hope that changes. I want to share everything with him.

Our month-long romance feels like a dream, too good to be true. I want to know it really happened but the memories are all I have left. I'm dying to send him a message but will refrain. I'm practicing patience. It's not easy for me.

I ran a mile and a half before my old knee injury started hurting, just as it had the day I stopped running two years ago. I'll probably have to walk forevermore. It felt great to get outside and get some exercise, though.

Church tomorrow, Rachel is serving, brunch and afternoon with friends, basketball tryouts. I love my time with the kids but have learned to enjoy the aloneness when they're with their dad. Rob's in China for the next two weeks so they're home for a long stretch. I won't have much quiet. Maybe that's good for now.

Sunday, October 12
I'm reflective again today. I want to write TIM but am respecting the silence, so here I sit. I hate this!

Monday, October 13
Rachel served for the first time at church yesterday. I enjoyed watching her, and she did a great job. Had basketball tryouts. Don't know how I can add one more

thing to the schedule but am giving her the opportunity to consider it.

Had coffee with Carmen this morning, and then more with Diana and Paula. Gigi, Cate, and I walked the dogs while the kids were at soccer. Cate's seventeen-year-old Jack Russell terrier ran like a puppy chasing a squirrel. So funny! We laughed until we cried. Afterwards, Gigi and I walked-ran around the track for half an hour. Good conversation. Love her.

Am having lunch with Bryan tomorrow. I'm clear about my feelings and our friendship but am not sure what he's thinking. I know I'm a welcome distraction from his ongoing divorce but I hope he doesn't want more. Why can't I be in control of my feelings for TIM that way? It's emotional, not intellectual, that's why.

I want to get through this day without contacting him and get busy with the week ahead.

Tuesday, October 14
Happy Birthday, Mary! Role model, surrogate mother, and friend. She's the replacement for the mother I never had. How ironic that it's my mother's birthday today, too.

It was a sad day. I cried all day. Not knowing what happened between us makes me crazy. I wish we could talk. If I understood, maybe I could fix things.

<u>Wednesday, October 15</u>

Saw my therapist Marilyn today and talked to her about my journal discoveries. She wants me to express my feelings of anger to my mother and TIM.

I'm mad at myself for writing TIM yesterday but I wanted to talk to him and wish him well. It's been almost a month since that night, since we've seen or talked to each other. He wrote back with thanks and a promise to talk soon. His reply didn't feel good. I don't want to be on his to-do list. I want him to be in touch by choice.

I responded to his e-mail, telling him not to worry about contacting me again. I'm taking control of my feelings and letting go of the outcome, so I can move forward. If I don't hear from him, I'll be sad but will understand it was nothing more than bad timing for him and for us. I can finally accept that. If I hear from him in the future, I'm not sure how I'll feel, but I know I can't go back to being emotionally invested.

Didn't think much more about it but tonight, I'm mad as hell. My emotions are spinning wildly. Tears and anger, I can't sleep. What he did wasn't fair. We haven't spoken in almost a month. He disappeared after our night together, treated me like trash. I understand he's in a bad place, but that's no excuse for his poor behavior. Did he ever consider my feelings?

I hate thinking about him! It frustrates me. I'm dying to tell him off, but since he's not calling, I don't have that option. So, I'll continue writing...

Cate, Gigi, and Carmen are furious with him for treating me the way he did. If I were my friend, I would be too.

Thursday, October 16

Had lunch with Bryan today. He hinted at wanting more out of our relationship, but I'm not interested. The vibes I send are clear, so he must get the message. I look like hell each time we get together, not because I'm intentionally trying to drive him away, but rather I don't feel like pretending everything is OK. I'm good with that for now.

TIM hasn't resurfaced. That's his way, avoidance. Still don't know why, but I need to accept he's simply not there. There is no relationship, just five weeks of fun, lots of kissing, and fifteen seconds of terrible sex. I wish he hadn't said so many things about our future that he probably never meant, but he wanted to believe in happiness after divorce and I wanted to believe in love.

He came into my life for a reason. Although I was uncertain of what it was previously, I believe he was the catalyst in healing my shattered heart, not the one responsible for breaking it. I never would have guessed it, but I needed someone to reach the sacred spot to start recovering. TIM was ideal for that purpose.

I'll move on from here. Not sure where he'll land, but I hope he heals his wounds and goes on to live a happy life. He has a good soul and I wish him all the best. I'm still mad at him, though. It's good for me, I guess.

More Tylenol PM. How much longer will I be living this nightmare? Processing these hurts is hard work, but I'm certain it's what's meant to be. I'm in a much better place now.

Friday, October 17
I sent him an e-mail last night saying good-bye, felt like something I needed to do. He replied back with the response I was expecting—his plate is full, his feelings crossed the line, I was beginning to attach...blah, blah, blah. It's nice to finally have closure so I can move on.

Cried again all day and went out to dinner with Cate in my sweats, no shower, and no makeup. Thankfully, we never see anyone we know at our beloved Branch (the Olive Garden). I'm sad because the ending of this relationship is the death of another dream, the dream of sharing romantic love with someone special. I still don't know if he was the one or if I was simply drawn to the idea of him, but the loss is more difficult than the divorce. For the first time in a long time, I was hopeful for passion, not resigned to loneliness, and wasn't ready for it to end.

As painful as this experience has been, the solitude and introspection into my emotional state have been immensely valuable. I'm learning things about myself, my mother, and my marriage, important things I've not been able to see previously. I'm acknowledging feelings and healing hurts deep within my heart. I'm proud of my growth and look forward to being much healthier once I get through the devastation.

I miss him...the idea of him...the dream I had for us.

Saturday, October 18
Dear God,
Please give me the courage to face my fears,
the strength to overcome them,
and the will to never give up trying. Amen.

Wednesday, October 29
Saw Gigi at school for pickup. I love seeing her. She told me I was glowing and I feel like I'm back from the darkness. Nine days of deafening silence, seven days of unstoppable crying, weeks of emotional turmoil, hopefully over. No crying for me today. Yay!

I went to see Cate while the kids were at soccer. It was rainy, muddy, and gross. We've repaired our friendship, which was strained while I was seeing TIM. She didn't like him and she really didn't like me with him, partly because she could see straight through him and partly because he was encroaching on her territory. We had a great conversation about our special bond and the importance of respect and open communication in our relationship.

Not contemplating life's struggles or world peace today, just trying to live an honest life.

Thursday, October 30

I've been reflecting on several recent events. My father was here a month ago for the Neil Diamond concert and we discussed my mother and his memories of my youth. He shared stories of her emotional and physical absence and lack of connection with me when I was a small child; how he couldn't wait to get home to hold me and how she disappeared as soon as he arrived.

At the same time, my dear friend Cate made hurtful comments regarding my intense investment in TIM, in her opinion quite "disturbing," and TIM observed what he considered an inappropriate "attachment." Finally, there were my journal discoveries about my present emotional state and its connection to my past.

These events inspired me to look into Attachment, the early bond between caregiver and child, and how it affects emotional development. As I began my research, I was amazed by what I found—a detailed description of me, my characteristics, and diagnosis. It was hard to believe anyone could understand so much without knowing me.

I've discovered more about myself in the last few weeks than I have in five years of therapy. It's painfully obvious that I've lived my entire life with a severely compromised Attachment, leaving me with the emotional capacity of a three-year-old child. This realization brings a sense of relief and acceptance, an internal peace that I've never before experienced.

My life finally makes sense!

<u>Monday, November 3</u>
I can't stop crying. My whole life is a lie and I don't know who I am anymore. The questions are endless and the reality, daunting.

My research and self-discovery have led me to the Evergreen Psychotherapy Center and the Attachment Treatment and Training Institute in Evergreen, Colorado, where professionals have the credentials and experience necessary to heal my Attachment disorder. I applied for a two-week intensive treatment program, and am praying they'll find me a good candidate.

<u>Friday, November 7</u>
Rachel's twelfth birthday. I didn't feel much like celebrating but she makes it easy to rise to the occasion. She's endearing and lovable, extremely emotionally intelligent. I hope to grow up to be just like her one day.

Monday, November 10

Johnny's tenth birthday. Went to the Olive Garden, his favorite spot, with his two best friends. He's predictable and very easy to please. I wish my own happiness was that simple.

Monday, November 17

I followed up on my treatment application with Dr. Terry Levy. He seems like a knowledgeable man. We had a nice conversation about my childhood and recent revelations, and he agrees that I likely suffered a compromised Attachment and would benefit from intensive treatment. I scheduled my session, but it's not until January, which feels like an eternity. Unfortunately, I see no other alternative, so I will do my best to survive until then.

Saturday, November 22

Many thoughts and feelings have been racing through me since I last wrote, so many I can't capture them all. I haven't seen TIM in two months and haven't heard from him in five weeks. I'm experiencing the full range of emotions and am surprised by how well I'm doing. One day I'm mad, one day I'm sad, and one day I'm glad.

I'm angry at him for rushing the relationship, and I'm angry at myself for believing what he was telling me. I haven't shared that much emotion with anyone in more than twenty years, but neither had he. I'm mad for the stupid e-mails sent and feelings exposed because it was too much to share under the circumstances.

I'm sad and I miss him—the conversation, the laughter, the dates, the tenderness, and the passion. I had hopes for a relationship, more hope than I'd like to admit. I want to share all of myself with someone, and I imagined him being that person. I was open to the idea, but he wasn't ready for me or my dream.

I'm glad we met, glad for this healing process. The task of overcoming the ill effects of my compromised Attachment felt overwhelming at first. For a couple of weeks, it seemed my foundation had been pulled out from under me and I wasn't sure where I might land. I couldn't stop crying.

I'm a different person now, healthier and more authentic. I'm still upbeat, happy, and independent, but the frustration and guilt I've carried all these years is gone, leaving me unburdened and alive. My emotions are free and I'm not afraid to be myself. Instead, I feel inspired and compelled to discover my true identity.

Sunday, November 30
My mother was here for the Thanksgiving weekend. Before her arrival, I did some research and discovered her behavior can be characterized by obsessive-compulsive personality disorder, not to be confused with the behavioral disorder. Traits include inflexibility, preoccupation with rules, orderliness, and control, lack of

generosity, and limited expression of affection. Don't know if that's what she has, but it would explain her behavior throughout my life, which helps me recognize that most of what I experienced was situational, not personal, though it didn't feel that way to me at the time.

We joined my friend Sally and her family for a Thanksgiving Day meal and celebration. It was a great holiday, but I miss TIM and wonder if he thinks of me. If so, what does he think? Does he miss me or has he found someone else to numb his pain? Is he working through the divorce or still hoping his marriage can be saved?

He'd have done anything to keep his perfect wife, perfect family, perfect life. Does he realize that dream isn't his reality, never was? For me, it was easier to live with the unhappiness in my marriage than recognize the death of the dream, so I understand the denial.

What was it about TIM? Why don't I feel that way about Rob or Bryan? How did I allow myself to get into this situation? Only time will tell what the future holds. In the meantime, I may never have the answers to my questions, though I'm determined to make sense of what happened. It won't change the outcome, but there is peace in knowing the truth.

<u>Monday, December 1</u>

I can't imagine seeing TIM, can't remember the details of his face, but if I see one more black Range Rover, I just might throw up. I'm not contacting him again, not now.

I'm tired of writing. It's too much work while I'm sorting through my feelings. I want to be present in the moment, stop analyzing everything. I can't wait for treatment to discover the truth through the eyes of professionals.

Tuesday, December 23
Seattle had a record-breaking snowfall last week, and Thomas, Rachel, Johnny, and I were housebound all weekend. It was a welcome break after recent gum grafting surgery. We took daily walks to Starbucks and the grocery store, they played around the house and in the snow, and I watched *House* reruns, one after the other, drank strawberry smoothies, and contemplated life.

The idle time isn't good for my state of mind. I can't stop worrying whether I'll ever be at peace with all of this. Can't imagine what that would feel like.

Monday, December 29
The storm left deep slush on our street for eleven days, and I haven't been able to get out. It's making me stir-crazy! I didn't even make it to Christmas church, first time ever.

I shoveled my driveway, with the help of neighbors, and tried backing out but my SUV got stuck on a small patch of ice. It seemed the back wheels weren't engaging, so once free, I drove straight to the dealership. There I learned the all-wheel-drive component was blown and my whole transmission would have to be replaced.

It's a fitting end to my year of awakening and repair. No one can save me from this journey, as it's mine and mine alone to bear.

Friday, January 9
I'm nervous and excited for treatment, but it's the only choice I see. I can't live in this emotional isolation any longer.

After living forty-four years with the pain of Mother's emotional abandonment and the guilt of our failed relationship, I embarked on a personal journey to repair the damage done to my psyche and soul. In January 2009, Rob cared for Thomas, Rachel, and Johnny while I sought intensive treatment at the Evergreen Psychotherapy Center and the Attachment Treatment and Training Institute (the Center) in Evergreen, Colorado. They provide Corrective Attachment Therapy and Corrective Attachment Parenting, treatment methods developed by Drs. Michael Orlans and Terry Levy.

Flying Southwest Airlines since childhood in the '70s, I had trusted them to get me to my destination safely many times previously and this trip was no different. Except, this time they were holding the lives of my three children in their hands. I felt in some ways as if I were returning home in spirit, though the putrid yellow plane I remembered from the past had been replaced with a red, white, and blue one flying the stars and stripes of the American flag.

I arrived in Denver, Colorado, on a direct, uneventful flight from Seattle, Washington. Upon landing, there wasn't a trace of snow on the ground, not even from the air on approach. Considering it was the middle of winter, that was an unexpected blessing for a girl from Texas who's terrified of driving in the snow.

Following a desolate highway drive, I checked into the hotel, where I discovered my room had been upgraded and my rate reduced. Similar to the Hampton Inn in Kansas City, where we stayed on return visits after moving to Seattle, the Quality Suites felt eerily familiar. Friendly and accommodating, with a daily continental breakfast, it was clean and more than adequate for my purposes. In addition, the suite had a living room with a large desk to support long afternoons and late nights of writing.

Within a block, there were two more favorite destinations, Walmart and Starbucks, leaving my home states well represented in my temporary setting–Texas (Southwest Airlines), Arkansas (Walmart), Kansas (Quality Suites), and Washington (Starbucks). Though I was far away from family and friends, I had all the comforts of home nearby.

24

The first morning, I awoke to a scenic snowfall with thousands of tiny, iridescent snowflakes pouring from the sky. Visibility was reduced and the ground, blanketed in snow. There were already four inches of accumulation, and before it was over there would be two more, a stark contrast from the previous night when the land had been barren and dry.

Having been recently trapped by Seattle's historic snowfall, the heaviest on record in over one hundred years, I was feeling a bit reminiscent and apprehensive. This time I wasn't stranded and I wasn't staying home. I had an important mission to accomplish and nothing was going to stop me, not even my fear of driving in the snow. It was just one more thing to conquer on my road to recovery.

I followed the well-seasoned Colorado drivers as best I could and arrived at the small office park with plenty of time to spare. Sitting quietly in my car, I watched as the snow continued falling and wondered if I'd made the right decision in coming. After all, I'd left my children, friends, home, and vital income, traveled alone cross country, and spent thousands of dollars on treatment from three strangers, in hopes of healing wounds I'd had since before birth. The thought only lasted a split second, as I believed with certainty this journey was meant to be and the signs I'd experienced along the way were the only confirmation I needed.

Upon entering the offices of Drs. Anthea Coster, Michael Orlans, and Terry Levy, I felt a sickness in my stomach and a pain in my heart, imagining what I might find. "Hello, Anna. I'm Terry," he said with a smile.

"Welcome to Evergreen." I returned the pleasantries, shocked he knew my name. They treated only one client at a time, so of course they knew my name.

While on hiatus from my busy life as a devoted single mother of three, my commitments over the next two weeks were limited to attending my daily appointment, going out for food, and soul searching, quite different from my normal life in Washington. Most days there were spent caring for children and pets, maintaining a household, running an interior design business, and fulfilling volunteer hours and personal commitments. A typical day involved three schools, three staggered meals, four to six hours of driving, and work inside and out of the home.

Being freed from the responsibility of the daily grind required some adjustment, because I wasn't accustomed to a leisurely pace or caring for myself. However, I found comfort in routines–Starbucks for breakfast, treatment 'til noon, adventure in the afternoon, and writing before bed. For meals, I'd wander down the hill to El Rancho restaurant, sit in the bar, and watch CNN on the big-screen TV while the owner catered to my every need.

My favorite activity was walking the mile loop around the small, frozen lake, taking in the energy of the town. At one end, people of all ages ice skated while children played hockey, and on the other, fisherman in chairs and tents encircled fishing holes that had been drilled through the thick ice. The lake had a beautiful waterfall leading to a meandering stream that flowed through the town's downtown district. There I strolled up and down the street and shopped for mementos at Evergreen Crafters, a locally-owned gift shop.

Treatment proved to be intimidating at first, three highly trained specialists and me alone together in one room, but I soon found myself feeling secure and at ease in their presence. It was a good thing, because I would spend the next two weeks, three hours a day, in their offices unraveling the truths of my childhood.

FROM THE OUTSIDE LOOKING IN

I HAVE FOND childhood memories of wide, tree-lined, picturesque streets; old, Southern, two-story mansions; and luscious manicured lawns in our family's neighborhood. Life moved at a leisurely pace in Highland Park, an affluent community in the heart of Dallas, Texas, though I could hear a beat and feel its rhythm. There were walkers, joggers, and bikes in the streets, children and dogs on the sidewalks, and gardeners and football games on the front lawns. The neighborhood was alive and well, and I loved being a part of it.

Our home was one of the smaller two-story brick houses, dated and in desperate need of renovation. Rich in architecture and character, it had hardwood floors, tall ceilings, crown moldings, large-paned windows, and a huge backyard. Across the street were a babbling creek with grassy banks, a narrow, arched stone bridge, community tennis courts, and an elementary school. They and the local pool, a short bike ride away, afforded me hours of endless entertainment.

Mother and Daddy moved my three younger siblings and me there the summer before I entered second grade to provide us a superior education and life experience. It was quite a jump from the little ranch-style house we'd lived in previously, but Daddy's growing private legal practice and Mother's family money kept the dream alive for our family.

While establishing his career and building a successful business, Daddy managed to maintain a flexible schedule for the children's extracurricular activities. When he wasn't attending our school or sporting events, he liked to run, make improvements to our house, and putter in the darkroom.

He had a passion for black-and-white photography. With the finest enlargers and equipment money could buy, he spent hours in our basement developing negatives and making prints, mostly of the children, our belongings and activities. Sometimes he'd print one picture a dozen times to get it right and still not be pleased with the outcome, usually something to do with the shadows or lighting, he'd claim.

I'd wake some mornings to find professional lights surrounding me, as if my room were a photography studio and my bed, a stage. When Daddy wasn't taking candid shots, he enjoyed documenting our lives: shoes by the back door, coat rack in the hallway, bulletin boards in our rooms, and toothbrushes on the bathroom sink.

He filled the house with the joyous sound of loud music, mostly Neil Diamond, Simon and Garfunkel, and

Barbra Streisand, which was projected from the enormous floor speakers in our living room. Clearly audible from across the street, the music shook the entire house and caused Mother's decorative knick-knacks to hop about the tables, occasionally crashing to the floor.

Mother didn't work outside of the home, though she was away during the day and kept busy on the weekends with projects. She enjoyed working in the yard while Daddy designed and built structures from scratch, including forts, fences, decks, patios, and bathrooms. Overly meticulous, he thought he could do a better job than the pros, but it usually took him ten times as long. We had scaffolding permanently erected on the exterior of our house for nearly two years while Daddy painted it, before Mother hired a contractor to complete the job.

Lillian, our caretaker, came Monday through Friday from 8:00 a.m. until 5:00 p.m., from the time I was two years old. In elementary school, I'd usually have breakfast with Daddy before she'd arrive, but at least once a week, she'd feed me and help me get dressed. Every morning, she'd fix my hair for school. Brushing it tightly into a ponytail with nary a hair out of place, she pulled the skin away from my scalp, giving me a terrible headache before I left the house. She'd kiss me goodbye and welcome me with open arms upon my return.

Lillian always greeted me, "Come here baby. Let me take a look at you." She'd shake her head side to side and proclaim, "Mmm, mmm, mmm. You sure do look purdy!"

A lovely, petite, African American woman with a sunny disposition, radiant smile, and beautiful skin, Lillian wore thick, black-rimmed glasses and a stiff though stylish wig to cover her short, curly, black hair. Her dress was an old-fashioned nurse's white uniform with hose and black shoes, but I didn't care what she looked like. She was beautiful to me on the inside and out.

In the afternoons, after completing a long list of Mother's chores, Lillian chain smoked cigarettes and watched soap operas on TV while awaiting our arrival from school. *All My Children, One Life to Live, and General Hospital* were the highlight of her day. She developed quite a reputation for it, so much so that Grandmom, Mother's mom, affectionately called her our "TV maid." It was more a statement about my grandmother's Southern upbringing than her feelings towards Lillian, but I didn't like anyone calling her "maid," as she was family to me.

Grinning ear to ear, Lillian frequently teased me, "If you don't behave, I'll hang you up by your toes!" Thankfully, I never found out what that was like.

On occasion, I'd help her crack pecans from the tree in our backyard or watch her polish silver while hanging out in our den. Whatever we did, we laughed and enjoyed the time together. We'd talk about our families and friends, hers she affectionately referred to as "colored folk."

She cleaned house and did laundry for all six of us without complaint. When we made messes, she'd quietly and humbly put things back in order before Mother returned home. Starching Daddy's shirts was one of her most laborious chores. The dry cleaners didn't press them well enough, he said, so she spent hours each week ironing them to perfection. After mixing the starch and boiling it on the stove, she'd let the pale lavender solution cool, pour it into a shaker bottle, and store it in the refrigerator along with a bag of damp shirts. Hours later, she'd place them on an ironing board, spread a generous amount of starch on each, and press them until the thick oxford cloth was silky smooth, shiny, and dry. It was undoubtedly a labor of love.

My built-in playmates, two younger sisters and a brother, and I entertained ourselves around the house. We'd build forts with blankets on the bunk beds in David's bedroom and play house and school there for hours. I'd assign myself the role of mother or teacher, a privilege of being the oldest, while my siblings—Amanda, David, and Susan—were designated subservient children or students.

We had dogs and cats running all over the place, mostly animals the children found and brought home, typically five to six at any given time. Amanda was the ultimate rescuer, though I once discovered a homeless mother kitty and her babies beneath our porch. They were constantly making messes. Sometimes the dogs fought, drawing blood and forcing an emergency trip to the vet. I learned to stay clear of them when they socialized with one another and wear shoes at all times to avoid stepping in their disgusting pee, poop, and vomit.

My siblings and I loved riding around the backyard on Chopperoos—plastic, sit-down, pedal-powered cars with a long nose and small front wheel, much like a dragster. We spent hours forming race tracks along the back driveway with chalk, toys, watering hoses, and yard tools, pretty much anything we could find. Refereeing the races, I usually controlled the outcome by assigning penalties to anyone I felt didn't deserve to win.

In the corner of the backyard, Daddy built a huge wooden fort on eight-foot stilts which provided us a second home and hours of activity. Amanda led David and Susan on scavenger hunts through the back alleys, where they rummaged through garbage cans collecting treasures to furnish our new place: stained pillows, smelly blankets, broken baskets, and an abundance of yellowed lamp shades. While I arranged these decorations to make our fort feel like home, the thought of the germs they carried made me cringe. However, Amanda only considered the gain received from someone else's leftovers.

When we weren't playing in the fort, we could be found across the street in the creek. We'd roll up our pants and wade through the stream, occasionally netting minnows and crawdads. We caught fireflies, too, hundreds of them over the years, and kept them in canning jars with fresh blades of grass, dirt, and nail-punched lids. I loved watching them light up the lawn at dusk and my bedroom after dark, before returning the survivors to their natural environment the following morning.

I was starting second grade when we moved into our home in the Park Cities. That same year, I took my first plane flight with Daddy, Mother, and her parents to New York City. We traveled on Granddad's private corporate jet and spent a week touring the sights of the Big Apple. Compared to what I knew in my little neighborhood, everything felt so grand, especially the Empire State Building and the Statue of Liberty. The torch was open at the time, and I vividly remember climbing stairs with Grandmom for what seemed an eternity, all the way to the top and back down. It was a memorable trip for obvious reasons, but more noteworthy to me was the discomfort of having to share the experience with my classmates upon my return.

As my siblings and I matured, we'd ride our bikes around the neighborhood searching for friends and fun, preferably a private pool, swing set, or trampoline. Many of our neighbors had those amenities, so they weren't hard to find. On Fridays, we'd ride our bikes to the Highland Park Village and spend our entire allowance on candy at the 7-Eleven. Bubble gum was only a penny in the early '70s, so our dollar bills stretched a long way at the time. Sometimes we'd go to the other side of town to the Highland Park Pharmacy for lunch. They were known for their famous grilled cheese sandwiches, with mayonnaise and pickles, and made-to-order milkshakes in stainless steel cups. David would usually forego the shake in favor of his favorite ice cream across the street, Ashburn's lime sherbet. No one could ever convince him there was anything better in this world.

During the summers, I was given great independence and spent much of my time away from home. I'd rise before dawn and ride a mile to the Highland Park Swimming Pool, arriving before they opened. Waiting patiently outside the heavy, seven-foot turnstile that secured the premises, I'd celebrate being the first one in line and greet the lifeguards as they clocked in for work. It was paradise to me—fun, freedom, and friends.

I proudly wore my metal admission tag as a badge of honor, uncaring that it scratched my skin and left rust marks on my swimsuit. I spent every day there, from sunup to sundown, swimming, hanging out with the lifeguards, and playing with schoolmates as they came and went with their families. Daddy joined me for a few hours on the weekends, but mostly it was my home away from home.

Over the holidays, we travelled to Houston to visit Mother's relatives: my aunt, uncle, cousins, and grandparents. Amanda, Susan, and I usually stayed with Grandmom and Granddad, while Mother, Daddy, and David stayed with Aunt Dee Dee, Uncle Frank, and their three boys. Besides Aunt Dee Dee, Mother had another sister, Aunt Louise. She'd join us occasionally but had three little ones who kept her busy and out of sight.

My grandparents lived in an affluent community, River Oaks, later home to several of the fallen Enron executives. Their beautiful, colonial, two-story, red brick house was filled with antiques, china, and rare treasures from travels around the world. It wasn't set up for child's play inside, but Grandmom had a custom playhouse built for the grandchildren in the backyard. Our house had a standard-sized exterior door, two windows, crown molding, carpeting, an air conditioner, and a shingled roof. Furnished with a game table and chairs, books, toys, a music player and TV, it was an ideal hideout for children.

Their backyard also housed Grandmom's flower gardens, Granddad's tomato plants, and a garage with separate living quarters that served as his office. I loved playing outside, mostly watching chameleon lizards as they turned colors and scurried about the yard. Across the street, we played tag and climbed trees in a grassy island parkway half the size of a football field.

Aunt Dee Dee, Uncle Frank, and our cousins lived in the same neighborhood just a few blocks away. She had been a debutante and sorority girl like Grandmom, and was well thought of and connected in their community. Uncle Frank was one of the top partners in a prominent downtown law firm. Though he considered our family beneath his in pedigree and social stature, they graciously invited us to their exclusive country club, held family football scrimmages on the front lawn, and hosted holiday meals.

Grandmom and Aunt Dee Dee prepared elaborate feasts made from scratch with fresh ingredients, very different from any meal Mother dished up at home, and served it on exquisite tables of fine china, silver, crystal, linens, and fresh flowers. After Grandmom retired from hosting our large family gatherings in her home, Aunt Dee Dee continued the tradition in hers. She'd prepare for days before our arrival, and with Mother's help, they'd complete the finishing touches and serve the meal.

Occasionally after Sunday church, we'd eat brunch at the River Oaks Country Club, where my grandparents and aunt and uncle were members. It was a formal affair where ladies were adorned in designer clothing, hats, high heels, and their finest jewels, and men sported a coat and tie.

Though there were several celebrities in their neighborhood, Grandmom was not one to brag or talk about others. The only one I ever heard her mention was Alan Shepard, one of the first astronauts on the moon. She was fascinated by his accomplishments and charity. He lived down the block and she'd point out his house when we'd drive by it. In those days, celebrities didn't have masses of security and paparazzi like they do today so I could have run into him on the street or approached tennis stars Bjorn Borg, Guillermo Vilas, and Ivan Lendl at the River Oaks International Tennis Tournament.

Grandmom was more interested in connecting with the staff at the club than its guests. She took a special interest in Lilly, a beautiful African American woman who greeted us upon arrival. Grandmom made sure we stopped and visited long enough for them to exchange updates and family photos. They talked for what seemed an eternity to me as a child, but I could see the love and respect Lilly and Grandmom showed one another and remember how devastated she was upon learning of Lilly's illness and subsequent death.

I wasn't exposed to country club life in Dallas except for an occasional invitation to a friend's club, so being treated like royalty on our visits to River Oaks was a foreign experience. While they provided all members and guests with only the finest service, I believe they extended special care to our family in return for the compassion and respect Grandmom showed them.

"Treat others as you wish to be treated and always be kind," she would profess. It wasn't just a saying, but her way of living.

I attended summer camp at Camp Little Oaks as a young child by way of an old yellow school bus that picked me up from Grandmom's house and took me less than a mile to the club. Loud, with the noxious smell of exhaust filling the interior, the rickety bus scared me to death. I arrived safely, nonetheless. There we played favorite childhood games like Ring around the Rosy, Duck Duck

Goose, and Red Rover. We made arts and crafts, shot archery, hit balls on clay tennis courts, and putted on the beautiful greens, where I won several trophies for my golfing abilities.

Each morning, Grandmom fixed me breakfast, combed my hair, and helped me get dressed, as Lillian had done at home. She liked to work "just a dab" of VO5 ointment into my hair, which felt like an entire jar of petroleum jelly. It turned greasy, heavy, and flat, but Grandmom liked the way it shined. I couldn't stand the unpleasant smell, however, the joy of sitting with her while she gently combed through my hair was worth every minute of discomfort. She was patient, caring, and tender, and I could feel how much she loved me.

As I grew older, I spent a couple of weeks by myself in Houston with my grandparents each summer. By the age of ten, Daddy would take me to Love Field Airport, walk me to the gate, watch me board the Southwest Airlines plane, and wait until it was in the air before returning home. Confident Grandmom was on the other end to receive me, he never questioned my safe arrival. Truth be told, she was at the airport in Houston before I ever left the ground in Dallas to ensure extra time for unexpected delays.

Grandmom and I scheduled our days around her favorite TV shows—*The Price Is Right, The Dating Game, Family Feud, and Jeopardy.* She loved a good crossword puzzle and solitaire, too, so we'd work on those between shows or during commercials. In her bedroom, where she spent most of her time, we'd spread out on the king-size bed with pillows, blankets, cards, magazines, newspapers, and tissue...lots of tissue. She had allergies which caused her nose to run, her eyes to water, and her skin to itch.

A day at Grandmom's house wouldn't have been complete without dark chocolate. There were stacks of Eskimo Pies in the freezer and several boxes of fine chocolates stashed around the house. I could always pinpoint her location by listening for the sound of rustling wrappers or raspy breathing. Though she tried to eat healthy and control her weight, Grandmom was a pleasantly plump woman incapable of denying her insatiable love of sweets.

"Don't you want a piece?" she'd offer and encourage, "A little bit can't hurt anybody."

She frequently took me shopping for clothing and necessities. I wasn't the easiest child to dress because I had long, skinny legs and narrow feet. Thankfully, she had the willingness and patience to drive me all over town to find slim pants long enough to fit and shoes that wouldn't slip off my heels. Once I started growing, she bought me a seasonal wardrobe twice a year. The hours of shopping, long lunches, and her attentiveness created many cherished memories.

I didn't see Granddad much on my visits, though he occasionally took me to the club for a swim. He'd sit poolside in the shade with a cigar and a drink or two, while I swam laps and flipped off the boards. Sometimes for breakfast, we'd share a meal at the pharmacy café on Kirby and Post Oak, where he'd buy me candy or a small toy afterwards.

A successful engineer and company president for a subsidiary of the Pennzoil Corporation, Granddad was a shrewd businessman. Tall and serious, with a flattop haircut, pants that rode up higher on one side of his waist, and a natural frown, his presence scared most people, especially young children.

In his retirement, he worked in his office over the garage, tended to his beloved tomatoes and yard work, and took their Pekinese dog on short drives around the neighborhood twice a day. By late afternoon, he'd retreat to his bedroom, have several drinks and watch the evening news, not to surface again until early morning.

Granddad taught me how to drive by letting me cruise the local church parking lot in his big, silver, two-door Cadillac. Once, I lost the muffler going over a speed bump and thought the car was going to explode. My cousin Patricia and I abandoned ship with both doors wide open, realizing after the fact that we'd left our poor granddad trapped in the back seat. It still brings tears of laughter when I think of him calmly awaiting our return, as we ran screaming hysterically from the car.

Every now and then, he'd give me cash, a $100 bill at a time. Delivered with solemnity and a grimace, he'd claim, "Your grandmother tells me you could use a little pocket change." It was difficult to get a smile out of him, but I could read his mood by looking into his eyes.

During my middle school years, Grandmom sent Patricia and me to Camp Mystic, an exclusive all-girls camp in south central Texas. Traveling from Dallas to Kerrville on a chartered bus each summer, I spent five weeks along the beautiful Guadalupe River with a couple of hundred campers, ages five to eighteen. It was a privilege for all who attended, especially those who had the opportunity to meet Lady Bird Johnson, the former First Lady, on trips to see her granddaughter Nicolle.

Camp Mystic was primitive compared to anything I'd been exposed to previously. Without air conditioning, campers and counselors lived in harmony with the outdoors during the sweltering Texas heat, typically over one hundred degrees. Our rustic stone and wood cabins had screened windows, bunk beds, and a single bathroom, which didn't leave much privacy for the twenty or so girls living in them. The open cabins allowed in the fresh air and warm breeze, but they also invited creatures from the outside, notably hairy spiders and scorpions. Often discovered at bedtime or first thing in the morning, hidden in campers' trunks, shoes, or sheets, they were frequently announced with frightening screams.

There were many activities from which to choose including arts and crafts, sports, swimming and diving, and canoeing, as well as dance and horseback riding, my personal favorites. I didn't like swimming due to the aggressive water moccasins in the Guadalupe River. All campers participated in organized team rituals and friendly but fierce competitions between the two tribes, Kiowas and Tonkawas. I was a Kiowa tribal member and Patricia, a Tonkawa. Amanda became a Tonk a couple of years later, leaving me the lone ranger in the family. It didn't stop my enthusiasm or support for my teammates, which typically took my voice within the first few days of camp.

We awoke each morning at sunrise to the vibrant call of reveille and drifted to sleep at night to the peaceful sound of taps. In between, we ate family-style meals in a dining hall filled with rows of long, rectangular tables and benches. Camp Mystic exposed me to the great outdoors, gave me the opportunity to make new friends, enriched my summers, and helped me appreciate the comforts of city living.

As a teenager, I began swimming competitively for the Dallas Swim Club. A scrawny, immature adolescent who had used the pool in my younger days as a social tool, I was not adequately prepared for the countless hours and relentless training it required. My coach, Richard Quick, the future Olympics swimming coach, was a highly dedicated and principled man. I imagine his character and training regime didn't change much over the years, only the quality of his subjects.

Missing the talent and aspirations of a competitive swimmer, I swam for a couple of years before leaving to participate in high school athletics. As a ninth grader, I ran both cross country and spring track but was never a serious threat in any event, unlike Daddy. He held the state record in the 440-yard dash during his high school tenure.

I excelled academically in one of the top public high schools in the country, though the exclusivity of the Park Cities made Highland Park High School more comparable to a private school, both scholastically and socially. While I wasn't one of the popular kids, I dated a star tennis player and hung out with a nice group of friends. Wearing fashionable clothing, compliments of Grandmom, helped me develop self-confidence and a sense of style. I matured physically my junior year and graduated an athletic, intelligent, socially competent young lady.

To celebrate my high school graduation, Grandmom and I ventured on a two-week extravaganza to Europe over Christmas break. Having toured the world by boat, train, and plane, she knew how to travel in style and this trip was no exception. We travelled on the Concorde from New York to Paris and spent the holidays living luxuriously in France, Austria, and Switzerland. We stayed in five-star hotels, dined on gourmet meals and delicacies, went skiing in the Swiss Alps, and spent New Year's Eve at the Palace Ball in Vienna.

From the outside looking in, I lived a fairytale life, better than most could have dreamed. Mother and Daddy had succeeded in giving me the stellar education and privileged upbringing they'd hoped for when moving into Highland Park. I lived in a lovely home with my siblings and parents, had a full-time caretaker and extended family who loved and supported me, attended an exclusive summer camp, succeeded in academics and sports, received a new Chevy Camaro on my sixteenth birthday, travelled to Europe first class, and was provided a debt-free college education.

It appeared I wanted for nothing.

1964

Dear Mommy,

We are connected in flesh and spirit like no two others, and I am with you always. Though you can't see or feel me, I hear your voice, experience your emotions, and share in your existence. You have given me life and I love you.

I'm growing really fast and I need rest. I want you to relax with me, talk to me, and caress me, but you seem unaware of my presence. Calculated and tense, your body continually bombards me with stress hormones, leaving me feeling anxious and unsettled. Even in silence, I can't find peace in your world. I must escape this unhealthy environment and find a way to survive on my own. I can't wait to meet you, Mommy.

What a shock to my system! The outside world is cold and bright, full of loud noises and strange faces. I recognized your voice immediately and it brought familiarity, but I need you to hold and comfort me when I'm scared. You nursed me as the doctors recommended, but your body felt stiff and your touch, mechanical. I could sense your discomfort and see the vacancy in your eyes. It made me feel invisible in your presence.

I'm so excited to be home from the hospital and in Daddy's care. He held me, talked to me, and gazed endlessly into my eyes. When he leaves for work, I miss him very much; his touch, his voice, and his smile. I desperately want you to love me in his absence but you don't spend any time with me or respond to my cries for help. Where are you when I need you?

I'm trying to find my way in this world but I'm feeling alone, confused, and frustrated. Daddy cares for me, shows me his approval, and gives me affection consistently. I feel safe and loved in his care. You, on the other hand, feed me, change me, and clean me on schedule, but are seemingly unimpressed with my existence. There must be something terribly wrong with me.

My stomach aches and my whole body feels weird. I scream to the point of exhaustion hoping you'll help me, but I can't get your attention. You are my mommy, the one who has the opportunity to know me better than anyone. Why don't you want to be with me?

If I'm the perfect child, if you understand me, or if I can please you, maybe you'll appreciate my company and value my life. I'll work tirelessly to earn your love and I won't give up trying. In the meantime, I'll strive to gain your approval and hope it feels like love to me.

Love always,
Your daughter Anna

FROM THE INSIDE LOOKING OUT

THE REALITY OF my youth was much different than it appeared to be, but I was unaware it had impacted my emotional development. According to Orlans and Levy (*Healing Parents, Helping Wounded Children Learn to Trust and Love,* Orlans and Levy, 2006, Child Welfare League of America), the beliefs we have about ourselves are based on how our Attachment figures, or caregivers, act towards us in early childhood. From before birth well into the formative years, the subconscious receives tremendous input from which we formulate attitudes about self, others, and the world around us. These develop into core beliefs—the mindsets, attitudes, and expectations that define who we are, how we relate to others, and what roles we play.

The experiences children have with caregivers in early childhood are the basis for what Orlans and Levy call a *"Life Script."* This unique emotional footprint is created by documenting these experiences from the viewpoint of the inner child, along with adult intimate relationships in terms of emotional responses, and the important people involved in both. In treatment, Drs. Coster, Orlans, and Levy and I spent several days dissecting my feelings, behaviors, and interactions with my primary caregiver to decode my programming. It reminded me that Mother, in her absence, had more power over my state of mind than the four of us combined.

My *Life Script* is based on the following questions and answers, pertinent to my circumstances. Keeping in mind that adults typically look back on their youth with rose-colored glasses to minimize the impact of painful memories, accuracy is extremely important.

1. **Where did you spend your childhood?**

   In Texas in the early '70s. Dallas was experimenting with busing, moving children from their local neighborhood schools to different schools throughout the city, in an effort to integrate the public school system. My parents learned if I attended elementary school within the Dallas Independent School District, I could have been bused thirty miles across town to a poor, crime-ridden neighborhood in South Dallas.

   To avoid a long commute and any potential danger the area posed, they decided to move to Highland Park, an independent community in the heart of Dallas where wealth was commonplace, real estate was costly, and taxes, exorbitant. It was a stretch for our family, but the Highland Park School District provided excellence in education, receiving top honors at the state and national levels, and my parents felt the superior education and safe environment justified the expense, especially given the alternative.

Our middle-class family was a social misfit in this privileged world, the "bubble," as it is known to those in the area. We had a roof over our heads, clothes on our backs, and food on our table, but we certainly didn't have the luxuries our neighbors and my classmates took for granted, including expensive clothing, club memberships, fine dining, extravagant vacations, designer homes, and disposable income. Those were things we simply could not afford.

Since I attended school with children from the founding families of Neiman Marcus, Haggar Clothing Company, and Dr. Pepper, just to name a few, excessive wealth was the rule, not the exception. It wasn't uncommon for my peers to have a $2,000 per month clothing allowance, a different Gucci or Louis Vuitton bag for every day of the week, or a brand new $60,000 car on their sixteenth birthday, and that was during the '80s. While I found the wealthiest families to be the humblest, I couldn't identify with them no matter how hard I tried.

Mother and Daddy weren't social creatures by nature and didn't care what others thought, leaving me without positive role models or support at home. Indifferent to social acceptance, neither appreciated how difficult it was growing up in a materialistic, unforgiving environment to which I did not belong.

Though I was sheltered from the harsh realities of the outside world—crime, poverty, and violence—I was not protected from the cruelty of my peers, which felt a worse fate at the time. I didn't look, act, or feel like the average Highland Park kid and was teased relentlessly for it.

2. Name your siblings and describe each as children.

Amanda was born two years after me: beautiful, manipulative, selfish, dramatic, and adored. She was the chosen one in our family and used it to her advantage. Playing the victim role well, she cried often to elicit sympathy from Mother and Daddy to get whatever she felt she deserved. She didn't argue with authority, instead doing exactly what she wanted without consideration for rules or the feelings of others. Relating better to animals than people, she brought home every stray she could find.

In high school, Amanda looked like a Barbie doll with beautiful skin, long, straight, blond hair, and big, blue eyes. She was older than her classmates and developed physically before they did, so the boys were enamored by her. Following her like little puppy dogs, they tried to date her but quickly learned she preferred keeping her options open. The girls tagged along as well, wanting to join in on the action, but soon realized Amanda wasn't interested in being their friend either. "They're just jealous," she claimed, gloating in the limelight of popularity.

David was born a year after Amanda: creative, considerate, athletic, quiet, and sensitive, a loner in our family. The only boy amongst three sisters, he was frequently outnumbered in family votes and activities, but Daddy made a special effort to include him and spend one-on-one time to assure he didn't feel left out. With Mother's dark brown hair and olive skin, David looked a different ethnicity than the rest of us during the summer months, though he had Daddy's blue eyes and slight frame.

As a young child, David played cowboys and Indians with the neighborhood boys. His daily uniform consisted of a coonskin cap, leather fringed jacket, cowboy boots, and a western belt to hold up his high-water pants. Gifted athletically, he enjoyed football, basketball, soccer, skiing, and running track. He was a team player who was well respected and befriended by his teammates. When he wasn't involved in sports, he enjoyed listening to music and harassing his baby sister, Susan, whom he treated like a little brother.

Susan was born two-and-a-half years after my brother: independent, athletic, intelligent, strong willed, and entitled. She looked like David with lighter coloring and a solid build. The stubborn one in the family, she wouldn't back down from any challenge, regardless of the consequences. Unhappy living in an environment beyond her complete control, she packed a bag weekly by the age of four, claiming to be running away from home forever.

Once, on a family trip to Mexico, Daddy offered to buy each of us a souvenir. Amanda, David, and I had purchased ours while Susan continued looking through dozens of shops for the perfect embroidered dress. We searched for hours before Daddy finally suggested she pick one, reminding her of several favorites, including one in our current location. She looked at him with absolute disrespect and shouted, "I don't want that f...ing dress."

While we had no idea what the "*F*-word" meant at the time, we watched Daddy's response and heard him loud and clear as we marched out of the gift shop without buying a thing. Susan was scolded and her spending money taken away for the rest of that trip. She was five years old at the time.

3. Name your mother and describe her in your childhood.

Mother was controlling, rigid, righteous, vindictive, and cold. She identified with her father, an authoritative dictator, and not her mom, a compassionate, gentle soul. There was only one way of doing things in her opinion, so it was her way or the highway in our home. "Because I said so," was her mantra.

Operating under a complex system of rules, Mother spent twenty-four hours a day, seven days a week imposing them to keep order in our household, without exception or compromise. I wasn't allowed to have friends over because Mother didn't like the noise or mess of children.

She was emotionally unavailable and incapable of compassion, nurturing, or showing love to humans. Rarely approachable, she spent the majority of her time behind locked doors or away from home. When she was there, she doted excessively on the family pets, putting their needs before ours.

Mother kept our house organized and stocked with the least-expensive food, toiletries, and paper goods available. Acquiring them at a discounted price was her full-time job. Far ahead of her time on recycling and conservation, she skimped out of cost principle, not resource preservation, by restricting our use of these products, along with water and gas.

She expected us to take military showers, turning on water only when necessary for wetting or rinsing our bodies. To keep from buying paper towels or laundering linens, Mother cleared food from the counters and tabletop, cleaned the kitchen sink and floor, and wiped our faces with the same dark brown washcloth day after day. She claimed not to see the filth on it, but I could smell the mildew from across the room.

The freezer was Mother's favorite appliance because it preserved things indefinitely. She filled it mostly with frozen foods, which she liked for convenience, and ice cream, her favorite food group. Items in the refrigerator had scraps of paper taped or rubber-banded to them long before Post-it notes were invented. She labeled things that belonged to her or Daddy to notify the children and Lillian which foods were off limits. While they enjoyed Smucker's jelly, fresh fruit and juice, and whole milk, we had generic jelly, canned fruit, and powdered milk.

The thought of wasting gasoline made Mother especially upset. She plotted her errands for the week based on proximity, and if a diversion of any kind presented itself, including necessities or social activities, it might not be considered. She was unwilling to drive me to friends' houses, birthday parties, and sleepovers unless they fit into her driving schedule, which usually left me to find rides there and back myself.

It was too far for me to walk to high school, and Daddy supported my decision not to ride a bike in a skirt and high heels, so Mother relented to a morning carpool my freshman year. On our days, she timed each girl from the moment we pulled into the driveway, as she'd read it was more efficient to shut off the engine and restart it if idling longer than three minutes. If anyone dared to take that long, Mother would degrade them in front of the entire carpool. "If Lee didn't spend so much time putting on all that makeup, maybe she could get out here on time, instead of looking like a tramp," she'd proclaim. "Next time, I'm not waiting. That'll teach her a lesson!" It was no surprise when we weren't invited back the following year.

Mother practiced gas conservation in other places, too. She frequently turned off the engine at stop lights she knew to be longer than three minutes and in the middle of the McDonald's drive-thru while waiting for our food. I always wondered why she felt her and my siblings' special orders were their fault when they graciously explained the wait in advance each time. Somehow Mother expected them to change their system to accommodate her needs and felt it was her right to make others suffer until she got what she wanted. She'd complain to anyone within earshot of the window, "I can't believe how long it takes to be served at this place!" Followed by, "What is taking so long? We've been waiting here forever." Regardless of their answer, her response was an exasperated, "They just don't know what they're doing. This is absolutely ridiculous!"

Mother didn't like anyone who disagreed with her or her ways. She'd argue her point until they were convinced of her superiority, and if they didn't come around to her way of thinking, she'd shame them and deem them incompetent. Whatever the case, the objective was always her winning and their humiliation. Consequently, I spent my entire childhood trying to avoid upsetting her.

It was clear when Mother was angry with me because she'd raise her voice and tell me repeatedly what a miserable human being I was. "What is wrong with you?" she'd pose rhetorically before answering the question herself. "Why are you such an ungrateful child? What makes you think you're so special?" Waiting for a response, she'd glare at me before eventually demanding, "Answer me!" "There are plenty of starving children in Africa who'd be thrilled to be in your shoes," she'd declare. "What is wrong with you? I swear!"

When I didn't surrender, she'd chase me around the house, threatening to spank me. This treatment continued well into my teenage years, as Mother believed punishment was an essential means of maintaining control. She'd grab me by the arm, throw me over her knee, pull down my pants, and slap my bare bottom as hard as she could, before sending me to my room for the rest of the day.

Nevertheless, Mother's physical harm didn't leave scars like the emotional abuse she inflicted— alienation, shunning, and punitive punishment. At times, she wouldn't speak to me, serve me meals, or tell me goodnight while going out of her way to make sure I knew she was extending that care to my siblings. "Good night, Amanda!" "Good night, David!" "Good night, Susan!" she'd announce loudly from the hallway. Her silence could last for days until I'd honor her wishes or find a way to please her.

Mother was a dreadful woman in my book.

4. Name your father and describe him in your childhood.

Daddy was loving, giving, personable, artistic, and impatient; a perfectionist and devoted father. Six feet tall with salt-and-pepper hair, fair skin, and blue eyes, he had long, skinny legs, narrow shoulders, a small potbelly, and no caboose. He was a sharp dresser who loved fine clothing and shoes, whether he was wearing a suit to work or sporting casual attire at home.

There was nothing more important to him than his children, and we knew it. Operating as a sole practitioner, Daddy's law practice allowed him to be there for our milestones and activities. He prided himself on missing only one event in all of our years, the result of some misguided directions, he claimed.

Once, Lillian couldn't wake Amanda from a nap due to a high fever, so she called Daddy to let him know and report the ambulance was on its way. Somehow, Daddy managed to arrive home from work before the emergency aid and took Amanda to the hospital himself.

Beginning my sophomore year in high school, Daddy drove me to school in the mornings, sometimes in a client's beat-up, rusted, '50s white pickup truck. I'm not sure why he had it, other than he occasionally used it to haul things to the house for projects—dirt, plants, equipment, lumber, and whatnot. It was cranky most of the time and frequently got stuck in first gear. When it did finally shift, it revved like a race car and lurched forward with great force.

The passenger door was smashed and disabled, so I had to get in and out of the pickup from the driver's side. Daddy would shift the lever on the steering column into neutral, which was no easy feat, open the creaky door, also a difficult task, and get out so I could exit the cab. Then, I'd then slide across the torn, jagged vinyl seat, hoping it didn't snag my pantyhose or tear my clothing on the way out.

As he drove off with smoke billowing out all sides of the truck, I'd wave to my peers as they arrived in their BMWs, Porsches, and Mercedes, and dash into the building smelling like car exhaust. While I later appreciated Daddy's unpretentiousness, this scenario caused me tremendous strife and alienated me from my schoolmates at the time.

A perfectionist, Daddy was frequently frustrated with himself for his humanness and intolerant of others for theirs. "Dammit to hell" and "Oh, come on" were his favorite expressions in the heat of the moment. It was different with us, though. He taught me how to develop film in the darkroom, and while he reprinted pictures dozens of times to get them right, he made me feel good about the work I did on the first try. "Way to go. That's exactly what you want," he'd offer lovingly.

I used to run several miles with him when I was ten years old, and though I couldn't keep up, it didn't stop him from inviting me. He'd run more than double the course by circling back to keep me company, though he never complained.

Daddy was an independent thinker, a successful litigator, and somewhat of a renegade. When taking Mother and me to the Dallas Cowboy football games, followed by dinner at Steak and Ale, one of my favorite childhood activities, we'd ride in his two-door tan Volvo that reeked of David's cap guns. Daddy loved driving it, darting in and out of traffic as we approached Texas Stadium, loud music blaring. When the cars finally came to a standstill, he'd go around them on the shoulder, claiming other drivers didn't know what they were doing. He was proud of his ability to get us to the stadium in a timely manner, completely indignant of the fact that he had done so illegally. "Now that's what I'm talking about!" he'd broadcast with great enthusiasm.

5. State your name and describe yourself as a child.

I am Anna: scrawny, smart, responsible, bossy, and insecure, a caretaker to my siblings. Born five weeks premature, after a full day of shoveling sand, I weighed five-and-a-half pounds at birth and grew into a small child with big blue eyes, skinny legs, and dirty-blond, wavy hair. I had Daddy's slight build and Grandmom's temperamental fair skin. I didn't look or act like other children.

Underdeveloped and sickly, I came down with strep throat accompanied by a high fever several times a year and missed school in one-week intervals. Mother didn't like the inconvenience or expense of the doctor's office, so I'd usually ride out the infection without treatment. On occasion, when Daddy insisted, she'd take me to a parishioner's house to get a prescription for antibiotics. While I ate regularly and drank protein shakes to gain weight, untreated lactose intolerance gave me frequent diarrhea, which eliminated the nutrition. I looked malnourished, and there was nothing I could do to change it.

Allergies and skin sensitivities plagued my body. I was highly allergic to cats and dust, which caused my nose to run and eyes to swell shut. Fresh-cut grass created welts and eczema left me with inflamed, crusty red patches on my neck, elbows, knees, and underarms.

Overly concerned with my appearance, I began changing clothes several times a day before the age of two. Lillian told stories of me disappearing from sight, returning a short while later in a fresh outfit with a big grin on my face. When I was eighteen months old, my parents say I routinely got up in the middle of the night and tried on every piece of clothing in my closet, leaving the evidence strewn about the floor for them to find the following morning. Mother eventually installed a lock on my closet to stop what she considered "madness."

Constantly organizing things in a fastidious fashion, I liked being in control of my surroundings. I tended to other people's needs and was uncomfortable engaging in the unknown, including most innocent childhood games that involved imagination or trickery. I was beyond my years in competence but physically and socially immature, which left me excluded from popular sports and group activities. Teachers liked me for being a model student and rule follower, though my peers mocked me for being skinny and smart. They called me "brain" and "bird legs," and told me I looked like a frog or a rat.

These childhood challenges left me feeling uncomfortable and awkward in my own skin. To make matters worse, Mother bought me outdated, worn clothing at the church's thrift store while my peers were shopping designer boutiques. When I wasn't interested in her selections, it justified her assertions that I was a thankless, undeserving child. Self-doubting and lacking social skills, I struggled to make friends and kept to myself or befriended children who were rejected by others.

I was four foot, eleven inches tall and weighed eighty-five pounds, without a trace of puberty on my body, when I entered high school, a definite handicap. I couldn't relate to my peers, who had matured much earlier, and boys weren't interested in dating me. My oil glands became overactive, producing an uncontrollable shine and mild cystic acne. I spent hours applying makeup to cover the knots and separating every eyelash with a pin to get them in perfect order.

I never got along with Mother, though some stages were worse than others. Complete opposites, we had different values, beliefs, and personalities, and neither of us could understand nor appreciate the other. As she exerted control, I pushed back, and as I looked to connect, she withdrew. The alienation was debilitating and the arguments, never-ending.

I trusted Daddy and Lillian to care for me, but I was unable to find peace at home and escaped as often as I could. Sometimes I'd drive around aimlessly for hours and others, I'd go over to friends' houses, where I picked up social skills and etiquette. I developed physically my junior year. Though I looked and acted more like my peers, I still didn't feel like them on the inside. I battled frustration, feelings of unworthiness, and hopelessness throughout my childhood.

6. Why did your mom marry your dad, and why did your dad marry your mom?

I didn't know the answer to this question as a child because I never saw Mother and Daddy happy together. They weren't like anyone else's parents, and I was uncertain why they were married at all.

When I asked Mother recently, she told me, "Because everyone else was doing it," explaining that eight other couples in their high school tied the knot that same year. She also once claimed health insurance was a good reason, stating, "People have certainly married for a lot less than that."

Her responses surprised me. "What about love?" I wondered. "How could anyone be married to the same person for more than fifty years without being in love?" The answer: her *love* was about duty and control, not respect and admiration.

My parents were born and raised in a small mining community of mostly uneducated potash laborers, in New Mexico. Mother and Daddy dated in high school before eloping across the border to Mexico the summer prior to Mother's senior year and Daddy's junior. Both seventeen years old, they returned home and kept news of their marriage a secret for a year while living separately with their respective families.

Mother graduated and spent the following summer preparing to attend Arizona State University. However, she dropped out within weeks of her arrival and returned home to begin married life with Daddy. Thanks to Mother's parents, who provided them an apartment, my parents spent their first year together as Daddy completed his high school education.

He was not from a wealthy, stable family as she was. His father died when he was eighteen months old, leaving his unemployed and unskilled teenage mom to raise him and his two-year-old sister. She married a mine worker shortly thereafter and had two more children. Working long hours to support their growing family, Daddy's stepfather and mother were rarely present in his life. The solitude left Daddy feeling alone and unwanted.

He dreamed of escaping his family's meager roots and their small-town life. A gifted runner, he eventually accomplished this goal through athletics. With the recruitment, encouragement, and mentoring of his high school coach, Daddy was the star athlete on the track team. He won the state championship in the 440-yard dash in record time, which earned him national recognition and a scholarship to Southern Methodist University, an exclusive private college in Dallas, Texas.

Although Mother may have married Daddy because everyone else was doing it, I'm convinced Daddy married Mother for her independence and picture-perfect family. They gave him the instant love, attention, and support he longed for while serving as the role model for his and Mother's future. Grandmom was as lovely a wife and mother as June Cleaver, and Granddad, a successful businessman who provided wealthily for his family. As Daddy devoted himself to transforming this vision into his personal reality, he was confident Mother could take care of herself.

7. **Were there any traumatic experiences in your childhood before the age of fifteen?**
   Mother's personality made it extremely difficult for me to find happiness at home. She believed she was right about everything and was incapable of seeing anyone else's point of view. As a result,

she criticized and corrected me constantly and argued relentlessly for the sake of winning.

Daddy tried to avoid her emotional torment, but he couldn't escape it either. It was the cause of their marital difficulties, which began early in my childhood. After months of unproductive "discussions," Daddy sought professional help from a highly regarded therapist and encouraged Mother to seek counseling as well. She tried several therapists but stopped going once she found they didn't agree with her. Her objective was one of solidarity and affirmation, not enlightenment or personal growth, which defeated the purpose.

After many efforts in vein, Daddy called a family meeting to announce their separation. His heartbreak was evident as he wept uncontrollably and comforted us in our sorrow, while Mother remained emotionless and statuesque. She was unable to see fault in herself and blamed everything on Daddy. When he wasn't around, she'd explain, "Your father is sick in the head and needs help. There is nothing I can do to change that." I knew from my own experience that her view was not the truth, and furthermore, I realized she blamed me for empathizing with him.

I was in third grade when he and I first shopped for apartments, which fueled my dream of escaping Mother. Though she refused to permit me to live with Daddy, she occasionally let me spend the night. When she'd pick me up the following morning, she'd come inside, snoop around, and interrogate me on the ride home. "Did he talk on the phone? To whom? For how long? Did he mention my name? What did he say?" The questions were never about Daddy and me, only his personal activities. If I refused to give her details, she would abruptly end the conversation and not speak to me again for days. The phony smile she'd used to obtain information disappeared and her angry face turned to stone.

On one of my sleepovers, I was loading the dishwasher when Mother arrived. Daddy stepped out to put my things in the car when she came inside to get me. I looked up to say hello, but instead of a greeting, she offered a warning. With loathing in her eyes and spit spewing from her mouth, she proclaimed, "You'll never be able to take care of him the way I can, so stop trying! No matter what you do, he'll always love me more."

I was nine years old, his daughter, not his wife. I wasn't competing for his affection. I was taking care of someone I loved the only way I knew how. I quit the dishes and started to walk off when Daddy came in. Looking away to keep him from seeing the tears in my eyes, I caught Mother gloating as if she'd just gotten away with murder.

Daddy would have done anything to be with my siblings and me, and Mother knew it. Having no intention of modifying her behavior to save their marriage, she was smart enough to know we were her only bargaining tool. Thus, she manipulated his visitation rights and made him pick us up in an alley a block away from our house. He eventually tired of her shenanigans and moved home to have unlimited access to his children, out of fear of Mother, not love.

This cycle occurred multiple times in my youth. Daddy would reach the breaking point with Mother and leave; she would control his contact with Amanda, David, Susan, and me; he would miss us and return home. Through all the comings and goings, one thing remained constant, Mother. She was void of emotion, incapable of responding to the needs of others, and impossible to live with.

Like her father, Mother sought revenge on anyone she considered to have crossed her, making them feared leaders. Granddad was known to carry a little black book with him at all times to document grievances, small and large. Imposing restitution on subordinates, friends, and family, he let no one go unpunished. Mother kept score, too, and ruled our family with the same iron fist.

Because she considered Daddy and me to be traitors, she continually looked for ways to extinguish our spirits and defeat our wills to live. She once paid a visit to Daddy's law partner, a prominent judge in our community, to report of his despicable character. Aware this partner was Daddy's main source of income, she threatened his livelihood by asking the judge to abandon and disgrace him as she believed he had done to her.

Terrified of her rage and vengeance, Daddy didn't want to find out what Mother would have done if he pursued a divorce. He'd seen too many in his legal practice and knew of the detrimental consequences, particularly to children. His fear paralyzed him and caused him to remain in their toxic relationship.

His leaving, my worry for his safety and mine, and an emotionally destructive relationship with Mother were traumatic for me throughout childhood. Daddy couldn't save me from her abuse, my siblings didn't suffer the same mistreatment or understand my circumstances, and I couldn't do anything to change them. An outcast in my own family, I was lonely, scared, and hopeless. Our home was not a safe or happy place for me.

8. **Describe what message your mother gave you about yourself and what she taught you.**

I grew to be strong, self-sufficient, and competent through Mother's abandonment, not her modeling. On the day I was born, I took Daddy's love and attention from her and she despised me for it. She intentionally neglected me, ignored my feelings, and treated me as the enemy. Her feelings of resentment only intensified as Daddy's and my relationship grew and theirs deteriorated.

I couldn't feel Mother's love, so I tried to gain her approval in its place, but nothing was ever good enough for her. She taught me love was difficult, painful, and unattainable.

9. Describe what message your father gave you about yourself and what he taught you.
Daddy let me know I was important to him, in word and deed. As an infant, he held me and cared for my needs. In adolescence, he talked to me and empathized with my feelings. I could see my happiness and sorrow reflected in his eyes, and knew he was carrying my joys and troubles with him. He spent time with me and told me he loved me frequently.

Daddy believed a good education was the foundation for a successful future. Confident I could be anything I wanted as long as I put my mind to it, he taught me there were no limits to my dreams and achievements. He persuaded me to be an independent thinker, not a follower, encouraged me to do my best always, and told me to share my gifts with others, regardless of the payment received in return.

10. What did your mother model for you regarding women?

Mother was a strong, independent woman, something I typically admired, but she used these strengths to defeat and alienate others, which I detested. She didn't have friends or value relationships and was unwilling to give freely of her time, affection, or talents.

Mother's appearance was not important to her, simply a matter of function, as evidenced by her outdated, worn clothing and un-styled, wavy brown hair. Though she bathed regularly, she didn't wear makeup or dress in anything besides wrinkle-free jeans and polyester sweats. Most of the time, she looked as if she had just crawled out of bed. When she dressed up for church, she'd put on a skirt, pantyhose, and red lipstick, which looked out of place on her otherwise unkempt body. She bought clothes for their cheapness and utility, two features not valued in Highland Park, where beauty, style, and designer labels were revered.

Mother had her parent's money and spent it without consideration for our family. While Daddy struggled to provide us a home, meals, and necessities, she purchased items she deemed appropriate, like custom leather sofas exclusively for the dogs' comfort. She didn't feel the children were her responsibility and left Daddy to satisfy our financial, physical, and emotional needs.

For these reasons, I've spent my entire life trying to be the antithesis of her, which has served me well for the most part. However, it has not allowed me to be true to myself or given me a sense of identity, because I only know who I don't want to be, not who I am.

11. What did your father model for you regarding men?

Daddy was a unique and rare man. Both father and mother to his children, he fulfilled Mother's role partly because it was his nature and partly because she was incapable of it. He took the role seriously, parent first and provider second. By participating in our lives, attending our activities, and coaching most of our sporting events, he set the bar high. He was my savior and role model.

Daddy escaped an unhappy childhood and lack of opportunity in a small town to accomplish great things, including a state athletic record, a scholarship to an elite university, service in the

United States Navy, a law degree, and a successful legal practice. I admired his ability to overcome obstacles in achieving success but felt sad he never obtained the love he desperately wanted and deserved.

While he relied on the safety net of Mother's parents for financial support, he took great pride in providing his children a superior education and life experience, supporting all four of us through the completion of our college degrees. Attaining these achievements with minimal aid was quite a triumph for an underprivileged boy from small-town New Mexico.

12. Who were your role models growing up? Describe them.

Grandmom, Mother's mom, was a sweet, loving, gracious, generous, and socially conscious woman. With strawberry hair, a fair complexion, kind blue eyes, and an innocent disposition, she was the picture of Southern grace. Somewhat naïve, she believed the best in all human beings.

A caretaker, Grandmom fulfilled my physical and emotional needs, made sure I had essential provisions, and took me to the doctor for regular checkups. Once, she found an abandoned, scraggly dog in the gutter, took him to the vet, bought expensive supplies and food, and shipped him and his belongings to us on an airplane, without considering the cost.

Grandmom would have done the same for anyone in an unfortunate situation, as giving to others gave her great joy. Coming from a wealthy family, she had oil royalties and income-producing rental properties, which afforded her financial freedom. She remodeled apartments and leased them to families in need for less than market value, and would have given a stranger her very last dime if she thought he needed it.

Lillian, my guardian angel, saved me from Mother's neglect and hateful ways. She taught me how to care for myself and others. From the time I was two years old through my departure for college, she was my guardian angel. A gentle, loving, patient, and nurturing soul, she always had a smile on her face and love in her heart. Though Mother called her "maid" and treated her like an employee, I considered her Mom.

Aunt Dee Dee, Mother's sister, was the mom I longed for: sweet, loving, graceful, well-dressed, socially connected, and involved in her family and the community. Having three boys of her own, she made me feel like the daughter she never had. "Anna Lee, why couldn't I have had just one of you? You're such a dear!" she'd say. I enjoyed sharing girl time with her, something Mother didn't know how to do. My favorite memories include playing dress-up with her pretty clothes, shoes, jewelry, and makeup while she got ready for the day. Watching her every move, I dreamed of growing up to be just like her.

Grandmom, Lillian, and Aunt Dee Dee were my role models, the ones who shaped my ideals of what a good woman was and who I wanted to be. A good woman is strong, yet sensitive, independent, yet connected. While taking care of herself and her personal needs, she nurtures her husband and children and is devoted to her family and friends. She shares her time, talents, and love with others, giving back to her community and those in need.

13. What was your favorite fairytale?

I can't remember having a favorite fairytale, as they all seemed unrealistic to me. I preferred real-life stories. However, my favorite childhood movie was *The Sound of Music*, the story of a handsome widower and his seven beloved children who find a beautiful, loving nanny to care for them and fall madly in love with their dad.

I used to watch it at Grandmom's house on each visit. I loved everything about it—the family, the caretaker, the home, the scenery, the music, the singing, the happiness, the harmony, and the formal matching outfits. It was the dream I had for my own family; the perfect motherless life, my version of a fairytale.

14. **Describe your significant romantic relationships, and name with whom you had them.**
    - Bobby - First Love, page 79
    - Derek - Obsessive Love, page 95
    - Rob - Falling Into Place, page 117
    - TIM - The Awakening, page 1

FIRST LOVE

––––––

MY BEST FRIEND Beth and I met on the playground in elementary school and developed a friendship after discovering we each had a disappointing relationship with one of our parents. She had an absent, alcoholic father, and I had Mother. Living with her mom and brother several blocks away, Beth was an easy walk or bike ride from my house. We'd play at hers or meet on the school playground and shared summers together at the neighborhood swimming pool.

In middle school, Beth possessed what I wanted– flawless, golden skin, wavy, Farrah Fawcett hair, and a toned, fully developed body. She was a natural beauty with a great smile, friends, and popularity. The boys were crazy about her charming naiveté, which I ultimately learned was not an act, as I had suspected, but rather a true lack of intelligence.

She struggled in school and asked repeatedly to copy my work, but I offered to tutor her instead. In exchange for my help, Beth promised to introduce me to a tennis player whom I had a larger-than-life crush on. Sean sat behind me in sixth-grade math class. Too timid to talk to him, I admired him from afar—his blond hair, blue eyes, kind smile, and sporty style. The mere thought of seeing him produced an instantaneous reaction in me. My heart and mind raced, my face turned a thousand shades of bright red, and my internal temperature soared as if I were in the throes of a panic attack.

Meeting Sean would have been a dream come true, one I'd have to wait a while longer to realize. Though Beth assured me she was looking for the perfect opportunity to introduce us, she neglected to uphold her end of the agreement that year. After helping her with schoolwork and receiving nothing in return, I finally voiced my disappointment in her unfulfilled promises.

She apologized and suggested getting me and Sean together over the summer. It sounded like the perfect idea until it was time for me to leave for camp and I still hadn't met him. Feeling the chance had passed by me, I was surprised and delighted to receive a handwritten letter from Sean during the middle of my stay.

He mentioned Beth had contacted him and conveyed my interest. He said he liked my big blue eyes, skinny legs, and blond hair but was shy around girls and had been afraid to approach me. Touching on my vulnerabilities, the letter made me feel as if he'd taken a special interest in me. He wished me well at camp and asked if we could meet when school resumed.

I was absolutely ecstatic! I read the letter over and over, practically committing it to memory. The idea that someone I liked was returning the sentiment was life affirming. I couldn't sleep or think of anything other than Sean. I called Beth as soon as I could to thank her for making the connection and apologize for having doubted her intentions. Barely able to contain myself without drawing the attention of others, I was embarrassed by the intensity of my emotions.

Four weeks later, I entered school nervous and exhausted from a lack of sleep but elated by the thought of seeing Sean. Searching everywhere for a glimpse, I was beginning to give up hope when I spotted him on the front lawn. He looked exactly as I remembered, except his hair had been bleached white and skin tanned by the summer sun.

Dashing across the manicured school grounds, I hurried to catch up with him. As I called out his name, he turned to see me and our eyes met for the very first time.

"Hi," I said, as he returned the gesture. "Thanks so much for the letter at camp!" I gushed.

"What letter?" he asked with a look of bewilderment.

In that instant, I realized it was too good to be true. The words were hauntingly familiar to have come from a stranger, but my excitement had prevented me from seeing it sooner. I knew then that Beth had written the letter herself.

"Oh, never mind," I quickly responded with a grin, as if it had been a joke. As I hung my head low and walked away with tears in my eyes, he offered, "I hope you had a nice summer."

I ran crying all the way home. Lillian was there to greet me, but I didn't feel much like talking, not even to her. Completely devastated, I was blindsided by my misplaced trust in Beth and humiliated by the confrontation with Sean. I stayed in my room except for meals and school the rest of that week.

When I saw Beth again afterwards, I recounted what had happened and told her I knew she had written the letter. "Why did you do that?" I inquired tearfully.

"I never thought you'd find out," she admitted, seemingly without regret. She had hoped to make arrangements for me and Sean to meet before camp, and when things didn't work out as planned, she devised the letter to appease me.

She was the only friend I had and I was terrified of losing her. Though what she had done destroyed my faith, we moved past the incident as if nothing had happened. Beth continued to attract all the boys, and I remained the smart, supportive, unattractive friend.

In eighth grade, Beth had a suitor, Bobby, who befriended me in an effort to gain her affection. He was charming and humorous, bold and fast, perfectly suited for her but not for me. Nonetheless, he and I developed a close friendship that carried over into high school. We talked several times a day on the phone, rode bikes around the neighborhood, took his black Lab for long walks, and went for swims in his backyard pool. By then, Sean was a distant memory, though Bobby teased me about him frequently, as they were teammates on the school tennis team.

By the age of fourteen, I was driving all over town without a license. Mother had me picking up groceries, running errands, and taking my siblings to their activities. While I hated being at her beck and call and was terrified of being caught by the police, I enjoyed the freedom the driving afforded me.

In between errands, I spent my time at Bobby's house, which kept me away from home as much as possible. I attended his club practices and tournaments, hanging out with his parents and sisters while watching him play. They included me in their celebrations— holidays, birthdays, and graduations—and treated me like a member of their family.

Beth, Bobby, and I hung out together our freshman year. Though he had been hopelessly infatuated with her for almost two years, she was clearly not interested in dating him and told him so repeatedly. He eventually got the message and began pursuing a dating relationship with me instead. Bobby and I were best friends but he was too loud and daring for my tastes. Knowing it made me uncomfortable, he had fun embarrassing me in public by shocking people and drawing the attention of a crowd.

"Isn't she cute? I just love her!" he'd say while pinching my nose. It made me self-conscious and turned my face bright red, as I wasn't used to that kind of affection or the glares it drew from others.

Although I didn't have romantic feelings for him, he had become my lifeline and escape from Mother. We began dating the summer before our sophomore year and I quickly learned that he enjoyed showing off his girlfriend, like a trophy. He held my hand, kissed me, and professed his love everywhere we went, in front of his parents, at school, and in public.

When Bobby invited me to the Homecoming dance, Beth let me borrow one of her favorite dresses, a white crepe, calf-length, A-line gown with a synched waist, spaghetti straps, and a chiffon floral wrap that draped across the shoulders. Bobby, dressed in his designer tuxedo, arrived to pick me up in his parent's big, blue, four-door Cadillac. I greeted him at the door, where he waited with a fresh corsage in hand. He looked like an Italian stallion and smelled divine, either Polo for Men by Ralph Lauren or Grey Flannel by Perry Ellis, the only two scents for pretentious Highland Park boys at the time.

Mother approached and asked Bobby if he would assist her, a frequent request when she spotted anyone capable of fulfilling her needs. It didn't matter how large or small the task, Mother had no reservation requesting help, often from complete strangers. Daddy had given up complying with her demands years earlier but Bobby politely agreed, not knowing what he was getting himself into.

Before I knew it, Bobby, Mother, and I were standing in the backyard in front of our detached garage. It was a warm, fall Dallas evening with the temperature in the mid-eighties. I feared she wanted to engage him in her favorite pastime, rearranging furniture, and pleaded with her not to force him into physical labor.

"Please don't make him move furniture in a tuxedo!" I pleaded.

Mother didn't respond but instead took Bobby into the garage while I waited on the driveway. I could see her pointing to the rafters and hear her talking to him as if he were a servant. "Do this...don't do that...blah, blah, blah..." As she explained the assignment in full detail, I couldn't imagine how hot he must have been in a coat and tie inside the garage when I was sweating outside in a strappy dress. The next thing I knew, Bobby was pulling down boards stored atop the rafters as plumes of dust filled the garage, covering his hair, face, shoulders, and shoes. Ten minutes later, he came out drenched in sweat and soot looking like he had just cleaned the inside of a chimney.

I was fuming mad at Mother, but he was far too well-mannered to say anything to her. She dismissed us with an obligatory thank you and sent us on our way. "See, that wasn't so bad," she stated matter-of-factly with a smirk on her face. "You can go have fun now," as if we had to earn her approval to attend the dance.

Bobby wiped up with a dry towel as best he could and took me to a five-star restaurant for dinner, something I hadn't experienced previously. Thankfully, he had been exposed to fine dining and knew how to handle himself, so I followed his lead. Neither of us was of legal drinking age, though Bobby looked much older than fifteen, especially given the shadow and crevices left by the grime. As such, he didn't have any problem ordering alcohol. The margaritas on the rocks were smooth and tasty, different from the Tickled Pink and beer I had sampled previously. They relaxed me and numbed the anger I felt towards Mother for what had just transpired.

We had appetizers and salads before our meal arrived, but I had already consumed six drinks by then. The effects of the alcohol hit me as I began eating dinner, and I immediately felt sick. After I threw up all over the table, Bobby, and myself, the restaurant staff helped me into the restroom, cleaned me up, carried me outside, and laid me across the back seat of Bobby's car. I passed out, we missed the dance, and Bobby drove around for hours before finally taking me home at 1:00 a.m.

Fearful of getting caught, I snuck in quietly, went up to my room, hid Beth's clothes in my closet, and got into bed. Mother and Daddy let me sleep in the following morning, though it didn't do much to alleviate the hangover I suffered the entire next day. Weighing only one hundred pounds, I'm lucky I didn't die of alcohol poisoning that night.

I made good grades, ran track, and spent the rest of my waking hours with Bobby. He wasn't comfortable or welcome at our house because of Mother, so we hung out at his, where his mom frequently cooked us dinner and bananas Foster, my all-time favorite dessert.

Bobby played tennis competitively and was ranked one of the top ten junior players in the state of Texas. While his teenage hormones were raging, I was well behind in development and didn't have any urges to explore my sexuality. Bobby, on the other hand, was physically and sexually ahead of the curve, and had the drive to go along with it. He wasn't shy talking about his appendage and proudly tried to show *it* off, but the mere thought of *it* and sex terrified me.

He spent several months taunting me before I allowed him to have his way. Almost sixteen, I had no idea what we were doing, but we were having sex, nonetheless. Uncomfortable in my own skin and conflicted by actions against my moral compass, I didn't enjoy it, but the emotional reward of pleasing Bobby made the intimacy worthwhile.

Bobby lived life with great zeal! He studied hard, practiced hard, and played harder. Eventually overwhelmed by our relationship, school, and competitive tennis, he needed a break from the intensity of it all. That's when he starting hanging out regularly with one of his teammates. They were both driven athletes who could relate to the demands of their sport, so I accepted my replacement as a positive outlet for Bobby's stress.

I thought this friend was a well-liked, charismatic guy, but he turned out to be a delinquent, often in trouble with his parents, the school, and the police. Instead of doing homework after school, they were smoking pot and snorting cocaine three to four days a week. It wasn't until Bobby began failing academically and on the tennis court that I discovered what they were really doing. They tried to include me in their fun but quickly learned I disapproved of their illegal activity and the negative impact it was having on Bobby's life.

Bobby's and my relationship was forever changed from that point forward. He began hiding his whereabouts, leaving me at home in tears on many a scheduled date night while he partied with his new friends. Sometimes I'd hear from him later that evening with an ill-conceived excuse explaining his absence, and sometimes I wouldn't hear from him at all.

"Did we have plans?" he'd ask innocently, trying to diffuse the situation. "I was just hanging out at Gwen's house. You could have come over and watched a movie with us." Pleading, "Please don't be upset with me. I promise we weren't doing anything."

87

He'd spend hours trying to convince me he was changing his ways, and I hoped endlessly that he'd honor his promises. Sitting by the phone night after night waiting for it to ring, I worried for his safety, wondered when he might resurface again, and dreamed of ways to regain his love. I couldn't function or think of anything else.

Bobby developed a drug addiction and had the financial resources to support it, which only exacerbated the situation. He didn't see any problems with his "recreational" use, but his family and I saw it quite differently.

Having committed myself to Bobby both physically and emotionally for life when we started having sex, I wasn't prepared to walk away and didn't know what to do. We had talked of college, marriage, and babies, but the current arrangement wasn't what I had in mind. My entire existence was dependent upon him rescuing me from Mother, and in return, I was certain he needed me to save him from his destructive ways. It was the only path I could see to unconditional love.

I hadn't experimented with drugs other than alcohol and didn't understand Bobby's apparent dependence on them but knew he needed support to overcome it. As I fought for his recovery, I leaned on Beth and confided my feelings in her. She knew of my vulnerability, the intimacy, and my commitment to Bobby. As he worked to regain control of his life and I struggled to understand him, the three of us began doing things together again on a regular basis.

Bobby never stopped using drugs. Instead, he invented new ways to convince me, his family, and friends he had. Though his life was rooted in deceit, I was determined not to give up on him or our relationship. By then, he was frustrated with my cross-examinations, I was tired of his pathetic lies, and there wasn't much love left between us.

When we returned to school in the fall, I learned through the grapevine that Beth and Bobby were dating. He and I were still talking daily and hadn't officially broken up, though our relationship had effectively disintegrated, and Beth was sharing their communications under the pretense that she was supporting me.

Crushed by the news, I confronted them both in an effort to get the truth. I started with Bobby. Deep inside, I knew he had always been in love with her and would have been too proud to keep any secrets. When he avoided answering me and suggested I talk to her, I knew something was up.

"It seems you and Bobby have been spending a lot of time together lately," I commented to Beth. Prompting, "Has something changed?"

"No. I'm still trying to get you two back together," she claimed. "We're just friends."

"Then why won't he answer me when I ask if you two are dating?" I posed.

"He won't?" she replied with a nervous giggle. "I don't know."

After a long pause, she inquired hesitantly, "What if I was dating him? Would you still be my friend?"

"Are you in love with him?" I questioned with reservation, not wanting to hear the answer.

"Yes," she admitted. Before the conversation was over, Beth explained that they had been friends but their feelings were too strong to deny any longer. However, they were both worried about losing my friendship and wanted to make sure I was OK with their dating before going public. I didn't need more detail, but Beth's guilty conscience led her to confess that they'd also been sleeping together.

In an instant, I lost my two best friends and the hope of one day escaping Mother. Overcome with devastation, I cried hysterically for weeks. I didn't have anyone to talk to or console me because I wasn't going to tell Daddy or Lillian tales of sex, drugs, and betrayal at the young age of sixteen.

The impact of this physical isolation and emotional abandonment was profound. "Something must be terribly wrong with me if my own mother and only two friends deserted me," I thought. "I must deserve to be treated this way." Feeling I had no reason to live, I lost weight and interest in school, activities, and life. I spent endless nights tossing and turning in bed, questioning what I could have done to earn their love. I stayed in that dark place for a couple of months before deciding I couldn't live there any longer. I forgave Beth and Bobby, wished them all the best, and moved past their disloyalty and deceit, though I never trusted either again.

By the time we graduated, Bobby's health was in danger, and he was wanted by his neighbors for stealing, by the police for possessing and selling illegal substances, and by several drug dealers for debts owed. Watching the devastating effect the addiction had on him, his family, and his life, I vowed to stay completely clear of drugs.

I matured physically my junior year and looked and felt more like my peers. While Beth and Bobby dated, I made new friends and developed a social life. We enjoyed innocent fun mostly, but occasionally drank alcohol.

One night, we'd been playing pool and drinking screwdrivers at one friend's house before moving to another's for a late-night movie and sleepover. Upon arrival, someone suggested munchies, and I offered to make a trip to the nearby 7-Eleven, the same one I had frequented since childhood.

En route, I approached a red light, stopped, and looked in both directions for traffic. While looking right, my foot slowly slipped off the brake and I began rolling into the intersection. I turned back to the left just in time to see the lights of a car T-bone my driver's door. It knocked me into passing lanes of traffic. Thankfully, the streets were barren except for a police officer in the oncoming lane, who witnessed the entire incident and came to my aid.

Extremely shaken and immediately sobered, I jumped out of my car and ran to check on the other driver. The front end of her car was damaged and my car was totaled, but neither of us was badly injured. I didn't feel drunk and neither the officer nor the other driver suspected my drinking, but my friends were amazed I had survived the crash. Having retraced my steps when I didn't return from the store, they rescued me and took me back to the gathering.

By the time I called home to let Mother and Daddy know what had happened, it was almost 2:00 a.m. Daddy was used to being awakened by clients from jail on occasion and answered the phone on the first ring. I was in the middle of my explanation when he stopped me, asked if I were OK, and offered to come get me. The details of the accident were unimportant to him, but my safe return was his utmost concern.

In the meantime, Mother had gotten out of bed and picked up the call from a landline in another room. She interrupted the conversation with loud interjections, "You didn't clean your room before you left!" "You did not have my permission to be out!" "It serves you right!" "You'll be punished when you get home!"

She hung up the phone without hearing of my condition or expressing concern for my wellbeing. It didn't feel like an appropriate response under the circumstances, but then again I never considered Mother's behavior "normal."

I had the exact opposite experience with Lillian when we'd been involved in a wreck years earlier. I was about three years old, riding loose in the back seat of her car, when a diaper truck rear-ended us. It shattered the back window, sprayed glass on the seat where I had been sitting, and knocked me to the floorboard. Lillian grabbed me from the car, hugged me, and assured me I was going to be alright. While I screamed bloody murder, she repeated the same thing she said every time I got hurt, "You're OK, baby. I'll take care of you. I love you!"

When Mother picked me up the following morning, she blamed and lectured me some more before telling me I was grounded for a month. Then, she didn't speak to me afterwards for a week. Daddy, on the other hand, took me to the tow yard that evening to check out the damage my car had suffered. Upon discovering the driver's door smashed in almost to the center console, we wept considering the tragic ending that had been averted.

I stayed out of trouble from then on but wasn't engaged academically. Exhausted by trying to please Mother and constantly failing, I needed a break. Though I had once been a star student, my efforts waned and my grades dropped significantly in one year. I fell from the top 10 percent of my class to the top 25 percent.

Work was the only commitment that provided me an escape, so I signed up at a nearby department store for as many hours as I could manage my junior and senior years. Earning money for clothing, necessities, gas, and entertainment expenses, I gained some financial independence and was able to buy the things our family could not otherwise afford.

When it came time to apply for college, Mother and Daddy offered to send me to Southern Methodist University, their alma mater. It would have afforded me an excellent education, but it was three blocks from home and the offer was contingent upon me living there. I didn't consider it a viable option for one second, as I couldn't have imagined anything worse than staying with Mother a day longer than absolutely necessary.

My good friend Charlotte and I made a pact to go to college together. We had hopes of attending Stephen's College, a private girls' school in Columbia, Missouri, but when she didn't get in, we agreed on the only school that had accepted both of us, the University of Arkansas. Having initially applied there only as a backup, I never dreamed it was where I'd actually land. Nevertheless, I wasn't reneging on my commitment and began making the necessary preparations to fulfill my end of the deal.

Two weeks before school started, Charlotte backed out and enrolled in a community college in Dallas. There was no time for me to change plans at that point, so I was left to go it alone. Though I'd not visited the campus in Fayetteville and didn't know what to expect, I was elated to finally be leaving home.

Daddy offered to drive with me and stay for a few days to help get me settled. I packed my car with all my worldly possessions the night before our departure and was ready to leave early the following morning. When I stepped outside, I found my belongings strewn all over the driveway and Mother reorganizing my trunk. She didn't like the way I had done it and was certain she could do a better job. Organizing my life her way, as she always had, was her attempt at sending me off with my best foot forward.

I secretly vowed never to return to Dallas except for occasional visits to see Daddy, but Mother had something else in mind. Because I hadn't lined up a job my first summer, she made me come back for work. Sanger Harris, a specialty department store in the Highland Park Village, rehired me, and I spent as much time there as possible. When I returned to college for my sophomore year, I found a job, several of them, and never lived at home again.

OBSESSIVE LOVE

IN THE FALL of 1982, I began college at the University of Arkansas in Fayetteville. Several girls I knew from Highland Park were attending, but my best friend and confidant, Charlotte, was not. Having been assigned a roommate and placed in a sketchy dorm across campus from my high school classmates, I feared the worst.

My roommate certainly didn't look or act like anybody I knew from home. A hippy from California with stringy, long, blond hair and fair, freckled skin, she didn't wear makeup or a bra and dressed in somewhat revealing, loose-fitting clothing. Though I was confident we could get along, she left school due to illness before we had the chance.

I wondered if it had been the funny cigarettes she chain-smoked daily, as they filled our small room with smoke and the stench of cloves. Oozing out from under our door, a thick fog contaminated the entire dorm wing. It invaded my respiratory cavities and permeated my bedding, clothing, and hair.

The second semester brought a new roommate. Though she appeared to be similar to the well-bred girls from my high school, she didn't act as respectable as she looked. Pretty face and hair, well dressed and manicured, she skipped class, partied every night, and ordered late-night pizza. She usually passed out before it came, leaving me to pay the delivery man and wrangle with her later for reimbursement.

I met my best college friend, Suzanne, in that dorm, too. She, her roommate Lindsey, and I developed a friendship over meals in the cafeteria. Practically the only girls there who dressed up for school, we were instantly drawn to one another. As it turned out, they were more like the girls I knew from Dallas than I had imagined. Lindsey was from a prominent doctor's family in small-town Arkansas, and Suzanne lived a few miles away in a tiny rural community. It wasn't long before they included me in their weekend trips home to spend time with family.

They had the same luxuries as my friends back home—nice cars, clothing, homes, vacations, and disposable income. The affluence was nothing new to me, but I thought Suzanne was kidding when she told me her dad developed and farmed land for a living. All the wealthy people I knew had professional jobs: lawyers, doctors, and company presidents who wore coat and tie, and worked in tall buildings. I was surprised to learn that physical labor could provide a quality of living more privileged than mine.

The Greek system at the university had a significant presence, but I wasn't prepared for the formal admissions process called Rush. Having planned to attend a girls' college that didn't have sororities and fraternities, I hadn't obtained the required recommendations from alumni members. It would have been difficult for me anyway because Mother didn't have friends to write on my behalf, and even if she had, the deadlines for submitting them in a timely manner had already passed.

Aunt Dee Dee and Grandmom were both Kappa Kappa Gammas and would have been ecstatic for me to join their sorority. Certain I was unworthy of their approval, I dreamed of it but never considered it a realistic possibility. How could I expect to be accepted by girls who didn't know me when I had trouble making friends amongst my peers in Highland Park?

Suzanne and Lindsey joined sororities while I made friends in several houses and became a little sister to a popular fraternity. Not being affiliated with a sorority, I could attend all the Greek functions as a guest, which was better for me than being limited to just one.

After Christmas break, one of my favorite sororities invited me to join through Spring Rush, which was a less-formal affair open to only those houses that had available spots. Through Grandmom, Mother caught wind of my desire to pledge and asked her, Aunt Dee Dee, and one of Amanda's friend's moms to write recommendations for the Kappa house. Unfortunately, they weren't participating in Rush, and I wasn't a good candidate for anyone because my grades had been below a 2.0 GPA my first semester in school.

Upon discovering her efforts were for naught, Mother became enraged. She had extended herself by asking for three unrequited favors that would have to be returned, because that's how her score keeping system worked. I had never known her to admit wrongdoing about anything, so I knew she had to find someone or something to blame. She chose me.

"You are a disgrace to me and my family. If you ever do anything like that again, I'll disown you!" she vowed. In a nasty letter, she told me I was a waste of her time and energy. Furthermore, she said, "If you *assume*, you make an ass out of u and me." I was shocked by her offensive tone and foul language, but didn't understand what she meant. Was she implying that *I* had assumed something? If so, *what*? Vengeance was her nature and always had been. It wasn't surprising, just extremely hurtful.

Academics in college were a challenge for me, as they had been my last two years in high school. Capability and rigor were not the issue, rather my inability to balance studies with activities. For the first time in my life, I was completely free from Mother's critical eye and controlling ways. I had many friends and a thriving social calendar and accepted every engagement that presented itself, which didn't leave much time for school or studying. I stayed out until 2:00 a.m. several nights a week and skipped half of my classes. Because I absorbed most of my knowledge by listening and taking notes, this routine did not benefit me academically.

If I weren't perfectly dressed and presentable, I'd drive my friends to their classes and cruise around campus, music blasting, while waiting for them to get out. My car's custom stereo system, with six speakers and a booster, could be heard from blocks away. Like Daddy's loud music at home, the noise distracted me from my unhappiness and provided me a sense of calm.

While my social life flourished and my studies suffered, I worried constantly about getting to class and making good grades. However, I was incapable of controlling my impulses and rarely honored my academic commitments. The internal turmoil created stress, which caused intestinal upset. On one occasion, the unpleasant symptoms were accompanied by sharp pains in my abdomen. After a trip to an emergency clinic and some noninvasive tests, a doctor concluded I had ulcers, potentially the bleeding kind. He prescribed medication and a special diet, which thankfully healed the condition.

Grandmom considered disposable income part of a girl's college experience and sent me envelopes of cash on a regular basis. Fearing funds from a check would take too long to access, she mailed bundles of twenties, three hundred dollars at a time. I spent most of it at a clothing store on the downtown square, trying to uphold the image of a Highland Park girl.

The friends I hung out with didn't use drugs, but we drank alcohol socially. While it was never my intent to get drunk, I'd consume until I couldn't drink anymore and wake the following morning with no memory of the previous night's events. I found myself unable to manage my intake, just as I had at the Homecoming dance in high school. I noticed others didn't have the same problem, but that didn't stop me from repeating this pattern each time I drank.

One night after having had way too much, I snuck out of a party and drove through a fast-food restaurant to pick up some late-night munchies. On my way to a friend's place afterwards, I attempted to make a short cut through a residential property. After turning off a winding, two-lane country road into a narrow driveway with deep culverts on either side, I drove past the front door and came to a complete stop in the side yard when my axle became lodged on a tree stump. With the front end of my car suspended in the air, my back tires spun out of control as I floored the gas, kicking up earth and spraying it across the yard.

While the engine revved and music blared, the lady of the house came running out to investigate the ruckus. Still half asleep in a sheer nightgown, she tried talking to me, but I was unintelligible by that point. She removed me from my car, took the keys, and drove me to my friend's apartment a few blocks away.

I awoke the next morning fully dressed, with hair and makeup almost untouched. Horribly hung over, I stayed curled up on the bathroom floor near the toilet in case I got sick. Having no recollection of the previous night's activities, I assumed one of my friends had driven me home from the party. When I couldn't find my keys, I called around but no one knew how I had gotten there.

Meanwhile, my friends heard the doorbell and peeked out the window to find an unfamiliar, scraggly woman and her two young children at the door. Pounding, she shouted, "Open up! I know that drunk girl is in there."

They opened the door to a tale of events, how I had driven into her backyard and landed atop a tree stump, and how she and her husband had dropped me off at the apartment. Knowing I'd have no idea where my car was, they removed it from the stump and drove it to the complex the following morning. She returned the keys, left her name and address, and my friends thanked her for the good deed.

As soon as the door closed, the laughter began. Though I'd heard an unfamiliar voice at the door, I couldn't decipher the conversation from the bathroom and didn't know the reason for the commotion. My friends described the poor woman and her two children, and explained what I had done. I knew it wasn't a laughing matter but we couldn't help but snicker at the absurdity of what had transpired. Only God knows how I escaped that night without an arrest or serious injury to myself, my car, or Vaquita's family and property.

The next time I had a car accident, I wasn't quite so lucky. With dismal night vision and remnants of alcohol in my system, I drove home one evening with a friend along the main thoroughfare through campus. I knew it like the back of my hand but wasn't prepared for the roadwork that had begun while I was out of town. As I crossed a small bridge and rounded a dark corner, we were engaged in laughter when I came upon a road closure sign and heavy equipment barricading the construction site.

Suddenly, Michelle's head jerked forward and she screamed at the top of her lungs, "Anna, watch out!"

It was too late. There wasn't enough time to react. I slammed on the brakes, but our family's van skidded head-on into a bulldozer. Michelle sprained her arm and I hit my head on the steering wheel.

After making sure she was alright, I went to ring the doorbell of the house across the street for help. Though I didn't know it at the time, blood was gushing from my forehead and running down my face. It wasn't until the residents opened the door and responded with horror that I realized something was wrong.

As the good Samaritans cleaned my wound in the bathroom, the police showed up and escorted me outside, where a small crowd had gathered. I knew the accident was more about my distraction and poor night vision than the one beer I'd consumed earlier that evening, but I was petrified of the consequences nonetheless.

While sitting in the front seat of an officer's squad car, explaining the circumstances of events, I could see an acquaintance motioning to me. "I need to talk to one of my friends," I announced, without appreciation for the severity of the situation.

"You can't right now. You're in custody," the officer replied firmly.

"Then I'll keep one foot in the car and one foot out," I defiantly declared before opening the door and proceeding without approval.

"Don't say another word and ask to be taken to the emergency room immediately," was the advice given, and I followed.

Upon arrival, the hospital called Daddy and he insisted I refuse both the breath and blood alcohol tests. As the doctors stitched up the inch-and-a-half, smile-shaped gash on my forehead with three layers of stitches, the officer waited outside the operating room for my release. He didn't have cause to hold me at that point, and I was allowed to leave in the care of a close friend.

My law instructor at the University pleaded to have the charges reduced to careless driving. Besides a nasty scar, Michelle's bruised arm, and a wrecked van, I escaped the precarious incident otherwise unscathed.

Though I was connected socially, I was failing in school. I had aspirations of obtaining an undergraduate degree but didn't know exactly how I was going to get it or what I wanted to do with it. Grandmom offered her opinion, "A business degree will provide a solid foundation for any career." With dreams of owning a clothing store, I could see the value in it; however, I enjoyed my freedom too much to approach school seriously.

My sophomore year, I met Derek, a six foot, two inch tall, blond, athletic junior. His rosy complexion, boyish grin, and piercing blue eyes put me in a trance at first glance. Some considered him a "player," but I was mesmerized by his shameless charm. He was from a good family, attended a private boy's high school in Little Rock, belonged to a fraternity and local church, and was driven academically. I admired his ambition to become a highly-successful, independent businessman, like Daddy.

Having recently split with a serious girlfriend whom he'd dated for several years in high school and college, Derek was uncertain if he wanted to get back together with her or date others. It wasn't completely his decision to make, as she was the one calling the shots. While he was healing from her rejection and considering his options, we hung out together, taking and kissing for hours. I offered empathy and acceptance as he struggled with his emotions.

"Have you ever been in love?" he asked.

"Of course," I answered, sharing details of Bobby and his and Beth's betrayal.

"I thought Kim and I were in love, too, when she suggested we start dating other people," he explained with a look of confusion. "How could she just change her mind like that?"

"Maybe she's testing your love," I offered. "If that's the case, I'm sure she'll figure it out and come back."

"I can't take her back now," he retorted. "I'm not going to let her control me like that."

"What if I talk to her and find out what's going on?" I replied. "Will that help?" Before long, I found myself trying to get Derek and Kim back together, in an effort to please him. Then, I spent most of that year looking for other opportunities to make him happy. I comforted him, helped him in school, and bought him gifts. For Christmas, I asked my family for money and spent $1,000 buying him the finest clothing money could buy, mostly from the Ralph Lauren store in the Highland Park Village. He declined the gesture but I wouldn't take no for an answer.

While he may have been uncertain of his feelings for her, I was sure of my love for him. My heart and mind raced with excitement as I fantasized about the two of us being together. I followed him to the clubs and fraternity parties, keeping a watchful eye and waiting for an invitation at the end of the evening. When he didn't extend one, I'd proposition him, "Are you coming back to my place or am I going to yours?" In our intimate moments, Derek was responsive, caring, and gentle, which made me feel safe and loved on the deepest level.

Though he didn't think of me as family, I considered him part of mine and was excited for my sister Amanda to meet him. She was a senior in high school at the time but came to Fayetteville occasionally on the weekends to visit my friends and me. She enjoyed the college atmosphere and the attention she attracted as the new girl in town.

One night, Amanda and I hung out with Derek and his friends in the clubs until 1:00 a.m. before returning to my apartment. I retired to bed only to be awakened a short while later by a roommate reporting, "Amanda just screeched out of the parking lot in your car."

Knowing she had been drinking and was in no condition to drive, I worried sick for her safe return. "Did she say where she was going?" I asked frantically.

"No, I don't think she saw me but I watched her leave," my friend replied.

While sitting by the front door, I was roused by another roommate several hours later. I pleaded to borrow her car and she reluctantly agreed. Almost morning by then, I retraced every step Amanda and I had taken that night, but I couldn't locate her or my car anywhere. Desperate, I drove to Derek's apartment at 5:30 a.m. to involve him in the search.

As I pulled up, I noticed my car in the parking lot. Angry, frantic, and confused, I knocked loudly on the door. No one answered. I knocked again, no answer. With both fists, I banged as hard as I could. Screaming, I cried, "Open the door! It's Anna."

Derek's roommate Jeff cracked the door ajar. I pushed my way inside and discovered my sister, asleep on their couch. He immediately began explaining, "Amanda was drunk when she showed up, so Derek and I put her to bed to keep her out of harm's way."

Noticeably uncomfortable with the situation, he didn't need to justify their actions to me, because I knew exactly what had happened. I had witnessed it numerous times. Amanda loved having her way with the boys and she especially loved a good challenge. The winning was so gratifying that it didn't matter if she had to sleep with strangers or steal a friend's boyfriend to get what she wanted. In fact, it was almost better that way.

Though I knew she was indifferent to what others thought of her or her indiscretions, I didn't realize she felt that way about me. Suddenly, it was crystal clear.

Derek poked his head out of his bedroom, "Is everything OK?"

"No, it's not!" I shouted without explanation.

I woke Amanda from her drunken slumber and escorted her back to my apartment. She packed her things and we left for the airport within the hour, as originally planned. Traumatized by her betrayal, I couldn't speak. I cried the entire two-hour drive to the Tulsa International Airport while she remained silent, offering no explanation or apology.

Amanda's and my relationship was irrevocably changed. Thankfully, she didn't succeed in sleeping with Derek, but my awareness of her intentions and lack of integrity completely dissolved my trust, respect, and loyalty. The reality that Amanda had pursued the love of my life was unconscionable. "I was her sister, her own flesh and blood. Did that not mean anything to her?" I wondered.

The following day, Derek apologized for not calling me upon my sister's arrival. "I'm not sure why she came to my apartment," he questioned, "but I think she was after Rick." Looking squarely into my eyes, he vowed, "Nothing happened. I promise. I would never do that!"

Derek had always been loving and kind, but we weren't dating, so I didn't get the respect of a girlfriend. We continued meeting secretly through the end of that year before he started seeing other people without telling me. My feelings were hurt for many reasons, mostly because he didn't acknowledge me or the connection we shared publically.

While this blatant disregard was hurtful, the loss of intimacy fueling my soul was life-threatening. I spent many sleepless nights searching for answers and two days in the fetal position on the bathroom floor, retching, throwing up bile and foam. I drove for hours on end, listening to music that expressed my sorrow and distracted me from thoughts of despair.

"Why doesn't he love me?" I struggled to comprehend. "What can I do to earn his love?"

Willing to accept whatever I could get to avoid losing Derek, I remained at his disposal, both physically and emotionally, night and day. My friends were frustrated by my desperation, but I couldn't change my pathetic behavior. Thankfully for both of us, he didn't allow that scenario to continue much longer, though my feelings remained strong. I'd drive by his and his friends' houses, around campus, and to the gym just to catch a glimpse of him or his car. Knowing I could find him brought great comfort and relief.

Once, I left a note on his car, "I love you, miss you, and can't live without you any longer!" It was an inside joke from a *Cosmopolitan* quiz, but I was never brave enough to question the status of our relationship. When running into him, I'd simply ask, "How's life treating you?" He was always pleasant in return, "Hope you're doing well. Take care!"

Too busy stalking Derek and looking for ways to earn his love, I failed to attend classes or study, and my grades reflected it. I knew this situation was unacceptable, but I was incapable of concentrating on schoolwork and managing my emotions at the same time. Aware others seemed to handle these tasks effortlessly, I questioned why they overwhelmed me.

By the middle of my sophomore year, I was placed on academic suspension and required to take a year-long break from school. Fortunately, there was a job opening at a local clothing shop. The owner, John, a young man who'd grown up in his family's retail business, was looking for someone to take over the women's department. An astute businessman who prided himself on knowing his customers, their trade and their purchasing power, he served a wealthy community in the land of Walmart, Tyson Foods, and J. B. Hunt Trucking. I was one of his best customers thanks to my love of fine clothing and Grandmom's generosity.

As I got to know John, I shared my dream of having my own clothing store with him and inquired about his background in the dry goods industry. He spoke of his family's history and his personal entrepreneurial experience. Through the good times and bad, his life was both enriched and burdened by being a sole proprietor, but he wouldn't have had it any other way.

He approached me with an invitation to interview for the job. It would supply hands-on experience, beyond academic knowledge, doing exactly what was required to run a retail business, including travel to New York and Dallas buying markets. I knew it was the perfect opportunity and frankly, the only option I had at the time.

He offered the job, and I accepted. At the young age of nineteen, I managed the women's department and was granted the freedom to make choices that impacted the company's success or failure. John was a great mentor who took me under his wing and exposed me to his knowledge and infectious love of the clothing business. I thought it especially generous of him given my youth and non-familial status.

As a self-sufficient, career-minded individual, I no longer received regular monthly income from Daddy or Grandmom. I budgeted and managed my own finances and didn't like the idea of throwing away money on rent when house payments were comparable. With Daddy's help on the down payment, my full-time employment, and a favorable recommendation from John, I qualified for a mortgage all by myself.

I began researching the local real estate market. Based on my findings, I selected a few desirable areas I thought warranted investment and sought the services of a Realtor. We set off in search of my perfect house, and before long, she found it. The house had good bones and a great floor plan but was in desperate need of cosmetic repair. Having watched my parents renovate our childhood home, I felt prepared for the task.

Truth be known, I had no idea what tremendous work lay ahead of me, though I quickly learned the job at hand wasn't quite as easy as I had envisioned. Thankfully, John, his wife, and my co-workers were there to help. They organized weekend work parties, where we removed carpeting from atop hardwood floors along with leftover tack strips, nails, staples, and glued-down padding.

After the group projects ceased, I began stripping wallpaper and woodwork and painting the interior one room at a time. It took months to complete, not weeks as I had planned, leaving me in a continual state of disarray. The paint remover I used on the wood windows left such a mess that my fussy neighbor thought I had intentionally frosted my windowpanes in preparation for the holidays...in July.

I loved my little 1,200 square-foot home. It had everything I needed, including a living room, dining room, kitchen, utility room, two bedrooms, and one bathroom. The rooms were good sized. There was storage in the attic, a large backyard, and a detached, one-car garage. The hardwood floors, moldings, old wood windows, and a covered front porch gave it the charm I desired. The work and expense were never ending, but Daddy and Grandmom stepped in financially when something beyond my capabilities needed repair, and Mother contributed to the landscaping and furniture annually.

While I felt safe there, Daddy worried about me and thought I needed protection. I considered an alarm system, but he had something else in mind. Without my knowledge, he sought a protector to watch over my little house and me. A twelve-week-old boxer puppy I named Ginger, she was a beautiful, flashy, brindled female with perfect markings and expressive eyes.

Ginger went everywhere with me in the front seat of my old BMW 320i. She sat in it as if she were human; bottom in the seat, shoulders and head straight forward, eyes on the road. We were inseparable, my seventy-five-pound faithful companion and I.

I fed Ginger only the finest meals, a mixture of uncooked ground chuck, raw egg, and cottage cheese with a splash of specialty dog food purchased at the feed store. When I couldn't afford anything besides macaroni and cheese, Ginger continued eating like a queen. She was from a long line of champions, had a lustrous coat, and was full of muscle and character. "Talking" with humanlike qualities, she attracted attention wherever we went.

While working at the clothing store, remodeling my house, and caring for Ginger, I had little time for anything else. However, my friends were invaluable to me, so I spent as much time with them as my schedule permitted. Sharon, a devoted wife and mother of two beautiful little girls, started working with me shortly after I took the job. Lonely for adult interaction, she didn't need the money but enjoyed the company and conversation. Though she was ten years older than me, we developed a close friendship that crossed age barriers. Observing her with her husband and family, I learned about commitment, marriage, and parenting.

John, Sharon, and I traveled to Dallas together for market. He made arrangements to stay in a hotel while I offered for Sharon to stay with me at Mother's house. There was plenty of room and it didn't make sense to pay additional lodging expenses when it wasn't necessary.

Sharon mentioned she was slightly allergic to cats, but she had never been exposed to five indoor cats at one time. Although Mother offered her the bedroom assured to be 100% free of allergens, Sharon had a serious allergic reaction upon arrival. I took her to the emergency room, where they administered medication to stop the asthma attack and provided a prescription to prevent another one. After waiting several hours for the inflammation in her lungs to dissipate, we returned to the house. I was afraid for Sharon to stay there, but she wasn't worried. Mortified by what had happened, I apologized profusely for what we later referred to as the "cat attack."

The following morning, Sharon and I awoke to Mother's account of events. "I don't understand. There's no way my home could have made you sick," she asserted. "It's perfectly clean." In a patronizing tone, she extended, "I'm so sorry for you, Sharon. You must be more sensitive to cats than you realize." Though Mother tried to convince us of her way of thinking, we both knew quite differently.

I worked at the clothing store for more than a year before realizing the hours and responsibility of the retail business were not for me. During that time, Derek and I maintained a distant friendship, though we didn't connect physically as we had in the past. He tolerated my psychotic behavior, calling and showing up unannounced, but had moved on long ago and I knew it. He eventually graduated and relocated, which put an end to the mania.

Once my academic suspension lifted, I returned to school to complete my education. With a newfound determination to succeed, I declared a business major in finance with a minor in accounting, combining my interest in real estate with my love for math. I attended classes and studied regularly, making As while holding down three part-time jobs to maintain the lifestyle I had created for Ginger and myself.

Before graduating from college, I lost Lillian. I travelled home to be with her when I first learned she was in the hospital, but no one in our family realized how sick she was. By the time I reached her, all the nicotine filters I had purchased in my youth and prayers couldn't save her from the lung cancer that took her life the following week. Nevertheless, she maintained her cheery disposition until the very end. I was distraught by her death but thankful to have seen her and told her I loved her one last time.

Our family attended Lillian's funeral. "The only white people in a sea of 'colored folk,'" she would have said. While Daddy, my siblings, and I stayed after the service to talk with her family and friends, Mother removed herself and waited from afar. With hands gripped behind her back and feet planted firmly on the ground, her body swayed to and fro as she stared catatonically into space.

She was surprised at how deeply affected my siblings and I were by Lillian's death, as she considered and treated Lillian like an employee, not a family member. However, it was not the first time Mother had encountered our strong feelings. In our youth, Daddy attempted to

113

scale back Lillian's hours to three days a week while struggling to support our family. To sustain herself and her children and stay close to us, she took another job working two days a week down the street. We were miserable without her and rode our bikes to visit on off days. Within a couple of months, she told Daddy she missed us immensely and wanted to return five days a week regardless of the pay received. He welcomed her back and all was right in our world again.

Lillian was the only caretaker any of us had known, and none was prepared to live without her, especially David. He withdrew after her death, so much so that he was diagnosed with clinical depression and admitted to a residential treatment facility, where he remained under a doctor's care for longer than a month.

If Lillian was my mom and guardian angel, then Grandmom was my protector. She provided me comfort, support, and unconditional love in good times and bad. A beacon of kindness, compassion, and wisdom, she was the one I depended on for guidance and strength. I talked to her weekly, at a minimum, and visited three to four times a year throughout my life.

When Grandmom's health began to fail from complications of diabetes, I heard from her less often. Shortly after noticing a significant drop in communication, I received word that Mother had been summoned to her bedside. I called Houston immediately, but Mother claimed Grandmom was disoriented and couldn't come to the phone, assuring me there'd be other opportunities. I could hear her voice in the background and pleaded with

Mother, but she refused to let me talk to her over the next several days.

Unfortunately, I was unable to reach Grandmom before she died. While I was comforted knowing she knew how much I loved her, I regretted not being able to tell her myself one last time. She and I had a special bond, a connection Mother was incapable of understanding or having with anyone.

Just as Mother had interfered in Daddy's and my relationship by limiting our contact, she denied me access to Grandmom in her final hours. Whether these actions were intentional or not was irrelevant because the outcome was the same. Mother's egotism, disregard for my feelings, and compulsive control deprived me of love and altered the course of my life.

FALLING
INTO PLACE

AFTER GRADUATING FROM college with a business degree in real estate finance, I took a retail sales job in Kansas City, Missouri. It was a step down from the buying and management positions I had held previously, but it allowed me to pursue a more diverse single life than Fayetteville had to offer. Still uncertain of my career path, I planned a year off before completing my education, either a graduate or law school degree.

Phillip, a colleague of mine from John's clothier happened to be moving to Kansas City at the same time. I hadn't known him socially because he was two years younger in school, but he seemed like a nice guy and I was happy to have a familiar face in a foreign place. A trust-fund baby from a respectable Oklahoma family, Phillip was opening a franchise burger restaurant with his family's support. While he wasn't in business yet, he was supposed to be managing the facility build-out and startup

117

operations. In actuality, he played golf more than he worked and frequented the bars late night.

Phillip knew several guys and gals in Kansas City, making him the perfect partner for a new girl in town. Consequently, I found myself spending most of my free time with him. In our togetherness, he was under the mistaken impression I had moved there to date him, though nothing could have been further from the truth. I wasn't attracted to him physically; he was short with dark brown hair and eyes and an oily complexion, like Mother. He was arrogant and abrasive and his behavior was appalling when he didn't get his way. Regardless of what he thought, friendship and geography were the only reasons for our relationship, but I couldn't convince him of that.

The best thing about Phillip was his family, particularly his mother. She was an elegant, generous, and socially acceptable woman, the mother I always wanted but never had. His father, a reputable doctor, established a successful healthcare facility in Oklahoma, earning wealth and the respect of his peers and their community. Phillip and an older sister attended elite schools and lived charmed childhoods.

Although he had the fairytale life I dreamed of for my own family, I didn't seek partners for financial gain, rather compatibility. I never understood how money could be more important than love, but I was aware others, including Mother and Amanda, felt very differently.

As I grew to appreciate Phillip as a friend, we slowly began a dating relationship. While I enjoyed his childlike spirit and sarcastic sense of humor, I was continually frustrated by his lack of responsibility and ambition. We dated off and on for more than a year before he broke off the relationship. Though it hadn't been necessarily rewarding, I wasn't ready to give up on the dream of finding love and became disillusioned by another unwanted ending.

Afterwards, I moved back to my little house in Fayetteville and continued my education as originally planned. To increase my chances of being accepted into the University's law program, I spent a year taking classes to raise my GPA, as it had been damaged almost beyond repair my first three semesters in school. The application process included an interview with the dean of the law school. That's when I learned my admission had been denied.

With a stalled career path and several failed relationships by the age of twenty-seven, it seemed my hopes for a successful life were eluding me. In contrast, however, my friends were well on the way to fulfilling theirs.

I maintained connections in Kansas City, including one with my retail sales manager, Julie. She had retired from the clothing industry and was in the business of restoring and selling antiques, her lifelong passion. We were like sisters but there was little space for me in her collectible-filled Tudor home, so I usually stayed overnight at Kristen's apartment when I came to town. She worked at a boutique patent firm, where I had been a paralegal's assistant, and socialized with my former co-workers.

Six months after my return to Arkansas, Kristen mentioned that one of the attorneys we knew, Rob, was interested in asking me out. Not having seen or heard from him in the two years since my departure from the firm, I found this news hard to believe. Besides, I didn't know him well. He'd say hello when I passed by his office but the conversation never lasted long. He was unusually quiet and I didn't want to overstay my welcome.

Kristen and Rob made plans for the three of us to attend a professional hockey game on one of my visits. Though she tried convincing me of his interest beforehand, he spent the entire game engaging with her and ignoring me. We stopped by his home later that evening, where I noticed two tickets to a charity ball openly displayed on his dining room table. If her assertions were true, as she claimed, I was certain it would have been the perfect opportunity for him to ask me out on a date.

No invitation followed, and Kristen didn't speak of Rob again. Having dismissed the idea completely, I was surprised when he called several months later. We talked about his work, my school, and the hockey game before he inquired, "Do you have plans to return to town again soon? If so, would you like to attend the Jerry Seinfeld show on Thursday evening, April 22?"

The delivery was somewhat awkward but I replied, "Sounds great! Thanks for asking."

Rob told me later he thought a long-distance invitation would be a conversation starter, never imagining I'd accept. Obviously, he didn't know me well. I rearranged my work schedule, skipped two days of school, and drove four hours to Kansas City the morning of the show. He picked me up at Kristen's that evening and treated me to the performance and a nice dinner afterwards, where we enjoyed good conversation and easy laughter. At the end of the date, he walked me to the door, thanked me, and left without a hug or kiss goodnight.

"Maybe he just wanted to be friends," I thought, which would have been fine with me. I contemplated our evening on the drive home the following day and couldn't decide if Rob liked me or not. Furthermore, I didn't know how I felt about him. He seemed like a really nice guy, quiet and reserved, with a dry sense of humor. Average height and slight build with dirty blond hair, he looked like a typical mid-westerner, unassuming and conservative in manner and appearance.

Rob began calling twice a week, but he didn't say much, which left me unsure of his intentions. Julie called, too, with news of a job opportunity in Kansas City. Her close friend and former Limited colleague, Barb, was opening a specialty home furnishings store and interior design business, and was looking for a manager. Barb would oversee company operations, store inventory, and the design studio. Julie would travel to Europe to buy antiques and the manager would supervise the retail business and be an assistant to Barb, as I had done previously with John. Given my work background and love for design, it was a match made in heaven.

After interviewing, I received an offer and gladly accepted. Once again, it happened quickly and the timing and fit couldn't have been more perfect. The door to my postgraduate education had been temporarily closed, I had a co-worker in Fayetteville wanting to buy my little house, and Rob and I were beginning a new relationship in

Kansas City. It seemed as if things were finally falling into place, as I had always hoped they would.

While I remained uncertain whether Rob and I were friends or more, he offered to help me move, which seemed a positive gesture in either direction. He and Kristen traveled to Fayetteville together, and the three of us spent the day packing and loading my belongings into a Ryder rental truck. From there, Rob, Ginger, and I followed Kristen to my new residence in Overland Park, Kansas. A two-story townhouse with a large grassy area out back and an unfinished basement, it was the ideal place for me and my best girl to call home.

Rob and I hung out together regularly, but he still hadn't kissed me a month after the move. It was in direct contrast with what I had heard of his promiscuity from one of the paralegals in the office. Rumor was he drank heavily, socialized in the bars, and entertained women after hours. In fact, one girl talked openly of their wild sexual encounters, knocking over furniture and straddling gear shifts, but it was difficult for me to imagine that scenario with what I knew of him. Reserving judgment, I waited until I had enough information to form my own opinion.

The Rob I knew was the exact opposite: a quiet, shy, intellectual guy who didn't socialize much or drink at all. When sharing his past, he explained he drank in college and his early professional career but was incapable of controlling how much he drank and stopped. "I woke late one morning and discovered I'd slept through an important client meeting. My secretary had been trying to reach me for hours, but I didn't hear the phone. It was almost noon. That's when I decided the drinking had to end," he claimed. It had been more than two years since his last drink. I could see his present behavior corresponded with his account and had no reason to doubt him otherwise.

Rob grew up in small-town Nebraska in a Catholic family with traditional values. His father was the town's general practitioner and his mother stayed home to raise the children. Rob was the oldest son, behind a big sister, followed by a brother and a baby girl.

He attended the University of Nebraska, where he joined a fraternity and served as president of the house his senior year. Graduating with a degree in mechanical engineering, he took a job in Washington, D.C., where he worked by day and put himself through law school at night. Upon graduation, he accepted a position with a highly regarded firm, purchased a condo in Alexandria, Virginia, and spent time with friends on Capitol Hill.

After realizing the fast-paced life of law and politics wasn't his speed, he moved back to the Midwest to be closer to family. By the time we started seeing each other, Rob was a successful and well-respected attorney. He had reputable friends, several of whom I had met, attended church on a regular basis, and kept in close contact with his parents and siblings.

Though I still questioned the direction of our relationship, I trusted him and was comfortable waiting to see where it went. One night while watching TV on my couch, Rob leaned over and kissed me. It was uncertain and impassionate, but the wondering was finally over. I realized then that he had been taking his time, waiting for the right moment to reveal his intentions. My heart didn't race and my emotions weren't spinning out of control. I was secure with myself and didn't need him to fill any voids, which allowed me to simply enjoy his company. It felt safe, different from any relationship I had ever experienced.

We talked every three to four days after that, though I would have preferred more contact. Assuming he was busy managing a thriving legal career and the social life that went with it, I didn't want to burden him with additional demands. In the time we shared, we went to restaurants and movies on the weekends, cooked dinner at each other's houses, and attended church regularly.

I'd grown up in the Episcopal Church but enjoyed sharing my faith and accompanied Rob to the Catholic Church. There I received the Holy Eucharist, the "actual" body and blood of Christ, until I discovered the church reserved that sacrament for Catholics only. I had taken Holy Communion, a "symbol" of the body and blood of Christ, my entire life and considered it an important expression of my faith. However, when I went to the altar knowing of the church's disapproval, I felt I was doing something wrong, and when I didn't receive the bread and wine, I felt something was missing. I couldn't win.

Rob and I ultimately agreed to search for a church where we both felt comfortable. The Episcopal Church was struggling in Kansas City at the time and after attending a service, we decided it didn't provide the environment we sought. Thus, we continued frequenting the Catholic Church where Rob had visited with relatives as a child.

Traditional in ritual, though progressive in thought, I found myself feeling more comfortable with it over time.

Rob encouraged me to explore the Catholic religion through Catechumenate classes, which provided an understanding of the church and its teachings and an opportunity for membership. Though it had only been five months since we started dating, we began attending classes weekly in addition to Sunday mass. We hadn't talked about the future, but I felt as if we were working towards one together whether it was mentioned or not.

I met Rob's parents, Doc and Clara, on one of their trips from Nebraska to Kansas City. Doc, a clean-cut, handsome man with a prominent jaw, crooked smile, and slight build, was a die-hard golfer who played the part well. He wore slacks and a short-sleeve golf shirt, sported a year-round tan, and scheduled his life around the game. Enjoying a private, understated existence, he worked part time in retirement at the local medical clinic when he wasn't on the course. Noticeably awkward around others, he used his dry wit to hold a conversation and avoided social gatherings at all costs.

Clara, a classic beauty with a square face and straight, silver, shoulder-length hair, had a quiet presence and traditional style. Gifted artistically, she took art classes and painted with oils and pastels when she wasn't volunteering at church, cooking, or gardening. Their home was filled with fresh flowers and the heavenly smell of home-cooked meals prepared with fruits and vegetables from her garden. Clara enjoyed spending time with family and friends, occasionally hosting them in her home.

Later that summer, Rob invited me to his brother's wedding in North Carolina, where he introduced me to his three siblings. His brother had just graduated from medical school and was preparing for a residency in orthopedics, and his new bride worked as an attorney. Rob's older sister, also a talented artist, was happily married with three young children in Nebraska, and his baby sister attended school in Wyoming.

When talking about the nieces and nephews and what he would say if they asked about us sharing a room, Rob stated matter-of-factly, "I realized then that I love you. I don't know why it's taken me so long to tell you."

"Thanks for sharing. I love you, too," I replied effortlessly.

For Thanksgiving, we entertained twenty-one of Rob's extended family in his small home. It was our first holiday together and the only one either of us had ever hosted. Our guests brought dessert. I prepared mashed potatoes, green beans, stuffing, and gravy from scratch, and he deep-fried a turkey, a relatively new tradition in my family. A friend had turned Daddy onto the recipe, and he provided the equipment and detailed instructions for Rob to follow.

Not realizing a twenty-pound turkey could be cooked in sixty minutes, the elders were traumatized by the sight of a raw bird an hour before the big meal. "Poor kids don't know what they're doing," they muttered. "Guess we won't be eating turkey this Thanksgiving!"

As we gathered to observe the sizzling pot of hot peanut oil, we stood in amazement at the sights and sounds of it. Besides the crisp, juicy bird that emerged, the novelty of cooking the turkey was the hit of our celebration, a family memory that is remembered with fondness and laughter.

That Christmas, Rob and I set up a fresh tree in his living room, adorned with white lights, crystal ornaments, and red velvet ribbon I'd meticulously positioned into place. Poking fun at my fastidious ways and discerning tastes, he affectionately called it the "designer Christmas tree." Alongside the fire, with festive holiday music front and center, we celebrated the season with Ginger, family, and welcomed guests.

Though Rob and I still didn't discuss the status of our relationship or a future together, I trusted it would be revealed in time. He dreamed of becoming a partner in the law firm and I enjoyed my career in home furnishings and interior design, especially working with clients and travelling to markets in Dallas and High Point, North Carolina. In the meantime, we spent evenings and weekends hanging out in each other's company.

On the anniversary of our first date, April 22nd, Rob surprised me by showing up on my doorstep at 7 a.m., the same thing I had done for his birthday the previous summer. In a robe, with no makeup and crazy hair, I opened the door and invited him inside. We sat down at my little red antique table for juice, pastries, and vitamins wrapped in wax paper. I wondered why he'd brought them, but I was still half asleep and hadn't caught on to his carefully laid plan.

While he poured the juice, he suggested I open the tiny package. "Why don't you get the vitamins out for us?" he said.

I could see there was more to his request than I realized by the nervous expression on his face. As I unfolded the paper, I felt his penetrating stare and gazed back at him with an inquisitive smirk.

There was something amongst the tablets, though I couldn't tell what it was at the time. As I looked up to question him, he took my hand and asked, "Will you marry me?"

"Of course," I replied without reservation.

Before he revealed the treasure inside, he proudly told the story of how he'd come upon it. Rob met a jeweler on a flight while traveling for work. After returning home, he drove two hours to the jeweler's store, where he learned about the grading of diamonds and handpicked the stone himself.

Elated over our engagement, I called Daddy to tell him the news, but he had some of his own to share. Rob had flown to Dallas the day before and asked for my hand in marriage. After receiving it over a quick lunch, he returned that evening in time for the proposal early the following morning. By noon, my co-workers were eagerly awaiting my arrival. They knew because Rob had arranged for the delivery of an engagement gift to my office, a large original pastel painting from one of our favorite local artists. Our dream day concluded with a small celebration of friends and colleagues at a jazz concert that evening.

Rob and I joked that the only reason he wanted to marry me was for my dog Ginger. She had human-like qualities, as I treated her more like a companion than an animal, and he loved her company. She and I hung out at his house on the weekends, and she stayed over when I traveled to market. Though she once ate a whole raw salmon off his kitchen counter, he learned to care for her differently than his family's pets, who were considered farm animals and treated accordingly.

I admired Rob's mellow disposition, strong faith, artistic interests, professional achievement, and personal success. He had overcome a drinking problem and earned the respect of his peers and colleagues. Quiet, creative, and intellectual, he complemented my social, emotional, and structured personality. I was thrilled to have found such a complimentary mate.

When discussing details of our wedding, we discovered neither of us wanted the attention and fuss of a formal affair. I feared the worst of my nervous stomach and sensitive skin and preferred not to expose them to family, friends, and guests. Rob claimed he'd rather not spend the money on a social event, and neither of us minded the idea of eloping. Unfortunately, we both wanted to be married in the church so it was the only option we considered.

Mother offered to buy my wedding dress, so I scoured the market and took her back to see my favorites. We visited several bridal shops before stopping at one last store on our way home. I was fairly certain I had already found "the one," but Mother insisted on seeing everything since she was paying for it.

I described what I wanted to the salesperson–an updated, elegant, off-the-shoulder, beaded, silk shantung gown with a draped collar. She escorted us to a dressing room and brought several dresses for me to try, though none of them matched what I had envisioned. Detecting my disappointment, she sent the owner, Caroline, to assist with the fitting.

Much to my surprise, Caroline was my age and every bit as glamorous as the girls I had grown up with in Dallas. Dressed like a couture model, she had delicate features, a chiseled face, and beautiful, long, curly brown hair. She graduated from Southern Methodist University, blocks from my childhood home, and knew many of my Mystic campmates and Highland Park classmates. The model of social grace, the true virtue of a Southern belle, she embodied Grandmom and Aunt Dee Dee's finest qualities. Furthermore, she lived with her husband and two young children just blocks from Rob's house.

Mother insisted we purchase the wedding dress from Caroline, even though her traditional long-sleeved lace gown wasn't my favorite. It was more expensive than the rest, but I didn't feel I was in a position to question her authority. At Mother's request, for logistical reasons, I charged the gown on my credit card and the wedding shop began making alterations to customize it.

Several weeks later when I tried to collect the payment she'd promised, Mother told me to ask Daddy for it. Confused by the apparent change in plans, I questioned, "But I thought *you* were going to pay for the dress?"

There was a long pause before she declared matter-of-factly, "Well, I know, but your daddy won't mind buying your wedding gown. Talk to him about it."

I never quite understood her reasoning but soon found myself explaining the $3,000 expense to Daddy. He was disappointed in Mother for recanting her offer but was understanding of my predicament and agreed to give me the money. Rob, on the other hand, was furious with her and demanded she not be involved in any more wedding planning.

While he was exposed to Mother's manipulative ways for the first time, I was learning about his family's dynamics as well. Rob feared his dad would show up drunk to the wedding, embarrass himself and Rob, and spoil our blessed day, so he insisted on a morning ceremony to stack the odds in our favor. Having witnessed the secrecy surrounding my Granddad's drinking, I was sensitive to his feelings and agreed to an 11:00 a.m. church service.

Besides trying to avert any unwelcome attention and humiliation his dad might bring, Rob was dealing with his own personal misgivings. Though he'd been president of his fraternity, was well-respected professionally, and had many social connections, he didn't feel comfortable sharing our "private" affair with any of them. Instead, he lobbied for a ceremony exclusively for family and close friends, followed by an evening reception for guests.

In September 1993, on a cloudy, cool autumn day, we married in the Catholic Church and enjoyed a festive outdoor celebration in our backyard. Filled with white-skirted tables and wooden chairs, a lighted tent for the buffet and bar, and welcomed guests from near and far, the reception exceeded my wildest expectations.

Rob and I retired for the evening to the Raphael, a historic hotel on the Country Club Plaza. Both of us, exhausted from the day's preparations and festivities, crashed upon arrival and slept through our wedding night. Before consummating our marriage, we departed on an early morning flight for a weeklong honeymoon to Maui, Hawaii.

We spent our first three nights in Hana, a remote town on the east side of the island, where the land's natural beauty and serenity remain untouched. To get there, we drove roughly sixty miles along the winding, famed Hana Highway as it paralleled the coastline and meandered through the island's tropical forests. In a convertible, with the ocean breeze in our hair, warm sun on our bodies, and scent of saltwater in the air, the drive was the beginning of a romantic stay in paradise.

At Hotel Hana, we were immediately submersed in the native Hawaiian culture, tropical architecture and landscape, fresh orchid leis, and greetings from islanders in customary dress. Our oceanfront cabin featured a wall of screened windows, wood floors, and French doors opening to a covered porch and private hot tub, marrying the indoor comforts with the outdoor environment. We relaxed under umbrellas on the hotel's white-sand beach, enjoyed spa services, and toured the island and caves on foot by day. In the evening, we dined in the hotel's five-star restaurant, where the local children serenaded us with traditional song and dance.

We travelled to Wailea, on the lower west side of the island, for our remaining days on Maui. There we stayed in a lavish honeymoon suite in a high-rise hotel overlooking the ocean and enjoyed typical tourist activities, including deep-sea fishing, sightseeing from atop Haleakala volcano, and the festive nightlife. Though Wailea offered the finest service and an abundance of activities, its man-made luxury couldn't compete with the natural beauty we encountered in Hana.

Upon our return to Kansas, we settled in Rob's charming brick house and life resumed as usual. Our careers continued at the law firm and home furnishings store, and we shared quiet evenings and weekends at home with Ginger. He enjoyed reading, drawing, and playing games on the computer, while I dreamed of our future and worked on home improvement projects.

MY THREE GREATEST GIFTS

I FOUND MY career in retail management and interior design challenging and rewarding, but professional aspirations were not my priority. Instead, I wanted to devote my time and energy to caring for a family, the one I had dreamed of since childhood. I imagined it would be happy and close, a desire Rob and I both shared.

At thirty-three and twenty-nine years of age respectively, we had exhausted our rich single lives and were ready for children by the time we wed. Six months later, our first child was on the way. I experienced some complications early in the pregnancy which caused the doctor concern and required me to take several days off work. Afterwards, I appreciated the delicacy of the process more than I'd imagined and cherished every moment. Taking exceptional care of myself, eating well, and exercising daily, my inherent stress level decreased and my skin glowed as my motherly figure took shape.

One morning while running, I began having sharp pains in my groin and legs and reported them to the doctor. It would have been too early for a routine exam, but she performed a check and discovered I was prematurely dilated at thirty weeks' gestation. I stopped running immediately, but within two weeks the dilation had progressed, leaving me on full bed rest for the remainder of my pregnancy. The doctor agreed to allow me to resume limited activity at thirty-seven weeks, but idleness was not my style and the thought of resting horizontally for five weeks nearly killed me. Nonetheless, I took a leave of absence from work and obeyed doctor's orders.

Halfway through the bed rest, I agreed to attend a baby shower that had been previously scheduled by Rob's law firm. I felt fully capable of sitting in a chair, having lunch, and visiting with guests, as it didn't seem much different from what I'd been doing at home. Tired of being incapacitated and bored out of my mind, I was thrilled to have an excuse to get out. I showered, dressed, and drove downtown to meet Rob and his colleagues, most of whom were my former co-workers. They decorated the conference room with trays of food, fresh flowers, balloons, and gifts galore. To keep from overexerting myself, I sat and mingled, ate, and opened presents before returning to my sedentary position at home.

Rob and a few others had packed my car with the many gifts, overwhelming for a first-time mom. While they sat in the garage and I lay inside the house, I grew impatient for him to come home from work and unload them. I wanted to look at our baby's new things and couldn't see any harm in getting a few from the car, but I hadn't realized there was a Radio Flyer wagon blocking access to the backseat of my coupe.

Determination took over rational thinking at that point, as I refused to let a silly little obstacle interfere with my plans. After unloading the car entirely by myself, I could feel my stomach tightening. I had felt it previously, but the sensations were stronger and more frequent. Concerned I was in labor, I lay back down on the couch and called the doctor.

By the time Rob arrived, the contractions were three minutes apart. We packed a bag and headed for the hospital, where they admitted me and connected monitors to track the baby's heartbeat and my contractions. The doctors ordered drugs to stop my labor, but the contractions continued every three minutes through Friday night, all day Saturday, all day Sunday, and into Monday morning, and so did the excruciating pain that came with them. The nurses administered pain medication as frequently as possible, but I was becoming immune to its efficacy. Emotionally and physically wiped out from the ordeal, I began refusing treatment even if it meant a premature delivery.

Mother arrived sometime over the weekend while I was incoherent and unintelligible from the drugs. Making no sense, I worried aloud about the things that had been left undone and spoke as if I were in the process of completing them. She knew I hadn't purchased diapers, shopped for clothes, or vacuumed the baby's room while in the hospital, but she dismissed me in front of the staff just the same. The disrespect made Rob angry, but he refrained from saying anything to avoid a confrontation.

"Don't listen to her," Mother announced. "She's crazy, has no idea what she's talking about."

Once I reached thirty-five weeks in the pregnancy, the doctors finally agreed to stop giving me terbutaline and allow my body to take over the birth. They believed the additional time and stress of the last three days had matured the baby's lungs, hopefully avoiding serious complications. Terrified of the impending delivery, I begged for an epidural, as I had since my arrival, but they claimed it could stall the labor and refused to give it to me. The contractions, along with the agony that accompanied them, continued every three minutes for several more hours.

Suddenly, I felt a surge of pain mixed with tremendous pressure as my water burst and gushed all over the floor. My bloodcurdling screams that followed attracted the attention of the nurses, who came running into the room.

"Let me up now!" I demanded, rolling towards to the edge of the bed. "I have to go to the bathroom."

The nurses stopped me and performed a quick check. I was fully dilated and the baby's head, crowning.

"You can't get up. You're ready to deliver," they said.

Against their opposition, I argued vehemently, "If you don't let me, I'm going to go all over myself!"

"Hold on just one minute," they urged. "Don't push!"

With my dreams of a painless birth shattered, I sobbed hysterically while the nurses sprang into action. They converted my bed into a delivery apparatus, positioned and strapped me into place, and turned on blinding-bright lights for the delivery. The doctor arrived within minutes and Thomas was born two pushes later, weighing five pounds, seven ounces.

I held my newborn baby boy for a short while before he was whisked away to neonatal intensive care, where he would spend the first week of his life. Instead of nursing him, I received a double breast pump and was told to pump milk every three hours. The staff said it was the only way for Thomas to get the nutrients he needed, as his tiny body was too weak to nurse.

When I wasn't pumping, I was holding and feeding Thomas in the nursery. I had to force him to ingest predetermined amounts of milk from doll-sized bottles every three hours to ensure weight gain, without draining his strength. Sometimes one sitting could take up to an hour. It was a difficult balancing act, but after a few days of success, he maintained his weight and the feeding tube was removed.

Following my release from the hospital, I drove forty minutes to and from Thomas for every meal, delivering milk and administering it as scheduled. I wanted to share that time with him just as I would have if he'd been at home. It wasn't how I pictured my first week with a newborn, but I was thankful for his safe arrival nonetheless.

Rob planned on taking a couple of weeks off work to care for me and the baby, but with Thomas in the hospital and Mother at the house, he returned to the office two days after the birth. He would meet me in the nursery for an evening feeding, come home for dinner, and leave for work again early the next morning. Taking after his parents, who placed their firstborn in a dresser drawer, Rob didn't have much of an interest in the preparations for Thomas's homecoming. Fortunately, Mother helped me shop for provisions and set up the nursery that week. I could always count on her to organize things, if nothing else.

This trip was different from her regular visits, which was a welcomed change, because I was ill prepared for her arrival. Usually, I cleaned in advance to remove allergic triggers from our home and sealed the windows to prevent new ones from entering. Fresh flowers, perfumes, candles, and down bedding products had to be placed in the garage and every particle of dust eliminated. I vacuumed drapes and lampshades, washed all bedding and throw rugs, along with my regular cleaning routine.

The measures seemed endless; however, I learned not to cook for Mother, as she typically didn't like my offerings. If I served her a meal, she'd look at me with the obstinacy of a child and ask, "What if I don't like it or don't want to eat it?" I could empathize with her because I'd been forced to eat plenty of food I detested in my youth.

As persnickety as she was, Mother's tastes weren't discerning. I realized this when she tried to convince me that Stouffer's frozen fettuccini alfredo could pass for my favorite restaurant's five-star version. "You'll never be able to taste the difference. I promise," she vowed. "And if you think you can, then your imagination is deceiving you."

While I can appreciate them both, frozen, processed food is never a match for fresh, in my opinion. To the contrary, it was her way of living. Her diet consisted of buttermilk, bakery sweets, or frozen cakes for breakfast, prepared or fast food for lunch, low-cal ice cream for dinner, and sugar-free, caffeine-free soda throughout the day. Most of these items were readily available at the grocery store, so satisfying her dietary needs didn't require much effort.

Mother was great with the arrangements for Thomas that week, but she wasn't as interested in visiting him in the hospital. When she did, she'd refuse to hold him, claiming she didn't want to take time away from me or the nurses. Standing with hands clasped tightly behind her back, jaw clenched, and body rocking back and forth, she watched while I fed and cared for him.

When Daddy came the following weekend, he wasn't into the accommodations but wanted to spend time with me and Thomas at the hospital. He marveled with awe at the miracle of life, especially one that was connected to his. Upon meeting his first grandchild, his eyes welled up with tears of joy. "Look how perfect he is. Can you believe his tiny little body has everything we have? It's one of life's greatest miracles," Daddy amazed.

Gazing into Thomas's eyes, he cooed, "Hi there. How are ya, little fella? Huh? How are ya?"

The day after Mother and Daddy left, Thomas was released from the hospital, and Rob and I took him home for the very first time. Following a week of twenty-four-hour supervision and expert care in the neonatal intensive care unit, Thomas no longer required individualized treatment. I was surprised they allowed us to take him without special instruction or training. The thought of sustaining him on our own was a little scary, but it was a privilege I was delighted to accept.

The next weekend, Rob's parents came to see our son, their fifth grandchild. While holding Thomas and sharing stories of their own children, it was clear Grandma Clara took great pride in being a mother and grandmother. She knew all the tricks of the trade and offered great words of wisdom, including ways to soothe him, suggestions to get him to sleep, and methods of time management.

Insisting they didn't want to get in our way, she and Doc stayed for a short visit before checking into a hotel on the Country Club Plaza later that afternoon. There they shopped, had drinks over a light dinner, and retired early for the evening. The following morning, they stopped by briefly to say goodbye on their way back to Nebraska.

With both sets of grandparents come and gone, Rob and I were left to settle into our new family life. While he worked sunup to sundown, Thomas, Ginger, and I spent our days hanging out together at home. Catering to our precious baby's every need, I attached myself to the machine I affectionately called the "Iron Maiden" and pumped milk every three hours, night and day, for six months. It was a new kind of exhaustion, different from the driving and preparations made for his arrival.

Thomas didn't like being left alone in his crib, not even to sleep, so sometimes I wouldn't put him down or get dressed until Rob came home from work. After dinner, I did chores while Rob held him. Thomas had colic, unexplained bouts of crying sometimes associated with premature birth, and screamed to the point of collapse for the first three months of his life. When Rob tired of it, he'd place Thomas in his crib and let him cry alone.

I couldn't stand the thought of not being there to comfort him and asked Rob, "Why are you allowing Thomas to suffer if it's avoidable?"

"He's not suffering. He's fine." Rob claimed, not understanding or appreciating my concerns.

I couldn't relax while Thomas wailed, so I'd eventually pick him up and hold him until he fell asleep in my arms. The colic eventually passed but Thomas had become accustomed to my touch and wouldn't sleep without it. At six months of age, the pediatrician convinced me it was time to let him "cry it out" to teach self-soothing and promote healthy sleeping habits. She assured me it wouldn't cause any long-term emotional damage, but I'm certain it left scars on me as I sat weeping in our kitchen while listening to Thomas scream. Every ten minutes until he fell asleep, which seemed an eternity under the circumstances, I was allowed to check on his wellbeing. Though it was sheer torture, the experiment worked and he slept peacefully through the night after the third attempt.

Rob and I took Thomas out with us to social engagements for six months before I was comfortable with the idea of a babysitter. JoJo, whom we'd met and visited with regularly at Royals baseball games, was the perfect candidate. She had befriended us, loved and worked with children, and was available on Fridays afternoons and evenings. While I trusted her implicitly, it was difficult for me to leave Thomas at first, so I stayed home and worked around the house until they became acquainted with one another. When I felt he'd be OK in my absence, I began running quick errands before eventually graduating to dinners out with Rob. It allowed us to spend much-needed, uninterrupted time together.

Ours was a fairly old-school marriage in the sense that he supported the family financially and I managed the children, our household, and everything else. Though I considered it a luxury to be home with Thomas full time, the work was more difficult than I'd imagined and I missed having adult interaction. While I did my best to establish friends and a support group during the early years of motherhood, I remained mostly alone. Rob went to work every day and escaped periodically for lunch, social activities, and golf outings with friends. Sadly, he didn't understand or empathize with the isolation I faced.

Caroline and I were the same age, though she was several years ahead of me in marriage and children. Knowing I didn't have anyone to share my experiences, she reached out with compassion and guidance. We developed a close friendship based on shared values, mutual connections, and Southern upbringings, which gave us an inherent sense of familiarity.

"Do you think people really understand what it was like growing up in the South if they didn't live it?" she asked. "Absolutely not," we both agreed. It left an indelible mark that had to be experienced to be appreciated.

Caroline had everything I wanted—a loving family, wonderful husband, beautiful children, exquisite home, her own business, a large circle of friends, and social stature. However, what I admired most was her authenticity and sense of self. Having come from a close-knit Catholic family of eight children, she learned when to fend for herself and when to accommodate those she loved. She gave love without expectation, compromised without disappointment, and forgave without resentment, and she extended the same courtesy to her husband, children, and close friends. She was genuinely caring, gracious, and compassionate, as beautiful on the inside as she was outside.

Caroline introduced me to her friends and Thomas's preschool, where I met and socialized with other moms. We'd gather for coffee after dropping the kids off in the morning, volunteer time at school and charity, and celebrate birthdays and holidays together. We took the children to playgrounds, the zoo, and the country club while sharing adult conversation and parenting experiences.

Caroline and her husband moved to Kansas City, his hometown, straight out of college. As a result, they shared a rich history with most of their coupled friends. Though Rob and I didn't have the same connections, Caroline graciously included us in their social events, as well as intimate family gatherings. Theirs was the closest thing we had to extended family in Kansas City, and I was grateful for their generosity.

"Please join us. You are our family and we wouldn't have it any other way," she'd say.

Before having a second child, Rob and I remodeled our little brick house to make room for our expanding family. The homes in our neighborhood were charming and well built, and the lots, large, making them prime targets for investment and development. Ours was conveniently located to Rob's work and in a good school district for the children, so an addition seemed more plausible than a move at the time.

I knew exactly what I wanted in our remodeled home— a second story with a master suite, French doors to a private deck, and a nursery. It would require rebuilding the stairs to code, taking off the back side of the roof to create a dormer, while reinforcing and finishing the attic space. I took measurements and drew up plans to scale before meeting with an architect. After reviewing them, he provided professional renderings, which I used to obtain building permits from the city. I consulted with subcontractors and scheduled the work accordingly, acting as the general contractor for our project.

After the drywall and trim were complete, my sister Susan came to stay with us for ten days to care for Thomas while I worked around the clock caulking, sanding, and painting our new space. Once finished, I decorated the nursery, and Rob and I moved up to the master suite. Thomas remained in his room downstairs, and we converted our old bedroom into a guest room. It was the perfect arrangement for our family.

Rachel was born nine months later, two years after Thomas. A repeat of my first pregnancy, I dilated early and was assigned five weeks of bed rest before her birth. It was more challenging this time because I had the added responsibility of a two-year-old. Mother, Rob's mom, and Susan came for one-week intervals, and Rob filled in as needed. None cared for Thomas or Ginger the way I wanted, so I took on small daily tasks. Luckily, I made it to thirty-seven weeks and was able to leave the hospital with

Rachel following an uncomplicated delivery and typical two-day stay.

Rob returned to work immediately afterwards, and Thomas, Rachel, and I adjusted to our new routines at home. We spent most of our days creating fun in a small porch that had been converted into living space. Rachel would lie on a blanket and bat at her activity center or bounce in the ExerSaucer while Thomas moved cars and toys about the room. The two kept Ginger and me busy watching over them.

While nursing Rachel, I'd hold Thomas in my lap and read books. He enjoyed playing in the sandbox, so she and I would sit outside and keep him company. We'd take strolls together up and down the street and occasionally walk to the local bagel shop for lunch. Wherever we went, Rachel could be seen carrying her blanket and baby doll clutched in her arms, and Thomas, wearing his red cowboy boots.

As I had done with Thomas, I held Rachel for hours, often in the club chair in the new nursery. After rocking her into a deep slumber, I'd try transferring her to the crib, but her eyes would open wide and she'd start screaming before her tiny body hit the mattress. I'd lay her down, swaddle her in blankets, rub her back, and tell her I loved her before backing away from the crib. After listening to several minutes of inconsolable crying, I'd pick her up and soothe her back to sleep, and the whole cycle would start over again. This routine left me sleeping many a night in the chair in her room. She, too, was spoiled by my holding and eventually had to cry herself to sleep to make it through the night.

Following Rachel's birth, Rob's and my date nights included an infant again as I took her with us everywhere we went for six months. Leaving Thomas at home with JoJo on Fridays evenings, we'd try to get out weekly, but it was difficult to maintain regular outings with a workaholic husband and two small children. The one activity we all enjoyed and could count on regularly was family walks around the neighborhood.

Rob was content, though overwhelmed, with two children, but I didn't feel complete. I wondered then what had happened to the guy who'd once told me, "I probably don't want more than *six* children." He was agreeable to having a third child but didn't want to delay the inevitable any longer.

With similar spacing to Thomas and Rachel, Johnny was born two years later. I dilated early again, but it was insignificant and didn't require bed rest, which allowed me to travel to Dallas to attend my sister Amanda's wedding and move into my dream house during the last trimester of pregnancy.

The house was similar in style to Grandmom's two-story colonial, and I imagined it would be the perfect childhood home for Thomas, Rachel, and Johnny. It had everything we needed including four bedrooms, separate family and living rooms, a finished basement for the children's playroom, and a large, fenced backyard for Ginger. The hardwood floors, crown moldings, tiled bathrooms, plantation shutters, and toile wallpaper gave it classic charm.

Johnny hung out with me wherever I went. Unlike the first two, he was on my schedule instead of his own. He had to take naps in the car while we ran errands and drove Thomas and Rachel to and from preschool and Mother's Day Out. I carried him on my hip until he was almost a year old and then attached him to my body in a backpack. We were inseparable, just as I had been with the other two.

Johnny grew to be a quiet, artistic boy who enjoyed drawing and playing by himself for hours on end. Well-adjusted, intelligent, and caring, he was admired by others though he preferred keeping to himself. As an infant, he didn't demand much, but he had reflux, a stomach sensitivity which caused him to throw up constantly.

Besides trying to keep him, our belongings, and myself clean, I had a newborn to nurse, three sets of diapers to change, laundry to maintain, meals to prepare, boxes to unpack, and a husband and elderly dog to care for. Life was in constant motion twenty-four hours a day. Although completely exhausted, I loved having a family and the rewards it provided. While I carried the weight at home, Rob worked long hours and wasn't around much to share in the joy and responsibility of raising our children.

Mother and Daddy visited annually, usually one at a time. He preferred travelling alone and she couldn't leave her animals without a caretaker. When Mother came, she kept busy with projects like reading old magazines, organizing our belongings, or shopping for antiques. We had different tastes, but she was helpful finding pieces that suited my needs and would offer to buy if it were near my birthday or Christmas.

She admired the children from afar when they slept or played quietly but was otherwise annoyed by their presence. One day, Thomas ran at her full speed with arms opened wide. As he wrapped himself around her legs, she stood closed with her feet firmly planted and arms tightly folded against her chest. "I'm not leaving. I don't need a hug," she said as she freed herself from his grip and returned to her chair.

"How could anyone turn away the pure and innocent love of a child?" Rob and I pondered with bewilderment. Thankfully, Thomas wasn't affected by her rejection, but we remained stunned for weeks afterwards.

Daddy, on the other hand, had a twinkle in his eye and a special place in his heart for the children, and they knew it. He'd play with them, walk and talk with them, take them to the toy store and swimming pool, and photograph their environment. As they got older, the children would fight over where he was going to sleep, each one wanting him in their room. The kids wore out Daddy, so he took naps in the afternoon and retired early in the evenings.

Though Doc and Clara were a short drive away, they didn't visit more than two to three times a year. They claimed they didn't want to intrude, but truthfully, Doc didn't want to disturb his routine and Clara wasn't comfortable leaving him home alone. He drank himself into oblivion every night and smoked two packs of cigarettes a day. Besides acting irresponsibly, he wasn't used to feeding or caring for himself.

When we'd invite them to stay for the night, they'd reply, "Thanks, but we don't want to impose."

"You won't impose at all," I pleaded. "In fact, Rob, the children, and I would love for you stay. Please consider it."

"Maybe another time" was the classic response.

When coming to see us, they'd usually arrive in Kansas City before noon, shop and have lunch, and check into a hotel before arriving at our home in the late afternoon. Rob's mom would come inside to see the children while Doc stayed outside to smoke and mix a drink in the trunk of their car. They'd offer to treat us to dinner occasionally, but more often than not, they'd stay for a short visit and return to the hotel for the evening.

Doc and Clara drove from their home in Nebraska to Sedona, Arizona, each February to escape the long, harsh winters. The never-ending snow and dry spell it left on Doc's golf game were unbearable for both of them. If I knew when they were leaving, I'd spend the day preparing the guest room and a meal, hoping they'd drop by to see us. However, we'd typically learn after the fact they'd driven straight through town or stopped to shop without giving us as much as a call. I didn't understand how Rob's parents could be in the same city as their son and grandchildren and make no effort to contact them. It was simply unimaginable to me!

When Rob mentioned my disappointment to them, they stopped informing us of their travel plans altogether. Though he accepted their absence from our lives without question or regret, it hurt my feelings for his sake and the children's.

After Johnny's birth, Doc and Clara offered to make the three-and-a-half hour trip to take Thomas and Rachel for the afternoon. They hadn't spent any one-on-one time with the children previously, and I was thrilled by the thought of it. Given the special bond I had with Grandmom, I would've loved for the kids to have had a close relationship with theirs, and it was clear by then they weren't going to have it with Mother.

Thomas was a busy four-year old who loved animals, tractors, Legos, and his best friend "Paddy," Paddington Bear. He was serious with a devilish streak and a contagious belly laugh. An independent thinker, he had an insatiable curiosity that compelled him to deconstruct almost everything he encountered, though it never inspired him to put them back together.

Rachel was a sweet two-year old, full of personality. A girly girl, she played dress up and took care of baby dolls she named "Momma Baby," "Daddy Baby," and "Baby." One traveled with her and her "blankie" everywhere she went. Attached to family and friends, she frequently offered hugs and kisses to those closest to her but was reserved around strangers.

I thought the children and Rob's parents might enjoy a picnic at the neighborhood park, a trip to the pet store, or lunch at the play structure at McDonald's. Since the Internet and cell phones were not readily available at the time, I prepared a list of these activities, along with hand-written directions and maps for every location.

Upon their arrival, I welcomed them with open arms. "Glad you made it safely. So great to see you!" I exclaimed.

"Nice to see you, too," Clara returned, as they came inside.

"Hello," Doc replied apathetically.

"Thomas and Rachel are really excited to spend time with you. Thanks so much for offering to entertain them for the afternoon," I gushed as Clara smiled and Doc snickered with a nervous laugh.

We visited for a short time before she acknowledged his anxiousness. "Well, I guess we should see the little one before we go," Clara declared.

"Don't take long," Doc grumbled. "We need to get going before traffic gets bad. I don't like driving in the city."

As she grabbed the children's things and they headed for the car, I presented my recommendations. "Here's a list of activities with addresses and directions," I offered. "You can decide for yourself, but I tried to pick ones I thought you and the children might enjoy doing together."

Clara took the paperwork before I could finish, without giving it a second glance, as Doc rushed her out the door. I waved good-bye, expecting to see them a short while later. Several hours passed before my relaxation turned to fret. Rob's parents didn't know their way around very well and weren't used to driving in town. Having no means of contacting them, I began fearing the worst. "Had they gotten lost or been in an accident?" I worried frantically. I even called the McDonald's to see if they'd been there, but no one had seen them.

When they finally returned, I was in a state of panic, though I remained outwardly calm. "I thought you were going to be back sooner. I was beginning to worry," I stated with a sigh of relief. "Everything OK?"

"Oh, yeah, we did fine," they said, seemingly indifferent to my concern, "but we'd better head home now."

"Did you and the children have fun?" I inquired. "Where did you go?"

"To lunch," they responded, clearly not interested in discussing the details. As they walked out the door, they extended, "Thanks again, kids. See you later."

I pieced together from my toddlers that Doc and Clara had taken them to admire perennials at a local nursery before stopping at the bar next door for lunch and a couple of beers. No longer appreciative of the grandparent's efforts, I was enraged by their disregard for my suggestions and reckless behavior with the children.

When I finally reached Rob later in the day and recounted my fury to him, he was surprised by my reaction. "It's what you wanted. What more could you have asked for?" he questioned. In his mind, the children had spent quality time with their family and come home in one piece. I should have realized then that the attention our children received from his parents that day was more than they had ever given him.

Rob and I discussed the challenges we faced with our quirky families and how we wanted ours to be different, but our expectations were influenced by our experiences. His parents were disconnected and that's what felt normal to him. They wouldn't accept invitations to spend time together or stay in our home and were noticeably awkward in social settings, including intimate family gatherings. We could always count on them making a brief appearance before removing themselves to avoid interacting with others.

Mine, on the other hand, were the exact opposite, to the point of intrusion. They didn't consider our plans when visiting, but would instead tell us what we were doing and when. Once in town, they'd take over our home,

154

leaving their luggage and belongings strewn about without regard for us or our guests, and expect us to accommodate them as if their needs were more important than ours.

Both our parents did what they wanted without care for social etiquette or the feelings of others. Though their methods were dissimilar, their detachment and disrespect were alike. Nonetheless, they didn't stop us from having all the elements of a fairytale life.

Rob had a successful career doing what he loved, and I was fortunate enough to stay home with our three happy, healthy children. We lived in my dream house, shared a strong faith, and enjoyed a charmed existence. Rob and I each found ways to connect with our peers, establish roots in the neighborhood and church communities, and give back to others. We had a trusted caretaker, two sets of grandparents, and extended family to enrich our lives, along with close friends who welcomed us and treated us like kin. The best part for me was the gift of my three beautiful children.

From the outside looking in, we had a perfect life.

2005

Dear Thomas, Rachel, and Johnny,

I've dreamed of you since I was a little girl. Before your births, I nurtured siblings, close friends, and wounded souls, as if they were family. I thought I knew what it was to love and be loved, but nothing could have prepared me for the joy you brought into my life. You fulfilled my childhood dreams of being a mom and answered my lifelong prayers for unconditional love.

Thomas, you are a contemplative thinker, rational and sincere in thought, reserved in judgment. I admire your ability to recognize your feelings and express them honestly. When I struggle with mine, you listen with your heart and reach out with open arms. Once you discover your life's passion, your determined spirit will drive you to happiness and success that extend beyond your wildest imagination. I can't wait for that to happen!

Rachel, you radiate positive energy, inspiring all in your presence. To those fortunate enough to call you friend, you are a trusted confidant and a loyal advocate. I marvel at your courage when facing fears and your tenacity in conquering them. Your compassion, cheerful disposition, and enthusiasm are enviable, but your capacity to love is your greatest gift. Always follow your heart; it will never lead you astray.

Johnny, you are steadfast in character and unwavering in principle, an old soul with wisdom well beyond your years. True to yourself and those you love, you are the first to defend my strengths and forgive my weaknesses. I appreciate your respect, understanding, and thoughtfulness. Gifted artistically, you have an innate sense of creativity that keeps you young at heart. You are going to make a lucky lady very happy one day.

Never did I imagine my reality being greater than the dream. I love you three with all my heart and soul, body and mind. Being your mom inspires me to live an authentic, purposeful life. You are the reason for my existence and my hope for the future.

Love you bunches,

Love you more,

Mom

PASSIONLESS MARRIAGE

———

ROB ENJOYED WORKING with inventors and writing and filing patent applications, though he detested the endless drudgery associated with billable hours in law firms and dreamed of becoming an in-house attorney with a corporation. It would reduce his client load, and the paperwork that came with it, from many to one.

When the firm assigned him to a small tech company's account in the spring of 1999, Rob was ecstatic. The work was far more interesting than hay balers and weenie rollers, and the company, his long-time favorite. He traveled to their headquarters in Washington several times that year to meet with inventors and strategize with corporate counsel on protecting their intellectual property.

Coincidentally, the company was looking to hire several patent attorneys at the time. Rob spoke of it nonchalantly, but I knew if the opportunity presented itself, he would have a difficult time refusing it. Working in house and ending a life structured in fifteen-minute increments, it was his dream job. I encouraged Rob to pursue the possibility, believing his personal success and our family's happiness greatly depended on his contentment at work.

"Would you consider moving to Seattle if they offered me a job?" he inquired.

"Yes," I reluctantly replied, though I immediately felt sick by the thought of leaving behind our friends and community in Kansas City.

In January of 2000, Rob and I traveled to Seattle for an interview. I hadn't been to the Pacific Northwest before and it didn't feel anything like home to me. The skies were cloudy, the highways crowded, and the architecture, contemporary and cold. I grew up in the South, where the weather was sunny and warm and buildings were stately and classic in design, not functional and sterile. I couldn't find comfort in anything there, not even Rob, who seemed to have morphed easily into this strange, unfamiliar environment.

After a full day of meetings, we shared dinner with several attorneys and their spouses from the company's legal team. They were overly welcoming, so much so that the seriousness of their interest in Rob and the excitement on his face hit me squarely between the eyes. Suddenly overcome with emotion, I excused myself from the table and headed for the restroom, where I wiped away tears and collected my thoughts before returning to the conversation.

We stayed at the Woodmark, a picturesque hotel on the Eastside of Lake Washington with views of the water,

Seattle skyline, and Olympic Mountains. Looking out the window at a monotone landscape of rain and fog, endless gray matter as far as the eye could see, I sobbed the entire weekend at the thought of calling this foreign land home. It would be the last time I cried over the potential move, as I chose to let Rob's enthusiasm overshadow my sorrow.

He received an offer as I'd expected, making my fears of moving far away from family and friends come to fruition. Though I was devastated to leave the wonderful life we'd built, Rob assured me the work would be less stressful and the hours, fewer, providing him more time and enjoyment with the children and me. It was an exciting prospect for our family, one I blessed with my full commitment and support.

While Thomas and Rachel stayed home with friends, Rob, Johnny, and I traveled to Seattle to look for housing. Restricted by water, mountains, and accessibility, the available land was limited and in high demand, and the traffic was horrendous. The real estate prices were double ours in Kansas City, leaving us to consider empty shells in distant, cookie-cutter neighborhoods or small fixer-uppers in closer, less desirable areas of town. Neither option appealed to me. In our depressing search, we drove around for five days looking at houses that lacked character, looked cheap, or desperately needed repair. Did I mention I detested their architecture?

Rob's salary hadn't increased enough for us to afford an equivalent standard of living in Seattle, and the company was falling on hard times. Nevertheless, Rob began his new job a month later while the children and I stayed in Kansas City to finish the school year and sell the family home.

Though I had no idea where we'd be moving and wasn't ready to leave my dream house, we listed it for sale immediately. Keeping it in immaculate showing condition while caring for our three small children and two dogs was a daily struggle, especially when we had to leave the premises to allow potential buyers time to browse. It happened multiple times a week throughout the first month, but thankfully decreased once the house was under contract.

Shortly thereafter, Rob and I made a contingent offer on new construction in Washington, a smaller house in an old, quiet neighborhood near Rob's work. Frankly, it was the only property I considered a remote possibility. Its proximity would allow Rob less time on the road and more availability for our family, as planned. The freedom to customize interior finishes and add moldings would help our new environment feel more like home.

The house's completion and our cross-country move were scheduled for the first of May, leaving Rob and me with a three-month separation. He came back to Kansas City for the weekend twice, but the children and I had adjusted to independent living, even celebrating the Easter holiday without him.

It was an extremely busy time for both of us. While he was becoming acquainted with a new job, I cared for our children, supervised the sale and repair of our existing home, and designed the interior of the new one. The company offered to orchestrate our move, but I didn't trust strangers to handle our family's heirlooms, so I boxed our belongings myself and made arrangements for a local mover.

As Mother, Caroline, Thomas, Rachel, Johnny, and I watched them drive away from our homestead with everything we owned in two trucks and my car on a trailer, I fought back tears. I was sad to be leaving treasured friendships, irreplaceable dreams, and reminders of my beloved Ginger. She'd been a faithful companion for thirteen years, through college, marriage, and the births of all three children, but had recently succumbed to old age. There was no time for sadness or regret because we had a plane to catch. It would be the final step in our untimely departure from home.

The children and I had suitcases, backpacks, car seats, a stroller, purse, and tote bag filled with necessities, snacks, and entertainment for the four-hour flight. While I counted on Mother's assistance, I quickly discovered she had responsibilities of her own and was unable to help. She could barely handle her two carry-ons, a suitcase and a housewarming gift she had purchased in Dallas and brought on the trip to avoid shipping charges. The large, arched, cane cat house was two feet tall and inflexible, an impossible task for the attendants to fit in the overhead bin. It was for our soon-to-be new family member, one more cherished than a human in her world.

While reading magazines on the plane, she alerted me when the children needed assistance. "Anna, Rachel needs you," Mother proclaimed.

"Well, I'm feeding Johnny right now. Can you help her please?" I requested.

Responding without checking, she said resolutely, "No. She needs *you*."

I survived the flight despite Mother's desertion and was delighted to see Rob at the airport on the other end. He helped me with the children and all our stuff while she complained of having to manage the cat house through the airport.

"How far is it to the car?" she asked, implying she might not make it another step.

After Rob's reply, Mother paused and regrouped before continuing. "You mean I have to carry this enormous thing all that way by myself?" she posed with disbelief. Pleading, "I'm too tired from the trip. Can't anyone help me? After all, it is yours!"

Following a painfully slow and labored journey to the car, we headed for the two-bedroom apartment where Rob had spent the last three months, our temporary home for the next few days. He and Mother had agreed to stay there with the children so I could help the movers unload the truck and organize our home. However, upon their arrival, Rob went to work and Mother brought the children to the house. Incapable of caring for them herself, she unpacked boxes and arranged our things, leaving Thomas, Rachel, and Johnny under my watch. I became the caretaker and meal provider for them and Mother by day and worked on projects at night while the rest of the house slept.

Shortly after the move, I developed a bad, itchy rash on my inner thighs. The spots were raised and circular in nature, like ringworm, a contagious fungal infection known to be associated with animals. Thomas picked it up once playing in the dirt, and I recalled it took several weeks to relieve him of it. Mine was spreading quickly into a delicate area, and the cream I used to treat it was ineffective, so I made an appointment to see a doctor for proper diagnosis and treatment.

Embarrassed by my condition, I left the clinic excited by the thought of ridding myself of the fungus creeping towards my private parts. Neither Rob nor I was happy about the circumstance, because all physical contact had ceased to prevent him from catching it. Hoping the prescription medication would soon show signs of success, I applied it liberally twice a day but the rash continued to spread.

One month after our move, my sister Susan graduated from medical school in Texas. Although I was planning to attend the celebration, the thought of leaving home wasn't easy for me. I didn't have a trusted caregiver and worried about who would stay with the children while Rob worked. Thankfully, a neighbor recommended a reputable service that introduced us to our beloved babysitter Marilyn, who's been part of our family for the last fourteen years.

In Houston, Susan insisted I let several dermatological residents assess my precarious rash. They had me lift my dress, and within seconds announced, "Nummular eczema!" Mystery solved. It was perfectly logical since I had had eczema in my youth, but I hadn't recognized it in its current form. Following a few days of proper treatment, the rings began to fade and cleared completely within a week.

Upon returning to Seattle, the first order of business was getting Thomas registered for kindergarten and Rachel signed up for preschool. Rob and I had contemplated the children's education since before their birth, public schools versus private, but remained uncertain if we could afford to provide three children a private-school education through high school. Since we'd leveraged everything we owned in hopes of a better life in Seattle, the chances of it seemed slim.

Our neighborhood public elementary school was conveniently located three doors down from our new house, so I used it as a starting point. The school had received significantly fewer applications than needed for kindergarten enrollment and had accepted children outside the district to fill the classes. Unfortunately, there weren't any spots left for Thomas and he would be bussed to an undisclosed location within the district. I wasn't comfortable sending my firstborn, six-year-old child across town alone and began researching private schools. It reminded me how much I relied on the guidance of trusted friends in Kansas City, who were unable to help me in this situation.

Talking with neighbors, greeters at church, and parents at Thomas's martial arts class, I sought input on schools, babysitters, doctors, hairdressers, and grocery stores. My objectives were establishing a trusted community for our family and securing a quality education for the children. Based on recommendations, I found a Catholic grade school for Thomas and a reputable preschool for Rachel.

The preschool was in a home in a residential neighborhood, which didn't appeal to me, but several parents mentioned it was the best in the area, so I decided to check it out for myself. With Johnny strapped over my shoulders in a backpack, I stopped by one afternoon to pick up some printed materials and tour the facility. Dressed in a skirt with pearls, fully done hair and makeup, not a typical Northwest look, I entered the front door in search of the office.

"Hello, anybody home?" I broadcasted.

A voice called out from the basement and invited me downstairs. As I approached, I could see a middle-aged woman with short, dark brown, curly hair and heavy-rimmed reading glasses working at a craft table. Her effortless manner, casual dress, and paint-smeared apron gave her instant credibility and a look of endearment.

She glanced up at me and Johnny. Peering over the top of her spectacles with a look of bewilderment, she asked, "What can I help you with?"

Feeling like a fish out of water, I hesitantly replied, "I'm looking for the office."

"You're standing in it," she said with a chuckle and hint of exasperation. She proceeded to politely explain that she was the administration, the preschool was full, and there was a long waiting list for admission. She had kind eyes, a warm smile, and a gentle disposition; I knew immediately it was the right place for Rachel. I thanked her for her time and requested an enrollment packet, undeterred by the discouraging circumstances.

Returning the next day with the completed application, I explained I'd be willing to wait until space opened even if it were in the middle of the year. As luck, or fate, would have it, a family cancelled the week before school started and we secured their spot by agreeing to tackle one of the worst volunteer jobs. I didn't care, though, I was ecstatic for the opportunity for Rachel.

The director, Mary, was my first and most treasured connection in Seattle. Having raised three children of her own and operated a preschool for twenty-five years, she was an expert on parenting. As a mentor, surrogate mother, and friend, I trusted her wisdom and relied on her advice immensely. Socially conscious, she and her husband Roger demonstrated selflessness and compassion by dedicating themselves to serving others. They adopted our family and graciously included us in their gatherings, holidays, and special celebrations.

Through Mary's preschool, I developed a social network and met my close friends Cate, Michael Ann, and Carmen. Cate, a petite blond with a God-given athletic build and a tailored, sporty sense of style, was a busy single mom with a son in first grade and a daughter in Rachel's class. She'd graduated from the University of Washington and had family history in Seattle, giving her many lifelong friends and relatives in the area.

Uncertain of me or my background, Cate was tentative at first. Besides being selective of including others into her inner circle, she worked full time and didn't have much room for socializing. An executive with personality three times her size, she befriended me at Mary's request, though my formal Southern manner didn't fit her casual Northwest ways. Unexpectedly for both of us, it was the beginning of a treasured friendship.

Michael Ann and I, on the other hand, connected immediately and became fast friends. A stay-at-home mom with three children, one in Rachel's class, she and I lived parallel lives. Her bubbly personality attracted me initially, but what I admired most was her advocacy for her child who had special needs. Together we volunteered in school, took the children on outings, decorated our homes, and shopped at Nordstrom's. Our love for quality and fashion was equal, though our style was different. She had a glamorous Floridian flair that showcased her long, straight blond hair and year-round tan, while I covered myself with conservative, tailored, coordinated outfits.

Her husband worked at the same company as Rob, and they shared interests in technology and sports. It was the first and only time Rob and I made a connection with another couple.

Carmen and I met two years later when Johnny and her son started preschool together. She had grown up locally, had family close by, and knew everyone in town. Full of charisma, her free spirit inspired me to enjoy the adventuresome side of life, and her unwavering dedication to her children motivated me to be a better parent.

Mary, Cate, Michael Ann, Carmen, and I are united by a common bond, the philosophy we share and strive to model for our children. Be authentic, practice humility, help others, accept differences, forgive hurts, have a sense of humor, and be grateful. It's what drew us to one another and it's what keeps us bonded today.

Though my friends had more disposable income, nicer things, and bigger houses than we did, I felt fortunate under the circumstances. After all, the increase in the cost of living from the Midwest to Western Washington was a tremendous leap for our moderate means. As much as I loved our little house, we'd given up a yard, playroom, and square footage to make ends meet, leaving the children with no place to play indoors or out, and no room for company. It was a difficult adjustment, one the kids and I dealt with on a daily basis.

When we were bursting at the seams and private school tuition was draining our finances, I began looking at larger houses in better school districts. A move could have resolved our space, education, and financial issues, but after searching for more than a year, I realized we still couldn't afford anything in the neighborhoods we desired.

Wanting our home to be the favored gathering spot amongst family and friends, I envisioned finding one with a great room, kids' playroom, and backyard for outdoor activities. After expanding our search criteria, I found new construction that had everything we needed, including a peek-a-boo view of Lake Washington. The lot had been purchased and permits issued, but the construction hadn't begun yet. It would allow us time to customize the house to our liking, just as we had done with our remodel in Kansas City and existing home in Washington.

After reaching agreement on the purchase terms, the excitement set in. We were finally going to be living someplace that could accommodate our needs, where our activities weren't limited by our lack of space, and I was going to be participating in the building process again. With Thomas, Rachel, and Johnny in school, I spent hours drawing floor plans, researching materials and design, and dreaming of our family's new home.

While I was planning for the future and establishing a social network in Seattle, Rob withdrew. He didn't make new friends or maintain contact with old ones, engage in the children's lives or mine, or support plans to visit relatives in Nebraska and Texas. He claimed he didn't care if he ever saw his family again, but that scenario was unacceptable to me, so I maintained contact for us.

Well into the routine of our married lives, Rob and I had unknowingly settled into what came naturally to us, the experiences we had had in childhood. Rob's dad worked long hours and was absent from their lives, intentionally escaping family gatherings and social events. He left Rob's mom to raise their four children and manage the household by herself. A dutiful caretaker, she kept Rob busy in activities and sports year round, but neither of his parents supported him or attended his events. As a result, he assumed the same arrangement in our family and lived accordingly.

The promise of coming home for lunch never materialized, and sometimes he didn't show up for dinner. When he was at home, he was either reading, watching TV, or playing games on the computer. While bathing our small children, he'd leave them unattended in the tub for up to half an hour and ensure their wellbeing by periodically calling out from down the hallway.

Doc and Clara appeared to have the perfect life: a successful doctor, dedicated mother, handsome couple, four beautiful children, the means to live as they pleased, the respect of their small town, and a strong Catholic faith. Nonetheless, they treated their children as if they were disposable, alleging to have had four so they could afford to lose one or two if tragedy struck.

My expectations were quite different. Daddy was both father and mother to my siblings and me, working by day and caring for us in the evenings and on weekends. He was invested in our lives, home for dinner, interested in our friends and activities, and present at every sporting event. He didn't pass up an opportunity to connect with us.

I wanted Rob to show me his love and treat the children as Daddy had me, two impossible tasks given his upbringing and Daddy's extraordinary care. Though Rob had good intentions of being an exceptional husband and father, the model he emulated was one of zero effort and participation. Therefore, he considered himself a great partner and dad simply because he cared.

Mother, on the other hand, was unavailable, but I had three exemplary role models to replace her. Grandmom, Aunt Dee Dee, and Lillian cared for me and tended to my needs. I followed their lead by welcoming any and all invitations to participate in my children's lives. I attended their extracurricular events, organized their social activities, and volunteered in their schools.

Though my parents were completely disconnected from one another, they joined Mother's family for holidays and special occasions and pretended ours was one big happy bunch. In contrast, Doc and Clara weren't big on recognizing milestones or celebrating. They isolated themselves from extended family by intentionally cutting ties when they married. Except for Doc's sister and her family, who initiated get-togethers, Rob and his siblings weren't exposed to their relatives. In fact, Doc didn't take them to see his mother, or visit her himself, more than a few times during her ten-year stay in a nursing home thirty miles from their residence.

Though Rob seemed completely comfortable with this detachment, his acceptance of it was extremely upsetting. I desperately wanted to connect with him, but he didn't have the same needs of me. Content existing without social interaction, he used work as an escape from our family and personal commitments. When I tried to reach him, he wouldn't return my calls or listen to my voicemails, which left me feeling completely alone and unsupported in our relationship.

I had imagined things would be different in our new house. Rob and I would be happy with the joyful sounds of our children and welcomed guests. Although he was amenable while I looked, I knew the dream was mine and not his. (He was in Washington for that!) I tried incessantly to make it "ours" by involving him in the decision-making process, but he wasn't interested in contributing. Moreover, he said what I considered "home" had no value to him because he'd have been happy living in a trailer.

I soon found myself spending hours each week on the phone with the builder, Sam, discussing floor plans, designs, and finishes. We met at his office to study blueprints, at the house to measure layouts, and in showrooms to review selections. Though I respected his input and enjoyed talking through the options, I missed sharing these experiences with Rob.

Both passionate about architecture and building, Sam and I never lacked for conversation. We gradually developed a friendship and began discussing personal issues that arose during the course of business. He frequently asked of Rob's opinions and when I tired of making excuses for his lack of involvement, I shared my disappointment and the strain it placed on our relationship. In turn, Sam discussed the challenges he faced in his thirty-year marriage.

Frustrated with Rob, I realized the way I felt about his participation on the house coincided with how I felt about our marriage. While I worked tirelessly to please him, he didn't make any efforts or express appreciation. When discussing how we met and fell in love, Rob would tell me we were together because I came into his life at the right time and place, just as his mother had for his dad.

Once Doc decided to marry, he proposed to several women within a year before Clara finally said yes. The circumstance of their union didn't feel like love to me, but Rob considered it ideal. Referring to our relationship in these terms hurt my feelings because the implication was that Rob's love was born of happenstance.

On our tenth anniversary, on our way to dinner, I prompted, "Ten years, can you believe it?"

"Yes, I can," he replied.

"Do you think it was fate? Were we meant to be?" I inquired.

"I don't believe there's one right person. I think we're together because we met when the timing was right for both of us," he stated. "I'm just glad I don't have to date anymore."

"What about Doc and Clara?" I pressed. "How do you feel about them?"

"They're married for the same reason and look how well it's worked out," he answered.

As the work on the house continued and my friendship with Sam grew, I found myself reaching out to share experiences with him instead of my husband. Sam was woven into my thinking at odd times of the day and night and my emotions were starting to spin, which caused me great concern. Worried over the estranged state of my marriage, I exposed my unwanted thoughts to Rob in hopes the heartfelt sharing would lead us to repair our relationship.

"I wish you'd been there to help me pick out the kitchen cabinetry today," I stated.

"Do you like what you got?" he inquired.

"Yes," I answered.

"Good," he replied, as if that's all that mattered.

"But I'm starting to feel like I'm building this house with Sam, not you. I want you to be involved, so our home will be a reflection of our family," I pleaded.

"I don't care what it looks like. This house is your deal, not mine. I told you that when we bought it," he declared.

"The more time I spend with Sam, the more I want to share with him," I confessed. "It scares me because I want that connection with you and we don't have it."

"What do you expect me to say?" he questioned, irritated but seemingly unconcerned.

"I don't expect you to say anything. I just wanted you to know," I replied dejectedly.

When Rob didn't respond to my pleas for help, his apathy left me sorely disappointed. I spent weeks driving around in the car while the kids were at school or in Rob's care, trying to sort things out. The escape brought a temporary sense of calm and soulful music quieted my fears, though neither resolved my hopelessness.

The thought of the situation we faced terrified me. I wanted to feel my existence mattered to Rob, but even our sex life, once gratifying, was perfunctory and mundane by then. Thankfully, Sam and I didn't connect intimately, but he was developing strong feelings for me and I had desires for him.

How could I become emotionally attached to another man outside of our marriage when it was absolutely against my moral conscience? Compelled to discover the truth of my disturbing and uncontrollable emotions, I immediately sought insight and guidance from a professional psychotherapist.

I was physically and emotionally exhausted. Feeling lonely, overwhelmed, and unloved, I woke in the depths of despair one day, began crying, and couldn't stop. Rob eventually asked, matter-of-factly, "What's wrong?" to which I replied, "I'm just not happy."

"I don't know why you're upset. I'm fine. I promise," he declared with a huge smile on his face and hands thrown up in the air. It was clear then that he felt my contentment was solely dependent upon his satisfaction, which completely missed the point of my distress.

After finally admitting to myself and Rob that I was discontented in the relationship, I was determined to resolve our marital discord. Unwilling to move our family into a home Rob didn't want, I withdrew my support and we rescinded our purchase agreement. It relieved Rob's financial stress and eliminated my communications with

Sam simultaneously. Rob proposed couples' therapy and we began the difficult process of dissecting our marriage.

In its inception, Rob and I lived parallel lives as independent individuals and compatible roommates. We were comfortable existing in each other's presence and didn't require anything more from one another. The distance felt safe because it allowed me to remain in control of my emotions, something I had never been able to do in a romantic relationship.

I wrongly assumed children would change our marriage, altering our lives in ways we couldn't predict. Our focus would shift from being self-absorbed to working together as a team to provide our children a dream existence. I imagined we'd become a family in the most ideal sense of the word.

Mothering came quite naturally to me through instinct and experience. I had received unconditional love as a child from Daddy, Lillian, and Grandmom, and long dreamed of returning it to my own children. Wanting only the best for them, my interests and priorities changed accordingly the day they were born. I couldn't wait to be invested in every part of their lives.

Rob's role models in childhood had been much different than mine. When spending time with his dad, Rob performed manual labor or was dragged to the local bar in his pajamas while Doc drank, smoked, and played pool. The town drunk, not the beloved small-town doctor, he used alcohol to control his unbearable social anxiety. It prevented him from connecting with others, including his own family.

While Doc did as he pleased, Clara managed the children in his absence. She'd get angry at his irresponsible behavior, but honored him as provider and leader of the family and performed her role as caregiver and supporter. She waited on him hand and foot, made excuses for his rude conduct, and caved to his every wish in the company of others. Privately, I was upset with Doc for treating her with utter disrespect but eventually recognized she enabled his atrocious behavior.

When Rob and I talked of our families, I was aware of mine's dysfunction and made it known that I wanted to do things differently. Though he acknowledged his dad's drinking and parents' lack of involvement, there was no recognition that their disconnection was unhealthy. Instead, Rob learned to accept their absence and appreciate their existence.

Doc and Clara lived in the same house and attended church together regularly, something my parents couldn't compete with, so Rob was convinced they were the couple to emulate. He referred to them as "rocks" for one another, describing them as strong, supportive, and unwavering. To the contrary, I imagined cold, inflexible, inanimate objects. It wasn't the first or the last time the two of us viewed things very differently.

Rob and I attended couples' therapy for more than a year, but it was difficult for both of us. We were forced to discuss our emotions, something neither liked doing. Though Rob professed to have strong feelings for me, he appeared indifferent. I wanted tangible evidence of his love—an acknowledgment when I walked into a room, a phone call during the day, or a conversation with eye contact. Instead of making an effort to show me this kind of love, he argued I should trust him implicitly without questioning his intentions.

"Why are you so needy?" he probed. "You're my wife. I don't have to show you my love. If you can't feel it, that's not my problem."

To his credit, he provided and cared for me and the children as best he could, but it wasn't enough. I longed for him to be present and connected, while he looked for excuses to escape. He offered to pay for babysitters and house cleaners to lighten my load, instead of sharing the responsibilities, and he purchased an electric foot massager in response to my suggestion for a romantic prelude.

Because I was incapable of honoring my feelings of disappointment or communicating my needs to Rob, my assignment in therapy was to ask for what I wanted and allow him to fulfill my needs. Specifically, I requested he attend the children's activities, teacher conferences, and sporting events, and be involved in important family matters. In addition, I looked to him to provide guidance and emotional support in raising our children. It wasn't a question of competence, but a desire for companionship and intimacy.

I'd ask questions like, "Don't you want to be there to celebrate Thomas, Rachel, and Johnny's successes and comfort them in their disappointments?" Assuming there was only one natural parental response, I was continually astonished when he claimed, "If I don't enjoy what they're doing or don't feel like participating, I'm not going to do it." And, he didn't.

Rob was incensed by my "expectations" of him. He had no intention of sharing in our lives as I suggested and considered it unfair of me to change the rules during the course of our marriage. Had I realized he felt that way in the beginning, I never would have married him or had children with him, but it was too late to do anything about that then.

Having been raised in an environment without parental interaction, Rob was self-absorbed and lacked empathy. He'd become an expert at gratifying himself at an early age and didn't need or want my help. As a result, I couldn't find a way to get his attention, please him, or connect emotionally. The harder I tried, the more frustrated I became. I attempted to convey my loneliness in the marriage, but he was incapable of understanding.

Appearing easygoing by nature, Rob was merely unaffected by and unresponsive towards others. No one had shown him consideration or affection, and he didn't know how to give it in return. In its place, he learned to express love through criticism. Especially critical of my cooking, he frequently questioned, "How was this dish *supposed* to have been prepared?" While arguing his intent was satisfying curiosity and providing inspiration, the patronizing tone he used indicated otherwise.

I should have recognized his insensitivity much earlier when he described an incident he witnessed in Washington, D.C. While out for a walk one afternoon, he encountered several dogs and their owners on a street corner; among them, a proud, fussy man with a little Chihuahua and a burly guy with a great big mixed breed. Though the larger dog wasn't aggressive, his size alone was enough to make him a danger to the smaller one. After their introduction, the Chihuahua's neck had been snapped and the owner was left standing in a pool of blood with a limp, dead dog on the end of his leash. I felt sick to my stomach imagining that horrific scenario, but Rob thought it was hysterical. He enjoyed mimicking the lifeless Chihuahua, with his head flopped over to one side, continuing as my eyes welled up with tears. I never saw the humor in it myself but that didn't stop him from recounting the story over and over again.

I thought I knew Rob well, having been with him for fourteen years, but was surprised by what I discovered in therapy. Amongst other things, he had terrible anxiety that accompanied his social awkwardness. Besides his preference for being alone, it was the reason he didn't interact with others, including family members. The quality one-on-one time he and I'd shared during our courtship wasn't indicative of his budding interest, as I had imagined, but rather his attempt to date without public socialization.

Though I'd have preferred more communication when we first started dating, I trusted Rob and didn't worry about his whereabouts, a welcome change from past relationships. Additionally, I didn't want to burden him with demands for his time. I assumed he was busy building a successful legal practice and entertaining the firm's clients, like my uncle who talked of company politics and client development, the very reasons Daddy became a sole practitioner.

However, I could never have imagined in my wildest dreams what Rob was actually doing when we weren't together. He was watching dirty movies and having sex with himself several nights a week. It had become a part of his identity after he stopped drinking. I was naïve to that behavior but thought an obsession was exclusive to adolescent boys, sexual deviants, and dirty old men. Whatever the case, it certainly explained why he wasn't pursuing a physical relationship with me at the time.

Rob admitted to being turned on by loose women who degraded themselves physically, and preferred using them for casual sex or pleasing himself to having intimate partners. It allowed him to take what he wanted and give nothing in return. Antisocial and self-satisfying, not relational, his sexual preferences were clearly the result of his introversion and disrespect for women.

He denied himself these guilty pleasures after marriage, but it turned our exchanges into a fulfillment of needs, rather than a bonding experience. The lack of intimacy distanced me, and the infrequency that followed frustrated him, leaving us both dissatisfied. The result was tension and unrest in the relationship.

When inexplicable, heavy menstrual bleeding put a damper on our sex life, Rob quit kissing me, responding to my touch, or snuggling in bed. His desertion intensified my feelings of isolation and despair, and contributed to my health issues. By then, my physical problems no longer impacted our sex life because the marital conflict superseded intimacy.

In therapy, I listened to him explain how he'd intentionally withheld love and affection at the time because his needs weren't being met, without any regard for my feelings. It was hurtful but not as disturbing as what followed. Rob admitted to deliberately moving me across the country to disconnect me from friends and family in favor of a secluded life, similar to the one his parents had chosen for themselves.

"I wanted to move because I didn't like the life she was creating for us in Kansas City," he told our therapist. "Seattle was a chance at a fresh start."

Funny, he'd never mentioned that to me previously. There I was building the life I thought we both wanted for our family, while he was plotting my demise in return. It was unimaginable to think I had willingly left loved ones in support of him pursuing his dreams under those circumstances.

In addition, I learned Rob regarded the close friends we had accumulated in our marriage as "my" friends, not "ours," even those who'd welcomed us into their hearts and homes, shared their lives, and extended love to our family, including Caroline and her husband, and Mary and hers. "Your friends are not my friends, and I don't enjoy spending time with any of them," he said.

These revelations were shattering and left me feeling our relationship was a complete lie. Rob wasn't interested in fulfilling my needs because he valued me as an employee, not a partner. He was a great employer. He paid the bills, stayed out of my way, didn't complain much, and helped with meals. If that's all I'd been looking for, it would have been the perfect arrangement.

As our feelings were uncovered, Rob and I learned a lot about ourselves, each other, and our marriage. Rob took me as his wife, someone to cook and clean, bear children, and take care of his physical needs. That's what he signed up for when he asked me to marry him, and when I tried to change the rules, he felt cheated.

In one of our heated discussions, he angrily declared, "I could have married 25 percent of the female population and been happy. What is *wrong* with you?"

Speechless by the hurtful comment, I didn't respond but thought to myself, "I've given you my heart and soul for twelve years, and you don't consider me special. *Why* am I married to you? What *is* wrong with me?"

After a year of couple's therapy, Rob asked our therapist what she thought of our progress relative to our efforts, and she shared her opinion. "It's time for our work to end," she said. "You aren't succeeding in repairing your marriage."

Though I disliked her answer and the implication immensely, it was clear that Rob and I didn't speak the same love language. There was no right and no wrong, just disagreement.

I wasn't ready to give up on my childhood dream of having the perfect family. Moreover, I wanted to be able to look my children in the eyes and tell them with certainty that I had done everything possible to avoid the atrocities of divorce.

Rob and I lived together for another six months before he announced, "I'm leaving and there's nothing you can do about it!"

Our marriage was over. There was incredible guilt, devastation, and relief all in that one moment.

DEATH OF THE DREAM

ALTHOUGH I WAS not the one leaving the marriage, the decision was mutual. Rob and I had both tried painstakingly to get back to our happy place of ignorant bliss, but too many differences and hurts had been uncovered for us to live in our "pretend marriage" any longer. What I feared most in facing the breakup was the effect it would have on the children; however, there was no way to spare them from our failure.

In advance of telling Thomas, Rachel, and Johnny of our plans to separate, Rob and I talked to the therapists—mine, his, and ours—before sharing the news. We avoided the word "divorce" and its negative connotation but made it clear we wouldn't be getting back together. It was neither their fault nor their responsibility to fix, and we both loved them immensely.

I worried that once the children learned Mommy and Daddy didn't love each other any longer, they might imagine the same thing happening to our love for them. I explained I still loved Daddy as their father, not as a husband, and assured my feelings for them would never change. It was more than they could comprehend at the time, but it was the truth.

Rob moved out one month later, on my forty-first birthday. Because he was incapable of orchestrating a plan himself, or he blamed me for his predicament, or he didn't recognize special occasions, or some combination of all three, he expected me to assist in the move without asking, apologizing, or expressing appreciation. While his selfishness incensed me, as it had many times before, I did what I would have done for anyone in need. I arranged for the children to spend the day with Cate and helped him move his personal belongings and half of our family's furnishings into a small rental home ten miles away.

Loading and unloading a seventeen-foot Ryder truck, we spent the entire day driving it and my car back and forth between the two houses. With the exception of new bunk beds for the boys, he had most of what he needed to make a comfortable home for the children and himself. As time wore on, the anger I'd felt towards him for his inconsiderate behavior was overshadowed by gratitude for the opportunity to set up the children's second home.

The separation wasn't a new way of life, just the formalization of our reality, as I had effectively been living alone with Rob for years. It was never the solitude that bothered me, rather the loneliness in our relationship. Instead of feeling a sense of loss from his departure, I experienced relief and the freedom to live an authentic life.

Before leaving, Rob vowed to take care of me and the children financially, offering to divide our assets and his income evenly. We didn't have much, the equity in our home and a little retirement, so it seemed a simple divorce. Rob suggested we use the company's legal program, which provided services to its employees at a nominal rate, to avoid costly attorneys' fees. I agreed and awaited his first move.

I should have realized Rob's unresponsiveness in the marriage would have carried over into the divorce. Moving at a leisurely pace, he took eight months from the date of separation to enroll in the program, meet with an attorney, and draft the initial paperwork.

Upon receiving the filing documents, his petition for divorce and my response to it, I sent them to Daddy to ensure everything was as proposed. Though he practiced law in Texas, he knew the basics of divorce, the legal documents involved, and the principals of community property states. I discovered that had I signed and returned the response, as requested, I would have relinquished my rights in the divorce and it would've been granted on Rob's terms. Thankfully, Daddy stopped me from making that detrimental mistake and assured me the documents could still be filed jointly with a few minor revisions.

After making them, I sent the unsigned paperwork back to the attorney for editing. He altered the language in my response, not as I'd requested, and Daddy confirmed, once again, that my approval would have surrendered my legal rights.

When I approached Rob about the discrepancy, he told me if I weren't willing to sign the document, then I should probably hire an attorney. "The company attorney is representing me in the divorce, so you'll have to get your own," he declared.

"I thought you said he could represent both of us in a collaborative divorce? Why do I need an attorney?" I questioned.

"The company's legal services cannot be used to bring action against an employee, as in the case of divorce," he stated.

"But I don't have any money to hire an attorney, Rob. What am I supposed to do?" I retorted.

"That's not my problem," he replied.

It alarmed me that Rob had failed to mention this fact prior to requesting my signature on the filing documents. Had I trusted the pretense of his word and our verbal agreement, the terms of the divorce would have been granted solely in his favor. An attorney himself, Rob was fully aware of the law and what he was doing.

With only one viable option remaining, having Daddy help me draft my own document, I contacted Rob's attorney and requested he file the petition without me. He instructed me on filing the response and the divorce proceedings were formally underway in April 2006. From that point forward, I was on record with the court as a "pro se" litigant, meaning "without legal representation." It certainly wasn't by choice.

The first matter, and most important to me, was the parenting plan, a document used to outline the care for Thomas, Rachel, and Johnny. Their safety was my utmost concern, especially considering Rob had been an unsupervised child and an absent parent, leaving him unfamiliar with the children's needs. He believed they'd learn to survive on their own, as he had, without realizing we weren't living under the same conditions he'd experienced in small-town Nebraska in the '60s.

He let our nine-year-old daughter and her eight-year-old friend go unsupervised to a nearby public park, a place where delinquents hung out regularly and registered sex offenders were known to live within blocks. Additionally, he argued that leaving our seven-year-old son home alone for several hours was an appropriate way to foster independence, and then left him in a store at an outdoor mall by himself for fifteen minutes.

"He's fine. Nothing happened," Rob claimed. "Just because you're overprotective doesn't mean I have to be that way to be a good parent."

His irresponsible parenting didn't stop there. Rob lacked reasoning skills, the result of having decisions made for him as a child. It left him incapable of making sound judgments or providing safe boundaries. Furthermore, his repressed anger towards his mother compelled him to advocate for the children's rights, irrespective of their wellbeing. For example, he'd let them choose to do their homework or watch movies and play Xbox until 2:00 a.m., bathe and brush their teeth at bedtime or not, and attend sporting practices and games or lounge around the house instead. Not surprisingly, the children ignored their responsibilities and did as they pleased on his watch.

"It's their choice. I'm not going to force them to do anything," he'd claim. "My role as their dad is simply to love them."

Thankfully, for Rob's sake, I valued his role because of the relationship I had with Daddy. I knew his presence was critical to healthy development, regardless of his parenting style, so I worked to accommodate his time while striving to maintain safety and consistency in the children's lives. Unfortunately, Thomas, Rachel, Johnny, and I had to suffer through Rob's poor decisions. The list of offenses was too long to document in the parenting plan but I had no intention of compromising the children's welfare and worked tirelessly to include as many precautions as I could, realizing at some point their time with him was out of my hands, just as he wanted. I eventually learned to trust that the benefit they received from that relationship outweighed the risk it posed, though I never stopped worrying incessantly for their safe return.

Rob and I reached agreement on the parenting plan over the summer without the help of evaluators or attorneys, and I began working on financial settlement, thinking the worst part of the negotiations was over. It seemed pretty simple. Our personal and family belongings had already been divided evenly with the separation, and we agreed to a 60/40 custody split. As the primary parent, I wanted to keep the house for the kids' sake and proposed he keep the retirement, roughly equivalent values. In addition, I sought enough monthly support for the children and myself until I could get on my feet financially.

I asked Rob to make me an offer. He didn't, so I initiated the first move. Several weeks passed before I followed up, hoping the silence was an indication of his thoughtful deliberation and not intentional disregard. Not surprisingly, Rob hadn't even considered my proposal and had no plans of making a counteroffer.

"I think we should meet with a mediator to reach agreement on a financial settlement," he suggested.

"Fine," I concurred and requested his W-2 along with detailed bank, stock, and retirement account statements, which he assured he'd bring to our appointment.

Though he originally proposed we meet together with the mediator, Rob requested separate rooms without mentioning it to me. The mediator took turns going back and forth between us, explaining the process and areas of financial settlement before the negotiations began. It became evident almost immediately that Rob hadn't supplied the required proof of income and asset valuation he had promised and contractually agreed to disclose for mediation. In fact, he brought two incomplete and misleading documents, utterly useless for settlement purposes. The conversation was futile under the circumstances. Without further discussion, I ended the mediation and we rescheduled a second appointment.

Our trial date was quickly approaching and it was becoming apparent a financial agreement wasn't in our near future. Helpless in this predicament, I borrowed money from Daddy and made an appointment to discuss my case with Cate's former divorce attorney and confidant, Judy. She agreed to counsel me as a favor to Cate, though I couldn't afford to retain her services.

"Your divorce will be settled at mediation or trial with whatever information is provided," she explained. "If that's all the documentation you have, then spousal and child support will be calculated on less than half of his income, the equity in your home will be divided in two, and his retirement and stock holdings won't be included."

That scenario would leave me without a home or the means to provide for the children and myself. Rob's scheme was finally clear. He was intentionally stalling and withholding evidence in order to receive the settlement he sought, just as he had attempted to relinquish my rights with the initial paperwork. He wasn't interested in the "fair" deal he vowed, but rather one that would grant him everything and me nothing.

Having been through many contentious divorces, Judy wasn't surprised by Rob's reprehensible behavior, but I was astounded by it. I thought more of his character and trusted his word. While his perpetual lack of response had become expected, I never dreamed he was capable of such evil.

Fear set in as my future looked beyond bleak under those circumstances. I hadn't worked outside of the home in thirteen years, and my previous career couldn't begin to support the children's and my current lifestyle in Seattle. Besides, defending myself against Rob's deviousness was my full-time job and I couldn't afford to give it up.

Reaching a financial settlement with the documentation Rob provided wasn't an acceptable option, so I set out to acquire proof of our income and assets. Judy offered the legal expertise of her assistant, Sarah, who helped me subpoena Rob's employer for his financial records and request a continuance of the trial date. It would allow me the means to obtain complete, accurate information and time to have a formal evaluation conducted.

The subpoena required a judge's signature before it could be filed with the court. Sarah prepared the necessary documents on my behalf and she, Cate, and I marched several blocks from her office to the county courthouse, where I presented them to a judge in the *ex parte* court.

Upon entering the small courtroom, Cate and Sarah took a seat on the churchlike pews while I submitted the paperwork to the clerk for review. Afterwards, I joined them and waited my turn in line. We watched as several others before me, some attorneys, were interrogated by the judge and rejected when they couldn't answer his questions of the law. Worrying what he might ask of me, I felt sick to my stomach, knowing I had no idea what I was presenting.

When Judge Carlos called my name, I rose and walked to the bench. Standing five feet in front of him, I feigned confidence with a nervous smile, a long skirt that covered my shaking knees, and a blouse that hid the red blotches on my neck. As he began probing, I stood paralyzed, unable to give him an intelligible response.

"I don't see an address. Where do you want these documents delivered?" he questioned.

When I couldn't answer, the judge quickly dismissed me, "How do you expect to receive them if you don't have an address?"

Though Sarah assured me she'd be able to provide the clarification needed, I walked away discouraged and in tears. Cate and I followed her back to the office, where we waited for the revised subpoena before returning to the courtroom.

As I approached Judge Carlos, he smirked as if surprised to see me back so soon. After review, the subpoena and extension were granted. "I see you made the appropriate change," he said with a smile.

I left the courtroom again in tears. This time they were tears of victory and relief, not agony and defeat. The subpoena provided me access to the financial records I desperately needed for an equitable settlement and the continuance gave me breathing room to prepare my case.

I spent the next months trying to collect documents from Rob. Sometimes he'd copy only two pages of a multipage statement or mix pages from one statement in between consecutive pages of another. He delivered them in loose, unorganized stacks, forcing me to sort through a huge mess to obtain the information I needed. It was his passive-aggressive way of paying me back for making him produce the documents in the first place.

As the deadline neared, I sent several e-mails to Rob's company attorney regarding the missing pages and statements. I knew him well by then, because he was included in all communication and a copy of every court filing had to be personally delivered to his office. I'm not sure if he was impressed with me or sympathetic to my case, but whatever it was, we had developed a friendly working relationship instead of an adversarial one.

Completely unaware of and unconcerned with Rob's partial and haphazard production, the attorney assured me they'd meet the terms of the subpoena. However, when the deadline passed, I didn't have half of what was ordered, so I made a list of the missing documents and provided it to him and Rob. They were caught off guard, because Rob didn't know I was tracking every page of every record and his attorney didn't realize Rob wasn't complying with the order. An instantaneous and apologetic reply from the attorney followed, guaranteeing me I'd get what was due in a timely manner.

Meanwhile, Rob had hired another attorney, known to be a "shark" in the legal community, to negotiate his financial settlement. Together they drafted a formal offer based on the information he supplied. Like mediation, it was incomplete, deceitful, and in his favor.

"I'm proposing to keep the house and rent it back to you for as long as you can afford to live there," he offered. "That way the kids will be able to stay in their home." Rob knew how important that was to me.

It sounded like a great plan, however, the spousal maintenance proposed wasn't enough to cover the house payments, and the monthly child support for all three children was equal to one penny for every thousand dollars he earned. Additionally, he wanted to retain full control of his stock and retirement. I knew in my heart it wasn't a fair settlement, and my forensic accountant Jake confirmed it.

"Did Rob not recognize that Thomas, Rachel, and Johnny would suffer the consequences of my financial ruin more than I would?" I wondered. "Or was he just too angry to care?" The thought of what he was trying to do to me incited fear and elicited my survival instinct.

When I didn't accept his offensive offer, Rob again recommended we resolve our differences in mediation, without representation, and I agreed. Three days before our scheduled appointment, he confirmed his and the shark's attendance, something specifically prohibited in our mediation contract. It required third parties be approved in advance by all participants and the mediator, neither of which condition had been satisfied.

Wise to Rob's malicious intent and enraged by his overt deception, I objected to his counsel's appearance and conveyed my position to him, both his attorneys, and the mediator. He neglected to tell any of them of our prior agreement, including the attorney he invited. Angered by his deliberate omission, she scolded him, apologized to me, and offered her withdrawal, all in the same email.

I came to mediation prepared to negotiate a settlement and proceeded accordingly, while Rob spent his time trying to contact his attorney over the phone. When our time was up, we hadn't progressed in any area of settlement, which left me feeling extremely discouraged. Unlike the first mediation, though, I was confident I had what I needed for trial if that's where we were headed.

Afterwards, I began copying the shark on all correspondence and soon learned she knew nothing of Rob's incomplete production of documents and disclosure of funds. In addition, the company attorney wasn't privy to the unreasonable settlement offer or the mediation snafu. It was finally clear to all that Rob had resorted to manipulating the legal system and both attorneys to get what he wanted, and none was pleased with his dishonest behavior.

His attempts to leave me with nothing failed, his stalling tactics were no longer a strategy to avoid the division of property, and his efforts to intimidate me in mediation were unsuccessful, so Rob began converting stock into cash and depleting it as fast as he could. If there were no assets in the marriage at the time of divorce, there would be nothing left to divide, and he knew it. Rob wasted nearly $200,000 in less than three months, money I didn't even know we had. It was from proceeds of company stock earned before the date of separation, making it joint property. I could have used my share to hire an attorney to defend myself or reduce the debt on our home, allowing the children and me to keep it.

The financial statements continued rolling in with the subpoena and I caught on to his endeavor to eliminate our marital assets. What Rob was doing was unconscionable, but by then I knew of his despicable character. With each turn of the knife he had plunged deep into my back, he was smiling and treating me with kindness in front of the children.

I would have fought 'til death to protect Thomas, Rachel, and Johnny, but the thought of intentionally destroying their father in the process would never have crossed my mind. The end result would have harmed them more than any benefit I could have ever received.

Swift legal action was necessary to prevent Rob from depleting our remaining assets and allow me time to prepare for an impending trial. That meant filing a restraining order and a second continuance. I felt confident with the latter because I had the first one to use as a guide, but the restraining order was a completely different animal. It was unusually complicated, requiring several documents that had to be signed and filed in a specific manner with the court. Sarah gave me a blank form, but she and Judy were unavailable to help and Daddy couldn't provide counsel because the procedures were different from those used in Texas.

I spent hours drafting the paperwork, double checking its correctness as best I could. After submitting the final copies to the court, I couldn't stop worrying I'd done something wrong. I didn't have the resources to know the answer, but I couldn't get the thoughts out of my mind. At 4 o'clock the following morning, I realized I hadn't attached an important document, a seal to protect confidential financial information. If the restraining order were denied because of it, Rob would be allowed to continue disposing of property and I'd have to submit new documents to cancel the previous motions and re-file, which I had no idea how to do.

Distraught and in a state of panic, I called Cate at 6:00 a.m. to seek advice. "Oh, my God! I forgot something!" I exclaimed. "What am I going to do? I have to fix it or I'll lose everything!"

"Call Richard and ask him," she urged.

I contacted our mutual friend and attorney Richard, who counseled me to make several copies of the seal and go directly to the court clerk to correct the error. With wet hair, no makeup, and sweats I wouldn't normally wear in public, I dropped the children at school and arrived at the courthouse in downtown Seattle before 8 o'clock that morning. First in line when the office opened, I shared my desperation and pleaded with the clerk, "I filed a restraining order yesterday but I forgot to include an important seal. Can you help me, please?"

"Well, you'll need to refile the documents correctly," she explained.

"Is there a form to cancel my previous motion or do I have to wait for the court to reject my request before refiling?" I inquired.

Perplexed, she tried to sort it out but was unaware of the process to remedy my predicament. "I'm not really sure how that works," she admitted.

That's when tears began quietly rolling down my cheeks. "I don't have an attorney and I don't know how to do this by myself," I confessed woefully.

Without explanation, the clerk retreated from sight. A short while later, she returned with papers in hand and offered, "I found your restraining order. Why don't you give me the seal and I'll add it to your paperwork?"

The motion was replaced and filed as if I'd submitted it correctly in the first place. Miraculously, Rob's access to our assets was frozen and the trial date was continued for another three months. Judy's calendar was free of conflicts, and she agreed to attend mediation or represent me at trial to reach a settlement, whichever was needed. It was the best of all scenarios for me under the circumstances, but not for Rob.

"Why did you freeze my accounts?" he snapped angrily. "You can't do that! I get to decide how to spend my money, not you!" Adding, "You're only hurting yourself if there's not enough money for child support."

"I'll let the court make that decision," I declared.

At the same time these contentious negotiations were taking place, my physical state was deteriorating. The eczema from my youth reappeared and left me with unsightly and painful red, itchy, crusty patches on my arms, legs, and neck. The allergens that had once elicited a runny nose, puffy eyes, and hives from cats, dust, and grass gave me asthma. It had progressed from an exercise-induced condition in childhood, to a secondary reaction to colds and allergies after moving to Washington, to a daily occurrence requiring maintenance medication during the divorce.

My elevated stress level also caused excessive uterine bleeding. There were times when I didn't leave the house for two days as it poured from my body, leaving me unable to make it through the night without waking in a pool of blood. It's no coincidence that my worst day occurred during the final divorce negotiations. After finding no identifiable cause for it, my gynecologist diagnosed me with menorrhagia, or heavy uterine bleeding.

My personal life was in a state of unrest as well, as I watched a dear friend lose her battle with addiction. Desperately wanting to help her overcome it, a mutual friend and I orchestrated an intervention for treatment. Throughout the six months preceding the event, there was tremendous worry for our friend's physical and emotional health. Afterwards, there was concern for the impact this confrontation would have on our relationship.

Two weeks later, Mary's husband, Roger, had health complications related to a mechanical heart valve. The medication used to control his blood's consistency caused him to have several life-threatening blockages and nine surgeries in one year. Besides accompanying the family to all of the procedures, Cate and I had the privilege of taking Roger to his doctor's appointments, driving him to job sites, and assisting in his care.

While in the hospital awaiting the final procedure to replace his heart valve, Roger's spleen ruptured. By the time Cate and I arrived at 7:00 a.m., the spleen had been repaired, but his body was weak and his temperature had dropped significantly. We watched and prayed with the family for almost two hours as doctors took turns performing CPR, working to warm his body enough to give him a chance for survival. Roger never recovered and died seconds after their life saving efforts ceased. His unexpected death hit close to home, because the children and I considered Roger family.

Cate and I cancelled our plans for spring break the following week and stayed home with Mary, the boys, and their extended family and friends. Our children were scheduled to be with their dads, leaving us free to provide support and help with funeral arrangements.

To escape the physical and emotional turmoil of the divorce, intervention, and death, I scheduled a trip to Dallas to visit Daddy. He worried for the children's future and mine, and wanted me to know I always had a place to call home. Though he'd been in a small apartment for more than twenty years, he knew Mother had room to spare in their four-thousand-plus-square-foot home. When I wasn't sure where we'd land, the idea of being in his care again was comforting, but the thought of living with Mother was not.

Daddy had offered our family home previously to Amanda during the construction of hers. Like his, her housekeeping was messy and cluttered, but living in constant filth and disorder didn't seem to bother her. However, it was more than Mother could bear, so she began organizing Amanda's belongings, as she'd done during the thirty years Amanda lived at home. This time her things included a husband, two full-time nannies, an infant and a toddler, and all their belongings. After Mother was done rearranging, there was a playpen with three toys in the corner of the family room and a high chair at the kitchen table. The remaining items had been removed from sight and use.

While Mother organized, Daddy enjoyed having Amanda and the babies at his disposal. He came the house every afternoon, spending hours holding and playing with them. Although Mother had always considered our family residence exclusively hers, she suffered through the intrusions for the sake of having Daddy back home.

On my visit, I stayed at Amanda's house because Mother didn't want guests in hers. Nevertheless, she needed me to take her to the doctor for a checkup early the following morning and planned my day accordingly. As we drove to the office, I listened to her explain how difficult her recovery from hip replacement surgery had been and the awful struggles she'd faced afterwards. She claimed the doctor had done a shoddy job and the nurses mishandled her, requiring a second surgery and a longer-than-expected recovery.

Even more upsetting was the imminent death of her beloved dog suffering from kidney failure. A lover of animals myself, I empathized with her heartbreak and offered my condolences.

"I'm so sorry!" I extended. "I'm sure they'll keep Lucky comfortable so she doesn't have to suffer, but I know that doesn't diminish your sorrow." It seemed an appropriate time to share my troubles as well. "If it makes you feel any better, I'm sad, too. I'm in the fight of my life with the divorce, defending myself and the children against Rob. He has two attorneys while I can't afford one," I stated.

I had mentioned it several months ago in a phone call. Her response, "Well, I'm sure you'll work it out," effectively ended the conversation. However, this time I was visibly upset in her presence. As I looked to her with tears streaming down my face, I found the same hollow eyes that had stared back at me my entire life. Following a long, awkward silence, she finally offered, "It's a good thing you have your daddy and Cate to help if you need them."

My mind immediately began racing. "What kind of response is that?" "Where is her compassion as a mother, grandmother, and human being?" "Why is she pawning me off on Daddy and Cate when I'm not asking her for anything?"

Though Mother had the means to provide financial assistance, I had learned long ago not to count on it and knew better than to expect an offer then. She had inherited a couple of million dollars from her parents but chose not to share it with Daddy, my siblings, or me. Instead, she spent the money on herself and her pets, and relied on Daddy to care for our needs.

After a few more minutes of my weeping and her silence, Mother began ranting about the injustices in veterinarian medicine. "Why is it that medical doctors can readily provide organ transplants to humans but animals aren't offered the same level of care?" she posed indignantly. "I would gladly pay $10,000 or more to keep Lucky alive if they'd just give her a new kidney!"

I'd never seen Mother cry due to human tragedy, but she sat on the sofa and sobbed uncontrollably the rest of that afternoon. Having experienced extreme sadness with the loss of childhood pets and my beloved Ginger, I understood her pain, but it was her insensitivity towards the inconceivable circumstances the children and I faced that stunned me. It struck me that she valued her dog's life more than ours, or at the very least she considered herself responsible for her pet, but not for us.

Her disparity in emotion was apparent at other times, the most memorable when Daddy was in the hospital for heart surgery. Scheduled for emergency angioplasty following routine testing that revealed a major blockage, he was admitted to a hospital in Houston, Texas, where Susan was in medical school.

As a team of nurses was getting him settled into a room following the procedure, Amanda, David, Johnny, and I waited outside while Susan discussed the procedure and post-op care with the doctors. We could see Mother standing over his bed and hear her reciting orders, "Do this...don't do that...blah, blah, blah..."

"My hearing is fine," he quipped angrily, "and I don't need your help, thank you!"

As she persisted, he became visibly agitated. His heart rate plummeted and all color suddenly raced from his face. The nurses asked Mother to leave the room immediately and began calling for help. Several doctors appeared, the door closed, and they began administering emergency treatment to get Daddy stabilized.

Susan assured us he was in good hands, but the incident scared the hell out of Amanda, David, and me. As Susan used her big medical words and wealth of knowledge to demonstrate her intellectual superiority, Mother offered her own explanation. "I told him not to... I knew this would happen. I just knew it!" she claimed. "Well, it's his own fault and he deserves what he gets!"

As soon as the door opened and we were allowed back into the room, she began explaining the error of Daddy's ways to him, never once considering the incident could have been the result of the surgery or his response to her unwelcome lecturing. She was determined to assign blame and there was not a hint of concern for his wellbeing. I found it disturbingly odd, but then again, it was Mother.

Incapable of empathy, she couldn't appreciate the toll getting divorced took on me or the children. Though she and Daddy had a relationship no one would want to emulate, they managed to escape my unfortunate reality, which entitled her to represent herself as a happily wed woman. It was shameful and quite pathetic to watch.

Daddy provided emotional and financial support throughout the divorce negotiations, which finally ended in July 2007, almost two years after Rob and I separated. Following a subpoena, two continuances, a restraining order, three attorneys, two mediators, one accountant, and tens of thousands of dollars in fees, Rob was forced to give me more than double what I had asked of him initially.

The journey was unexpected, but the one he chose because he could. Thankfully, I survived his attempts to annihilate me and received the fair settlement the children and I deserved. In the end, justice prevailed.

2007

Dear Rob,

I'm deeply saddened by the death of our marriage. With high hopes and good intentions, I fully expected us to be together until the end of time and never imagined we'd face the harsh realities of divorce. It seemed we were perfectly suited for one another; independent and competent with similar tastes, faith, and values.

When the children arrived, I looked to you to be the leader of our family and my partner in life. You provided well for us financially but otherwise left me alone to care for myself, you, and the children while you lived a solitary existence. Because I was unable to speak up for what I wanted, I managed accordingly and allowed you to remain uninvolved, compromising myself and our relationship in the process. This arrangement left me living in a lonely, unhealthy place for many years before our marriage began unraveling.

I don't regret our union for one second because it produced the three greatest loves of my life: Thomas, Rachel, and Johnny. As their advocate, I recognize the significant roles we both play in their lives. For that reason,

I will honor you as their father though there are times I do not agree with your judgment and am ashamed of your character.

I believed you had high moral standards and the utmost integrity, but you proved me irrefutably wrong. Instead, I discovered the one whom I trusted with my life was seeking my demise while professing to have my best interest at heart. By attempting to take my dignity and forcing me to beg for what was rightfully mine, you committed emotional rape.

Conversely, I take great comfort in being able to look the children in the eyes and tell them honestly that I loved you as best I could and did nothing to deliberately harm you during our marriage or the divorce. I accept responsibility for my part in our relationship's breakdown, without regret for its demise.

The truth is, we didn't know ourselves or each other like we thought and we were both incapable of acknowledging our feelings. However, our true colors were revealed during the divorce. I'm extremely protective of those I love, I know how to survive, and I never give up trying.

I choose not to defeat myself by seeking justice for the harm you caused me but hold my head high, stand strong for the children, and treat you with the respect I deserve, knowing inside I'm the one who earned it. I pray Thomas, Rachel, and Johnny never suffer the same ill fate when placing their trust in your hands.

Anna

IMPROPER
COMMUNICATION

I TRIED TO imagine life after divorce but couldn't. My family was my life and I knew that would never change. Though Rob and I were no longer married, we were still a family: a mother, father, and three young children. As their parents, we were responsible for providing them a safe, secure, and loving childhood, and separately we had personal lives to live. It wasn't any different to me than it had been since their birth.

I realize others may not have seen it that way, including peers who began treating me differently. Some thought it socially acceptable to be married and miserable, but not divorced. They treated divorce as if it were a contagious condition, one that could potentially destroy their own marriage or downgrade their social stature if they associated with it. Where I had once been an equal and confidant, I was unexpectedly not worthy of their attention or respect. Furthermore, the life I'd known for the last twelve years became irrelevant to my current existence, as if I no longer had anything in common with married folk.

With the change in marital status came the perception that my character had somehow transformed overnight, too. I didn't understand. I was still a devoted mother and my family was my priority, as it had always been. My goals and values were the same. I didn't hate men, celebrate my independence, or parade around footloose and fancy free, all threats to the institution of marriage. In fact, the exact opposite was true. I had learned so much about unhealthy relationships that I had greater respect for those who'd succeeded.

I couldn't do anything about these perceptions except live my life as I had in marriage, faithfully and responsibly, with my children at the center. Thankfully, I had the love and support of close friends moving forward.

Knowing I wasn't looking to replace Rob as the children's father or insert another into our sacred environment, I envisioned eventually sharing my free time with someone who could be available when I was, on Thursdays evenings and every other weekend. I'd devote myself to Thomas, Rachel, and Johnny while they were in my care and have the remainder of my time and energy to invest in a dating relationship.

While operating as a single parent, it became clear that arrangement wasn't a realistic possibility. Life with the children couldn't be compartmentalized so easily, as it flowed during my free time as well as my scheduled time. There were activities and sporting events to attend, volunteer commitments to fulfill, and experiences to share. The children needed me and I them, and it wasn't limited to our time together. Rob and I encouraged open communication in both directions which left me at their disposal twenty-four hours a day, seven days a week.

Whoever I dated would have to respect the relationship I had with my children and Rob, and they'd have to be willing to participate in it or watch from the sidelines, whichever was needed at the time. It was the beginning of a different vision for the future, but I was uncertain what it looked like because I couldn't fathom another person in our intimate world.

Dividing my time between the children and girlfriends, I wasn't actively seeking dates or a relationship after the divorce, though everyone else was looking for me. Several mentioned a guy who came to church on Sundays with his three beautiful children. They described him as caring, committed, and successful, a great role model and devoted father. He sounded like a dream, but I had no interest in meeting him or dating anyone and continued enjoying my life as a single mother.

The following year when Thomas graduated from the children's small private school after fifth grade, Rob and I transferred him, Rachel, and Johnny to our parish school. Its enrollment overlapped the church community, so I knew many families before our arrival and met others along the way. In addition, several from our previous school made the same transition, including Cate, whose son had been there the preceding year. We became familiar faces in the school community, though I'd been warned by Mother that if I extended generosity to others, they would take advantage of my time and resources.

At pickup one afternoon in the parking lot, I spotted a dad who immediately caught my attention. Vince had blond hair with bright eyes, a rosy complexion, and a great smile. Built like a teddy bear, he looked to be a kind soul with a gentle nature. I didn't know the first thing about him, his family or his marital status, but I could tell he had a sense of charm and style.

Admiring him from afar that day, I didn't think much more about it until Cate reminded me several weeks later of their previous meeting. Judy, our divorce attorney and a child advocate specialist, had introduced Vince and Cate when Cate's oldest entered middle school. Having represented both, Judy knew them well and admired them as individuals and committed parents. She hoped their connection would lend each support as they raised children in the same community. Cate was more than happy to oblige, but Vince hadn't acknowledged her since their coffee meeting the prior year.

Though Judy continued to assure Cate he was a nice guy and exceptional father, Cate considered his behavior rude and unacceptable. "He's an arrogant ass," she'd say. Her opinion didn't diminish my interest, though, because I was enamored by him, not the prospect of a relationship.

Vince's and my paths crossed regularly, as two of his children were in the same classes as mine. Before long, our daughters became friends. They were in the school play and extracurricular sports together, which led to play dates and afterschool activities. The exchanges that followed allowed me to see into his private life, piquing my curiosity.

I later learned he was the same guy everyone was talking about from church. It was obvious he and the children were embraced by the entire community and I understood why they thought highly of him. Besides being a well-liked member of the school and parish, he was a fabulous dad to his three darling girls. He took them to and from school, coached their sporting activities, and attended Sunday services on a regular basis.

Vince represented what I wanted and didn't have in Rob—a willing participant and committed father. Besides being handsome and charming, he was accomplished, respected, and socially active. I realized then that someone like him could enrich the children's lives and mine, not take away from them as I had initially feared.

Though I wasn't looking for a relationship at the time, the thought of sharing my life with someone who possessed those qualities was beyond exciting. I got butterflies in my stomach, my heart raced, and my emotions spun out of control each time we met, even if it were only in passing in the school parking lot. I hadn't experienced these feelings since Derek in college and was delighted to know the hope of finding love again was still alive. It wasn't Vince, or I was uncertain if it were, because I didn't know him well, but he came to symbolize my ideal of the perfect companion after the divorce.

One Sunday at church, Vince and I had plans to exchange our daughters following a sleepover. While the boys and I sat with my friend Carmen and her two children during the service, as we frequently did, Rachel sat with Vince and the girls. Afterwards, Carmen and I headed to the back of the church to meet them.

As we approached, I attempted to introduce Vince and Carmen but it was apparent none was necessary. They were both noticeably uncomfortable in each other's presence. Vince folded his arms across his body and leaned back as far as he could without falling over, and Carmen lost all coloring and expression from her face as if she were suddenly ill. The three of us made small talk for a few minutes before I thanked Vince, grabbed Rachel, and disappeared into the church parking lot. Carmen followed us out, and we parted ways from there without mention of the encounter.

I pondered the awkwardness and wondered what had caused it. Given the palpable tension between the two, I sensed familiarity mixed with aversion. In my wildest thoughts, I imagined they had known each other in college, had too much to drink one night, hooked up, and never spoke again. He was ashamed facing her and she was hurt by his rejection. It seemed farfetched, though plausible. Whatever had happened felt distant and removed from their current lives, as they were both responsible adults and devoted parents.

I called Carmen that night to tell her about my infatuation and find out what she knew of Vince. Not typically one to ask personal questions of my friends, I found myself uneasy addressing the issue and attempted to diffuse it with humor. In the middle of our conversation, I boldly blurted out, "Did you get drunk and sleep with him or what?"

There was dead silence on the other end of the phone and I knew instantly I wanted to take back my comment, but nothing could have prepared me for her response. "We dated off and on for three years in high school and college but haven't seen each other in the ten years since," she stated calmly. Adding, "I didn't know he was still living in the area."

Her pokerfaced tone let me know there was more to it than she was admitting. Though Carmen was happily married with two beautiful children and Vince had three of his own, their reunion was naturally awkward. In hindsight, it made perfect sense.

I apologized profusely for my insensitivity. I would never have posed the question had I considered that scenario, but it was too late for that then. Not only had I asked something inappropriate and stupid, the manner in which I asked it was disrespectful. Thankfully, my friendship with Carmen was strong enough to survive my blunder.

While their past prevented me from wanting a romantic relationship with Vince, it didn't stop the flutters from racing through my body each time I laid eyes on him. He embodied the father I imagined for Thomas, Rachel, and Johnny—dedicated, involved, and loving. Though I wasn't looking to provide the children with a replacement, these qualities earned my respect and admiration.

Vince and I had several things in common. We both had attorney fathers and domineering mothers, our former mates were incapable of caring for our children, and we'd each been affected by a loved one's substance abuse. His girls resembled Amanda, Susan, and me in our youth, close in age with blond hair and blue eyes. His oldest and Amanda even shared the same name. As the daughter of an absent mother and a single parent of three children myself, I identified with the challenges he faced in raising the girls, though our individual struggles were not the same.

Our similar experiences, shared community, and Carmen, Cate, and Judy's relationships allowed me to feel an improper connection to Vince. As such, I reached out over email to offer him praise and support through flattery and encouragement. "Judy thinks the world of you." "The girls are lucky to have you as their father." "It's evident you're well liked and supported in the community."

I didn't say anything I wouldn't have said to a close friend, but he was barely an acquaintance. He replied with a thank you, and our passing relationship continued throughout the following year, as did my schoolgirl crush. My girlfriends learned of it and referred to him as my "pretend boyfriend." They knew it was the "idea" of him, not him, that interested me, so the jokes were made in good fun and I played along while instigating some of them myself.

In marriage, I discovered it was difficult to discuss my feelings with Rob, and when I tried, he was incapable of empathy, which made matters worse. Determined not to let my discomfort interfere with future relationships, I experimented with professing my thoughts of adoration to Vince. It felt safe because I knew he wasn't interested in me and I wasn't planning to betray my friendship with Carmen.

"I want you to know that your efforts are not going unnoticed. I think you're an exceptional father, man of character, and model Catholic," I professed. "While I'm not looking for a relationship, these qualities are very attractive to me. Maybe that's why I find you both handsome and charming." I followed with words of encouragement, "Keep up the good work for those beautiful girls!"

Having never exposed myself like that to anyone previously, I felt a sense of exhilaration and relief after sending the obsequious e-mail. However, my bravery and triumph quickly turned to humiliation when Vince didn't respond. Though I didn't expect him to return the feelings, a simple acknowledgment would have been nice. I told him so a few days later in another e-mail and received a brief reply thanking me for my kind comments and requesting follow up over the phone. Discussing my feelings wasn't what I had in mind, so I let him know his response had been sufficient.

Later that year, Cate had a gathering for Judy and Lewis, a prominent forensic accountant and Jake's dad, to honor them and celebrate their work with clients in our social circles. When discussing the invite list, Cate and I agreed it would be inappropriate to exclude anyone within our school community, including Vince. Unfortunately, the thought of sharing an evening with him under the circumstances was mortifying, to say the least.

As the event neared, I was faced with the possibility of encountering him and my friends in the same intimate setting. I knew his appearance could subject the two of us to unwanted ridicule, so I tried to avert any embarrassment by filling him in on the jokes ahead of time. Though my humiliation from the recent e-mails was still great, I drafted another one and attempted to communicate our amusement. How the "pretend boyfriend" was not really about him, but rather the "idea" of him. I apologized in advance for any poor behavior that might occur, hoping he would appreciate the humor in the situation.

Not surprisingly, he didn't reply and cancelled thirty minutes before the evening began.

"Cate's residence," I answered.

"This is Vince. Is she available?" he asked.

"Oh, hi, Vince. It's Anna," I replied. "She's busy at the moment. May I take a message?"

"Let her know that something's come up unexpectedly and I'm not going to make it this evening," he explained. "Please give her my apologies."

"I'll let her know. Sorry we'll miss you," I offered.

I was crushed knowing I made him so uncomfortable he couldn't be in my presence and the company of close friends at the same time, though I understood he was wisely avoiding an unpleasant situation and didn't blame him for not attending. Cate, on the other hand, considered my forgiveness a denial of his rude and unacceptable behavior, which infuriated her. Already convinced he was an arrogant ass, she added "spineless" and "disrespectful" to the list of offenses.

Overly protective of me, Cate treats me like a beloved sister and I return the sentiment. We spend much of our available time together when we're without children, more one-on-one time than most married couples have. Sharing the joys and struggles of life and single parenting, we jest that we'd have the perfect marriage if only we liked each other in that way.

During the divorce, I spent more time at Cate's place on some weekends than I stayed at my own. A beautiful Northwest contemporary home designed for entertaining, it was the preferred gathering spot amongst close friends. It became my safe haven for support, companionship, and peace, but that all changed when Vince bought a home across the street.

The thought of running into him in my private circles was upsetting, but not as disturbing as the change in Cate's behavior. She had gone from disliking Vince immensely to being a gracious friend and neighbor. They were exchanging pleasantries on the street and at school and swapping kids back and forth. Cate's efforts seemed contrary and hypocritical to me, but I accepted their friendship after coming to terms with my failed attempts to connect with Vince and his blatant disregard for my existence, neither of which had anything to do with her.

Because Vince and I shared friends and community, I wanted to feel comfortable when our paths crossed. That meant an apology was in order. It seemed silly to write again, as that had been the origin of my disgrace, but it was the only form of contact I was comfortable with at the time. Instead of the exaggerated sincerity I'd used unsuccessfully, I opted for a light, sarcastic approach to ask for forgiveness for my inappropriate communication. I joked about the embarrassing e-mails ("OMG! Even my daughter knows not to hit the send button on that one!") and my schoolgirl crush ("The infatuation is over but the thought of sex does occasionally cross my mind! LOL!"). The zinger wasn't intended to be a proposition but rather a desperate attempt to connect with the only thing I hadn't already tried, his reptilian brain.

Several days passed and again, no reply. If Vince misread my intentions, he may have been put off by what could've been considered an unwanted advance. Though I'd never pursued anyone for sex and never would, he didn't know that, so it was within the realm of possibilities. Whatever the case, it was clear Vince had been rendered speechless. I followed up to let him know the apology was sincere and hoped he wasn't offended by my sense of humor. However, there was nothing I could do to take back my foolish comments or actions.

A false sense of familiarity allowed me to feel a connection to Vince that didn't exist, making the expression of my feelings improper and unwarranted under the circumstances. While I didn't blame him for his discomfort, his lack of response was hurtful and his disregard, demoralizing. It left me feeling vulnerable, misunderstood, and unloved.

Though the integrity of my character was not in question, my behavior was, and I was not proud of it. I had exposed my greatest weakness, my childlike emotional side.

THE
ENLIGHTENMENT

———

TO UNDERSTAND MY insecure feelings and behaviors in intimate relationships, I had to first analyze my emotional development and relationship with Mother in early childhood. Though I had other sources of love, she was my primary caretaker and I depended on her to meet my needs. At a minimum, I required unconditional love and responsive care for survival, both of which she was unable to provide.

No matter how hard I tried, I couldn't find a way to connect with my mother, the one person who was supposed to love me above all others. In fact, my attempts exasperated her, as she considered them unreasonable demands for attention. From her point of view, I was asking her to give of herself, an uncharacteristic task, while robbing her of her prized possession, Daddy. I deserved to be punished for that injustice, not rewarded.

To evade Mother's retribution, I learned to read her emotions, anticipate her moods, and react preemptively, but her emotional abuse made me feel undeserving of life. She taught me love was painful, required endless effort, and was unattainable. It caused great frustration and unrest. This was how I experienced the most basic form of love.

I became extremely proficient at avoiding the pain and disguising my insecurities from most, including myself, and didn't realize the profound impact the missing Attachment bond had on my state of mind. Nevertheless, Mother's incompetence and neglect, effectual abandonment, left marked deficiencies in my physical and emotional development. My emotional center, the limbic brain, was embedded with unhealthy interactions from birth, and my instinctive responses played out accordingly. Their pervasiveness was due to familiarity, not success.

My entire existence was based on forming connections that could sustain me, but the absence of secure love and feelings of unworthiness caused me to reject suitable mates and seek those who replicated the relationship I had with Mother. In my unconscious fight for survival, I obsessed over finding and keeping unattainable love, which prevented me from functioning in other important areas of my life. I gave away my soul in the process, leaving me emotionally depleted and unbalanced.

Outwardly, I grew to be a happy, smart, well-adjusted woman blessed with more than most: three incredible children, good health, supportive friends, a budding career, beautiful home, and idyllic life. However, the successes came with the sorrow of an emotionally unavailable mother, the dysfunctional relationship of my parents, the betrayal of a close friend and sibling, the death of loved ones, the intervention and recovery of a beloved friend, the breakup of my marriage, and financial ruin. Through all of it, I managed to survive forty-four years without facing the wreckage of a broken Attachment.

In treatment, Drs. Anthea Coster, Michael Orlans, and Terry Levy helped me recognize my emotional responses were actually coping mechanisms developed in infancy as defenses to Mother's indifference. I tried to be perfect so she couldn't find fault in me, feigned happiness so she'd want to spend time with me, and explained myself incessantly to gain understanding. When my efforts didn't elicit a positive response, I worked tirelessly to please her, hoping her approval would substitute for love. Refined throughout childhood, these behaviors were repeated over and over in my relationships with romantic partners.

To lay the groundwork for a healthy future, Anthea, Terry, Michael, and I reconstructed reciprocal interactions between caregiver and child. By reenacting my first three years of life through my inner child, Little Anna, I replaced past harmful experiences with secure exchanges and created a sound emotional foundation.

Anthea, a genuine and loving woman, acted as Mother. Cold, hateful, and apathetic towards me, she acknowledged her absence and confessed her inability to respond to the needs of others. She was admittedly self-absorbed, lacking interest or compassion for anyone other than herself.

"Don't bother me, you ungrateful brat. I don't have time!" she exclaimed angrily. "I have to take care of my animals and go shopping." Walking away, she called out gingerly, "Here, ducky, ducky. Here, little ducky." Then, she turned and threatened, "Clean your room and don't make any messes. Otherwise, you'll be punished when I get home!"

After attacking me with hurtful rhetoric and a dismissive demeanor, she apologized for her behavior and showed me the care I should have received. "I'm sorry I wasn't there for you when you needed me. It wasn't your fault. You were just a baby," she explained tenderly and pleaded, "Please forgive me."

Anthea held me in her arms, looked deep into my eyes, and responded attentively to my feelings. By giving me the love I desperately needed, she validated my existence and convinced me I didn't deserve to be neglected or abused. This realization released me from the hatred I'd felt towards Mother for the way she'd treated me my entire life.

Terry, a kind and gentle man, played the role of Daddy, an empathetic listener with a calm presence and quick wit. Needy, pathetic, and weak while defending his relationship with Mother, he was sorrowful when conceding his helplessness in preventing the damage she'd caused.

"Well, I wish I could help you, but I just can't," he claimed listlessly. "Your mother has been impossible to live with since the day I met her, and that's never going to change." Adding emphatically, "God knows I've tried."

While taking responsibility for his actions, he asked for mercy for his role in their dysfunctional relationship and my insecure life. Seeing Daddy in this new light opened my eyes to a different way of thinking.

"I wasn't strong enough to stand up to your mother and protect you like I should have. Instead, I turned my back on your suffering," he confessed with regret. "You were an innocent child. Please forgive me for not being there."

Michael, a soft-spoken and jovial man, a contemplative thinker, served as the voice of reason. Peaceful, comforting, and rational, he made observations and provided insight into the harsh realities of my childhood, the negative effects they had on my development, and the positive outlook for my future.

"Your mother wasn't capable of taking care of you, and your dad didn't protect you. That's not the way love is supposed to be. You deserve to be treated with kindness and respect."

Replacing unhealthy, destructive experiences freed me from deep-seated unworthiness and allowed me to honor emotions I'd disregarded my whole life, the most powerful step in my healing process. Though I knew the toxic relationship I shared with Mother was not my fault intellectually, I carried the burden and shame of it in my heart, much like the victim of child abuse. I couldn't get past thinking that if I'd done something differently, I could have prevented it, or if I'd been worthy of love, she would have loved me.

Truthfully, there was nothing I could have ever done to change our relationship. It wasn't personal. Mother was simply emotionally incompetent and mentally unbalanced. However, she used her authority and control to disguise her inability to connect with others. By imposing hierarchy, she distanced herself, fed her inflated ego, and created a false sense of reality. Unfortunately, it became my living nightmare.

Mother had children because Daddy wanted them, four in five years, none of whom she could care for. By her own admission, he was such a great caretaker that she made a conscious decision not to participate. She claimed we were too much to manage and he loved being with us, so she willingly turned the reins over to him. As a result, I bonded with Daddy in the evenings and remained under her absent care during my waking hours. This inconsistency resulted in an anxious pattern of behavior.

By the age of two, my brain had been permanently altered from the disrupted Attachment bond that had formed between Mother and me. Thankfully, my sisters and brother didn't suffer my same fate, because Amanda, David, and Susan formed secure Attachments with Lillian, who took over as the primary caregiver when Amanda was born. Lillian enabled Mother to admire my siblings from afar without accepting responsibility, much like the role of a grandparent. While they were bonded to Lillian and didn't rely on Mother to fulfill their needs, I still looked to her for caregiving and demanded things they did not.

The lone sheep in the family, I couldn't identify with my siblings and they didn't understand me, which left me feeling like an outsider in my own home. Daddy witnessed Mother's neglect and emotional torment but believed his love could overcome it. Because he consoled me, offered compassion and support, I considered him my savior. His care made me feel safe and loved on the deepest level. It prevented me from recognizing Daddy hadn't actually rescued me from Mother, but had exacerbated the situation by allowing it to persist. His choice to stay in the marriage, whether out of fear or in the best interest of his children, was significantly more damaging to our family's emotional wellbeing than if he'd been strong enough to leave.

These revelations were unexpected, overwhelming, and life changing! Daddy wasn't my knight in shining armor, as I had always imagined. In reality, he couldn't get what he needed from Mother and relied on me to provide him empathy, moral support, and unconditional love, an unhealthy burden for any child to bear. Though his emotional dependence on me was misguided, it may have been the very thing that saved my life. I could have died from failure-to-thrive syndrome, but the desire to keep Daddy out of harm's way gave me reason to live.

Besides having identical frustrations with Mother, Daddy and I share other likenesses—a similar tenderness, compassion, and sense of humor. Both perfectionists, we are detail oriented and easily frustrated with ourselves, and our emotions tend to overpower us. I assumed these characteristics were genetically influenced, like our eyes, smile, and build, but learned they were the result of compromised Attachments, something I was unaware Daddy and I had in common.

When he was eighteen months old, his father died, leaving his nineteen-year-old mother alone to raise him and his two-year-old sister. Working full time to support their family, she was unavailable to provide adequate care.

Daddy overcame his underprivileged childhood by setting lofty goals and working hard to achieve success. Cognizant of the challenges a low-income family faced, he vowed never to bring children into that environment and strove to provide us a superior life. While he succeeded in accomplishing that goal, he didn't achieve the same fulfillment in his personal relationships. His low self-esteem allowed him to marry an emotionally-void woman who thrived on controlling and demeaning him.

As I recognized Daddy's insecure Attachment, I began to understand the truth of his and Mother's marriage and how his role in it impacted my intimate relationships. Though I knew she was the reason I disregarded myself and accepted maltreatment from partners, I hadn't recognized Daddy influenced the men I chose and the manner in which I loved them. The enlightenment was beyond belief at first, but it became grotesquely obvious upon reflection.

Daddy was incapable of standing up for himself, which showed me men were incompetent and weak, unable to hold respect or protect those they loved. As a result, I sought men perceived to be needy, who benefited from my care, comfort, and support. If they accepted my efforts and exposed vulnerability, like Daddy had, my feelings of love blossomed.

My first love, Bobby, and I had a mutual liking for one another as friends long before a romantic relationship developed. While he was personable and had a good sense of humor, he was too brazen for me and didn't resemble the clean-cut, all-American boys I preferred. Nevertheless, as he shared his hurt feelings over Beth's rejection, I was honored to be the one he looked to in times of need. His trust made me feel appreciated and loved. I listened, empathized, and offered words of encouragement, just as I had done with Daddy.

Publically, Bobby showered me with affection to the point of embarrassment, the exact opposite of Mother, who hadn't acknowledged my presence privately. Having tried unsuccessfully since birth to get her attention, I was thrilled to be the focus of anyone's interest.

However comforting finding that love was, the fear of losing it was debilitating. Feeling whole for the first time, I tried everything to keep Bobby's and my love alive. I overlooked the way he treated me and focused on being the perfect girlfriend to prevent him from leaving. Though painful and unhealthy, our relationship perpetuated my existence. Bobby's love satisfied my longing for Mother's acceptance and freed me from seeking her approval, and my care of him replaced my desire to protect Daddy. Consequently, I was willing to surrender my soul to an undeserving mate in hopes of fulfilling my lifelong dream of unconditional love.

Thoughts of Bobby, my feelings for him, and the preservation of our relationship consumed me to the point of incompetence in other areas of my life. Incapable of balancing emotions, activities, and school, I alienated my peers and lost interest in athletics, activities, and academics.

Promiscuity was against my moral code, but rejecting his advances would have been the equivalent of an addict turning away a fix. I wasn't mature enough physically or emotionally to have sex, but gaining his love was more critical to my survival than upholding my personal values. Although it made me feel dirty and cheap, degrading my sense of self, the physical interaction satisfied my cravings for emotional intimacy.

Watching my teenage son now, I can clearly see how disturbing my behavior was then, but I wasn't in control of my emotions, they were in control of me. As Thomas discovers himself and the wonder of girls, he's more interested in developing a peer group than having a serious relationship. It's typical behavior for a sixteen-year-old boy, just as it was for Bobby at the time.

I gave away my soul again in hopes of finding love with Derek. Instantly drawn to his good looks, smile, and gentle nature, I couldn't get him out of my mind at first glance. His trust made me feel special, and consoling him gave my life meaning, another repeat of my relationship with Daddy.

There was something beyond our physical contact that fulfilled a primal need and led to obsession. In his arms, I could look into his eyes and see the reflection of his soul, hear his heartbeat in synch with mine, feel the warmth of his skin, and smell the essence of his being, the same innocent sensations a newborn baby experiences for the first time with its mother. I craved those moments, not sex. The connection replicated the Attachment bond and perpetuated my existence.

Derek and I both took what we wanted from our relationship. He satisfied physical desires while I received the emotional intimacy needed to survive. To sustain it, I worked tirelessly to please him, as I had Mother; provided compassion and support, as I had Daddy; and showered him with presents to express my love.

Derek's denial of our relationship was hurtful, similar to Mother's disregard, but I knew how to survive under those circumstances. However, when our secret affair ended, I found myself utterly devastated, in self-preservation mode. My emotions were completely out of control, and there was nothing I could do to contain irrational thoughts or behaviors. Tossing and turning in bed for months afterwards, I wondered how I might survive. I lost interest in taking care of myself and spending time with friends, and couldn't concentrate on my studies. My grades plummeted, requiring me to take a leave of absence from school.

Uncertain I could manage another failed relationship, I stopped dating, focused my energy on friends and Ginger, and immersed myself in projects at home, school, and work. It was several years later before my friendship with Phillip grew into a romantic relationship. He was unattractive to me, having physical characteristics similar to Mother, but he had the perfect mom and the ideal family. While I dreamed of becoming a member, I was never in love with him the way I had been with Bobby or Derek. Nonetheless, the breakup was unwanted and difficult in my never-ending search for love.

I dated a few others but they were nice, healthy guys who weren't dysfunctional the way I needed them to be. They treated me with respect and didn't require my support, leaving me unable to connect.

By the time Rob and I started dating, I'd been on my own for several years and was in a good place emotionally, thanks to close friends and a rewarding career. Competent, secure, and happy, I didn't need anyone to complete me and wasn't looking to replace Mother's love. Ours was different from any relationship I had ever encountered, convincing me it was true love at long last.

Rob and I lived independent, parallel lives under one roof. Although I expected our marriage to evolve naturally into a partnership when children arrived, each did what we felt was in the best interest of our family, irrespective of the other. I took care of the children and looked to Rob to provide emotional support, be invested in our lives, and share in its joys and struggles. He provided for us financially but otherwise lived a life of physical and emotional isolation. Unknowingly, we had both settled into the roles of the caretakers we most identified with.

While I aimed for perfection and explained myself incessantly to receive love, as I had with Mother, I couldn't get Rob's attention or understanding, which frustrated me and irritated him. No matter how hard I tried to connect, he preferred existing without human interaction. He purposely withheld love and remained unaffected by my presence, leaving me feeling unappreciated, unworthy, and unwanted. I was continually upset by his lack of effort but shied away from communicating it to avoid conflict. He allowed me to carry the weight for our family, and I didn't demand his involvement, which only fueled our dysfunction. Once we finally recognized we had conflicting expectations of one another, it was difficult for us to resolve our differences and find happiness in the relationship.

When considering whether the breakup had been a terrible mistake, mine to eventually explain to the children, I learned of the dynamics of our connection. Why it worked in the beginning and failed in the end wasn't exactly what I expected. My mistake wasn't the divorce, as I had feared. It was choosing Rob as an intimate partner in the first place.

After past wreckage, I protected my survival by locking the door to my heart. Rob didn't knock on it, and I didn't offer to let him in. I enjoyed his company, admired his artistic ability, shared his traditional values and faith, and respected his professional success, but I wasn't in love with him. Confusing comfort for love, I thought we'd be happy sharing the life and family we both desired without realizing it was naïve to think we could have had a successful marriage under those circumstances.

Rob wasn't a bad person; he just wasn't the right one for me. I would never have intentionally chosen a mate similar to Mother but intimate relationships instinctively mirror ones we have with our caregivers in early childhood. It's the reason many inadvertently end up with partners resembling their mothers or fathers, for better or worse.

Looking back, it was no surprise to discover Mother and Rob shared likenesses, though their traits were manifested differently in their personalities. For example, Mother didn't value interpersonal relationships, making her insensitive to others and their feelings. Her disregard felt hurtful, the same way it felt when Rob neglected me.

Though his lack of consideration was the result of introversion and social discomfort, my feelings of rejection were one and the same.

Mother and Rob both lack soul. They are equally self-centered, emotionally void, and socially inadequate, with addictive qualities and incomplete childhoods. Having missed out on her youth by marriage, Mother didn't develop close friendships or abide by parental rules. Thus, she never learned to compromise or respect authority. When she didn't get her way as an adult, she resorted to throwing temper tantrums—screaming, stomping, pouting, and occasionally throwing things.

Rob held onto immature behaviors as well. His therapist likened him to an adolescent in the throes of his teenage years. Feeling he hadn't been granted the freedom to make choices as a child, Rob acted like a caged animal. He rebelled against authority and held on tightly to injustices he believed had been done to him. It caused him to clench his teeth so hard that he had to have every tooth in his mouth crowned simultaneously to prevent from losing them.

While harboring tremendous anger against his Mother for decisions she'd made on his behalf, Rob quietly admired his father's disregard of her. The latent disrespect grew into contempt for all women. I heard it when he admitted using them as sex objects and talked negatively of his sisters, and later encountered it during and after the divorce. His suppressed anger created tension in our relationship, similar to the stress I suffered when dealing with Mother's rage. The association caused me to project childhood hurts onto Rob, compounding my unhappiness and contributing to the failure of our marriage.

At a time when I felt unwanted by Rob, Sam appeared and showed me the only love I'd ever known. He adored and trusted me, I admired and flattered him, and we commiserated over the disappointments in our respective intimate relationships. This replication of experiences with Daddy caused my emotions for Sam to spin out of control.

I respected my wedding vows and didn't want to get involved, but I couldn't stop daydreaming of the joy he brought into my life. Sometimes I didn't think I could face another day without his support, though I knew I couldn't work in good faith to repair my relationship with Rob while being emotionally invested in another, whether intentional or not. I compartmentalized my feelings, separating self-preservation from my marriage, but the intense and wanton emotions scared me to death. It was only later that I learned my inappropriate feelings for Sam had originated in the ashes of my childhood, not the death of my marriage.

Instantly attracted to Vince's boyish charm, I fantasized he was the perfect father and ideal mate. However, that image was in direct contrast with qualities I didn't like. He acted aloof, was rude to me and Cate, and had treated Carmen poorly in their relationship. The women he dated were young, superficial, and materialistic, not what I would consider good role models for his children. And, he flaunted a car costing an obscene amount of money, offensive in my book.

None of these traits was appealing to me, but my interest persisted nonetheless. It angered Cate because she considered him undeserving of my affection, but I was certain his dismissal was my fault and continued to look for opportunities to connect. It was a repeat of the pattern I had used to seek Mother's approval.

Even a three-year-old can figure out when someone doesn't want to play, but Vince's rejection didn't diminish my compulsive thoughts or communication. Instead, the dream of caring for him and his girls gave me a purpose for living. Without it, I felt lost.

Before treatment, I realized Vince was the father I had envisioned for my children, a doting and invested caretaker, but I hadn't recognized the parallels between him and Daddy. They both had three little blond girls and unstable wives. An amazing coincidence, I thought, before realizing my child-like emotional brain had already made that connection. Vince left the marriage and rescued his children from their mother's neglect, my lifelong dream for Daddy. By associating Vince with its fulfillment, my subconscious mind saw him as my redeemer. Though he and I didn't have a romantic relationship, or any relationship at all for that matter, the unfounded attachment fostered intimate feelings and behaviors.

My respect for Vince as a father and adoration of the girls remains, but I no longer need to rescue them to validate my existence. I'm not looking for his acceptance and the spinning in my head, racing in my heart, and compulsive sharing have all ceased.

Making peace with my improper connection to Vince was almost as important as discovering the truth of my intense emotions for TIM. After living a lifetime without love, I was certain he was my dream come true but wondered how I could have become emotionally invested in such a short period of time and not in twelve years of marriage.

TIM was *"The Ideal Man"* to me, from the way he looked to the car he drove, from the company he kept to the lifestyle he lived, from the work he did to the causes he supported. He offered care and consoling, as Daddy had, and accepted mine in return. My emotional support of him and his unabashed affection for me sparked feelings of unconditional love.

Reaching the depths of my soul, he spoke to me physically, emotionally, and spiritually like no one ever had. When we kissed, our eyes and lips locked while our bodies molded effortlessly into one. It seemed our spirits were intrinsically united through the physical connection. The passion fulfilled a yearning for emotional closeness that had only been briefly satisfied by Derek. While this attachment created unwarranted familiarity and overinvestment in the relationship, my longing for love led to extreme desperation.

After treatment, I understood the feelings I had for TIM were real but the person I envisioned was a figment of my imagination. Instead of seeing the superficial, conflicted guy I met while vacationing in Roche Harbor, I saw the person I needed him to be, my savior, like Daddy.

In actuality, TIM lacked self-confidence and was emotionally unavailable. A bragger, he made it known he attended a private college and was a commercial pilot, licensed captain, and the proud owner of a successful contracting business, all on the first day we met. He liked to drop names of wealthy acquaintances and list assets including a $2mil waterfront property, $1mil condo, multiple pieces of $400,000 machinery, Lexus, Range Rover, Mercedes, sixty-foot yacht, extravagant vacations...blah, blah, blah...

I'd been exposed to material wealth many times in my life and wasn't captivated by it. While I was enamored with his career and success in real estate, I was more impressed he had built himself and his business from scratch, like Daddy had. I didn't consider him a better person because of the money, and quite frankly, found his need to catalog it appalling. I was interested in getting to know his charitable spirit, not discussing his balance sheet. Yet my feelings of unworthiness allowed me to identify with his insecurities and overlook these shortcomings.

When our brief affair ended, I was distraught and emotionally bankrupt. Losing TIM was worse than the breakup of my marriage because I had renewed hope of finding unconditional love after a lifetime of failure. To survive the loss, I justified my emotions by comforting him, without seeing that I was the one in need of consoling.

"I know we came into each other's lives for a reason and I'm thankful for that. I'm not sure what happens next, but whatever it is, we'll both be alright," I extended. "For now, I wish you, the girls, and your family all the best."

I'm in awe of how two emotionally compatible, completely incompetent, perfectly suited souls were able to connect in a world full of strangers. TIM truly was ideal for me, just not in the way I expected. Instead of sharing years of happiness, he began the process of healing my compromised Attachment.

Intimate behaviors don't typically surface in friendships, but they exist between Cate and me. While we are not involved romantically, our bond is closer than most, more rewarding, but more complicated and intense. She was a partner through the divorce and again during my healing journey. When I didn't think I could go another step alone, she'd carry me until I could catch my breath and find my feet again. Nevertheless, that's not what makes our relationship intimate. It's the replication of experiences we each shared with our primary caregivers.

After uncovering the truths of my childhood and understanding my compromised Attachment, I discovered that many of my personality traits resulted from my shortcomings. While I'd been aware of them previously, I hadn't recognized their origin. Some were deficiencies in emotional development, some were compensations for the missing bond, and some were desperate attempts to connect.

Because my basic, innate human needs were not met by my primary caregiver early in life, I learned I couldn't rely on others. It caused me to become exceedingly self-sufficient but left me incapable of trust. Feeling unsafe, I was extremely cautious when exploring my environment, something necessary for healthy development. I became hypervigilant and controlling of my surroundings. I looked to my home and belongings for refuge, and it was difficult for me to feel secure outside of my comfort zone.

I created a safety net of friends, "chosen family," who welcomed me into their homes, hearts, and lives, in good times and bad. Consequently, I placed tremendous importance on these friendships, as the support they provided was instrumental to my survival. While this reliance made me vulnerable to mistreatment from those closest to me, Mother's abuse and my low self-esteem were the reasons I tolerated it.

At times, I was controlling and bossy, overly demanding and clingy, superficially engaging and charming, and easily irritable. I used sarcasm and humor to convey my feelings and offered compassion to complete strangers. I couldn't afford to be overlooked, so I learned to speak loudly and blamed it in jest on my second-grade teacher who was hard of hearing.

Two characteristics, being a pleaser and a perfectionist, have become part of my identity. Before the age of two, I tried on clothes in the middle of the night and changed every few hours during the day. I did favors to earn friends in elementary school, tutored classmates in junior high, and picked apart my eyelashes in high school. During college, I skipped class if not styled head to toe. As a stay-at-home mom, I wore skirts and pearls, kept an immaculate house, and overextended myself on volunteer commitments, all to uphold a flawless image. I worked harder than most to make others happy and wouldn't accept less than perfection from myself.

I experienced sleep disturbances and intense emotions, was sensitive to criticism, had inappropriate sexual attitudes and emotional responses, and lacked impulse control. To silence intrusive thoughts, I occupied myself with excessive busyness. For example, I held down three jobs while being a full-time 4.0 student, stripped and repainted a house in the idleness of a 60-hour work week, and orchestrated a cross-country move, including the sale of one home and design of another, with three small children in tow. Achievement gave me a sense of accomplishment and distracted me from self-doubt.

However successful I was at managing on my own, I was unable to attain the same fulfillment in intimate relationships. I hadn't realized it previously but my goal was replacing Mother's love, which caused me to engage in unhealthy behaviors and allowed partners to treat me disrespectfully. The physical and emotional closeness I experienced in romantic relationships replicated innocent exchanges between mother and child, something I desperately needed for survival.

While I learned some valuable lessons from losses along the way, it didn't prevent me from acting irrationally or getting into detrimental situations. I wasn't promiscuous, but I disregarded my moral values and acted irresponsibly to obtain intimacy, leaving my thoughts and emotions at odds with one another.

I was sexually active at the young age of fifteen, allowed men to disrespect me throughout my life, had unprotected sex on occasion, and eventually became pregnant. Unable to care for myself, much less a child, I couldn't imagine how I'd survive and have a baby at the same time. My partner was unwilling to support me, and even if Mother and Daddy had, returning to Mother's control or subjecting an innocent child to her abuse would have been a fate worse than death. Adoption wasn't an option either, because I wouldn't have knowingly abandoned a child as Mother had me.

It felt an impossible dilemma. Seeing no other viable options, I made the decision to terminate the pregnancy, which conflicted with my spiritual beliefs and moral values. Though it may have been the path of least resistance at the time, the internal conflict created turmoil and left emotional scars that still haunt me today.

My insecure foundation also left me vulnerable to improper social behavior, but Mother's antisocial morality (selfishness, vindictiveness, and lack of remorse) gave me reason to be the exact opposite of her. I developed my own set of moral standards based on what felt good and right to me. Thus, I'd never intentionally hurt, disrespect, or compromise another, not even my worst enemy. Instead, I loved others as I wanted to be loved, intensely and unconditionally. I took on their emotions, finding that easier than living in my own despair. It gave me a purpose while draining my energy and hindering the intimacy I craved.

Unfortunately, I didn't treat myself with the same respect. Only by the grace of God was I able to resist drugs and avoid physically abusive partners, recreational sex and communicable diseases, a physical affair in my marriage, and alcoholism. Though my drinking was out of control at times, my life could have been seriously endangered if I'd been born with the addictive gene or used food or alcohol for comfort. Because my body is incapable of regulating itself, I've learned to limit food portions and count drinks to manage my intake in place of self-monitoring, however, if my system is ever tested, I fail miserably.

I recently drank well beyond my limits at a social function when a friend jokingly filled my martini glass every time I looked away. She meant no harm, thinking I could stop, but I drank myself into oblivion without realizing I was severely intoxicated. The excessive alcohol in my system left me incapacitated for two days afterwards.

Besides physical challenges, a biochemical dysregulation prevented me from balancing thoughts, feelings, and behaviors. My emotions consumed me, which prevented me from functioning in other areas of my life. Though I had every reason to be a confident, secure adult, worthlessness and worry plagued my state of mind. The insolvability of this situation created tremendous frustration and hopelessness.

I can see my emotional responses were misguided by my experiences, not irrational thoughts or loose morals. The unhealthy relationship I had with Mother, the insecure role model I had in Daddy, and the coping mechanisms I created to survive were the basis of my intimate relationships. While I hid my insecurities from most, partners were exposed to my instability from the time I attached.

Many of the coping mechanisms I developed in childhood were counterproductive, but some have served me well. I learned to satisfy my own needs, which fostered independence and competence, providing me strength and tenacity when I need it most. Instead of wallowing in despair, I sought hope and positivity, which gives me a sunny disposition and comforts me in periods of darkness.

The suffering gave me empathy for the human condition, allowing me to identify with most everyone I meet.

Though five years of traditional psychotherapy didn't reveal the extent of my Attachment disorder, there's no doubt it affected my emotional health and brain development and left physical features as unique as the psychological scars that remained. As my inherent stress expressed itself physically, my attributes mirrored my mental health, evidenced by a premature birth, underdevelopment and chronic illness throughout childhood, intestinal upset in adolescence and ulcers in college, an inexplicable rash upon my departure from Kansas City, and uncontrollable uterine bleeding during the death of my marriage. Childhood ailments evolved into chronic conditions—asthma, overactive oil glands, irritable bowel syndrome, and heavy menstrual bleeding.

After four years of menorrhagia, I elected to have surgery to permanently end it. During the procedure, my physician discovered a malformation called bicornis unicollis. Instead of developing a triangular uterus, I formed a heart-shaped womb with a septum partially separating the uterine cavity, a fitting depiction of my disorder. The doctor claimed it was a miracle that I'd been able to carry three children almost to term without major complications, as this deformity could have created obstacles in conception and caused miscarriages, neither of which I faced.

My struggle to survive had a significant, if not paralyzing, impact on my wellbeing, but I was never happier and healthier than when I was pregnant with Thomas, Rachel, and Johnny. They answered my lifelong prayers for unconditional love, filling my heart with joy and eliminating my need to seek it elsewhere. My mind rested, the bleeding stopped, persistent ailments faded into obscurity, and all suffering ceased. It was the only peace I had ever known.

2009

Dear Anthea, Michael, and Terry,

I am infinitely grateful for your wisdom, care, and understanding. By healing my insecure Attachment, the primal wound, you restored my soul and lifted my burdens, giving me eternal peace.

Regardless of what the future holds, I now have the building blocks necessary to construct a healthy, balanced life. While the road ahead will not be without strife, I trust my new foundation to steady me when I stumble and catch me when I fall. With this support in place, I can be mindful of the journey without fixating on the outcome.

I believe in the perseverance of the human spirit, though I never imagined my life without continual strife. Thanks to you, my faith has been affirmed and my hopefulness, renewed. You have given me the power to realize my dreams for myself and my family.

By sharing my journey, I want to spread your message of hope and forgiveness to the world.

All my love,

Anna

TRUE LOVE

WHILE UNCOVERING THE truth of my Attachment disorder and its effect on past relationships, I discovered the only love I'd known was conditional and demanding and partners, insecure and weak. Treatment opened my eyes to the presence of true love in my life, the very thing I desired most but didn't know how to receive or give in return.

The greatest of these appeared in college while I was obsessing over Derek. As I looked for opportunities to see him, I spent hours hanging out at his apartment with his roommate, Jeff, waiting, watching TV, and small talking. He didn't seem to mind the conversation or company, and if he did, I would never have known because he was too nice a guy to say anything about it.

Jeff was the perfect gentleman: kind and thoughtful, soft-spoken, with a sense of humor. Tall, dark, and handsome, he dated some but was more selective than his philandering roommate. They'd both grown up in Little Rock, attended private high school together, pledged the same fraternity at the university, and shared an apartment, though they weren't necessarily close friends.

After I stopped seeing Derek, Jeff and I talked over the phone occasionally, saw each other in the clubs regularly, and invited each other to social events. I considered him a close friend and confidant, spending as much time with him as I did some of my girlfriends, and he became protective of me and my feelings. He eventually made it known he was interested in a romantic relationship, but I was still pining over Derek and was uncomfortable with the thought of dating his roommate. Nevertheless, our emotional connection led to physical closeness, which fueled his interest and created sexual tension between us.

While I remained ambivalent about my feelings, he didn't pressure me. Instead, the amount of time we shared and our conversations remained the same, leaving me uncertain of his intentions. He didn't impose them on me and I certainly didn't ask.

As our friendship blossomed, Jeff began sending clear messages through love notes and roses left on the windshield of my car. I was afraid of losing him if a dating relationship failed, so I avoided his feelings as if they didn't exist or pushed him away when he got too close. Though I secretly adored him and hoped we'd get together one day, it was the only way I knew how to respond to his thoughtful gestures at the time.

Jeff graduated from college and returned to his childhood home to study patent law at the University of Arkansas at Little Rock, while I remained in Fayetteville. We kept in contact through phone calls and weekend visits spent walking the boardwalk, dining at Cajun's Wharf, or traveling to the horse races at Oaklawn Park in Hot Springs. One of us typically made the seven-hour roundtrip at least once every couple of months that first year. It was as if we were dating, except we didn't discuss our feelings or the status of our relationship.

His parents would invite me to stay in their family home, where I slept in the guest room and was treated to his mom's Southern cooking and hospitality. Lovely, gracious people, they welcomed me and made me feel like family. All the while, I remained confused about my feelings for Jeff and he acted as if we were best friends, preventing me from seeing his growing affection.

One weekend, he asked if we could get together on an upcoming trip to Fayetteville. I told him I'd love to see him if it worked out but was wallpapering my dining room and wasn't planning to stop until it was completed. He called Saturday morning while I was in the middle of a great big, unfinished mess. Having been up all night and not showered, I was dead tired with dried paste in my hair and all over my clothing. The job was half finished and I had no intention of leaving it, not even for him.

Jeff stopped by that afternoon and found me working, frustrated, and unkempt. As I continued my efforts in his company, he was hurt I wouldn't stop to share a few moments, much less a conversation. He didn't display anger but calmly explained he was disappointed I wasn't making myself available.

"I just wanted to see you," he said. "That's all."

I couldn't understand why he was upset. I'd warned of my project in advance and hadn't agreed to go out with him. Thus, his wishful thinking felt like an unrealistic expectation, one that irritated me when it caused him feelings of discontentment.

"Well, I'm sorry but I have a lot of work to do. If I stop now, I won't finish," I offered defensively.

Though I could have taken a break to talk with Jeff or repair the damage from our miscommunication, I was incapable of handling my frustration or his emotions. Instead, I ignored him and continued wallpapering. He watched patiently for a while longer before getting in his car and driving three-and-a-half hours back home.

I recognized my inconsiderate behavior after he left and felt terrible to have hurt his feelings. I phoned his mother immediately and asked that he return my call as soon as he arrived. When he did, I told him I was sorry for my rudeness, and in turn, he apologized for leaving in a huff. We made amends, agreeing the upset had been a gross misunderstanding.

The very next day, Jeff drove seven hours to prove his sincerity by taking me to lunch. He mentioned his dad had tried to talk him out of making the whirlwind trip but realized Jeff was *in love* and needed to figure out how to manage the feelings himself. It was the first time he'd used the "*L*-word," and it scared me to death. I wasn't sure I could love him that way and didn't want to risk losing a friend to find out, so I continued evading his feelings.

Afterwards, he was hesitant to pursue a relationship with me and I was somewhat distant with him. We still made arrangements to see each other on occasion, but our inability to connect had strained our relationship. He dated other people and when I flirted with the idea of engaging him, he wasn't interested. By that point, our friendship was little more than an unsynchronized dance.

Having graduated number one in his law school class, Jeff had many opportunities for work and accepted a job with a large, reputable firm in Dallas. We'd get together when I was in town to see family, so he knew of Mother and Daddy's unique living arrangement, though he was genuinely astonished by it each time he visited.

Daddy had resided in an apartment for more than ten years but came and went from the family home as he pleased. Amanda and Susan were college students living at home; Amanda in a private room inside the house and Susan in a guest house over the detached garage. He'd come over in the morning to prepare himself breakfast, return after work to see the girls and scrounge up something for dinner, and work in the darkroom while Mother rearranged everyone's personal belongings, took care of the family pets, or watched TV. For all intents and purposes, they appeared perfectly content "playing house" together.

Daddy maintained a completely separate social life and rarely provided Mother details of his whereabouts; however, my siblings and I were privy to his activities. Though he didn't ask us to lie, he strongly encouraged us to avoid sharing with Mother, which allowed him to enjoy a single man's life while she lived in an imaginary state of wedded bliss.

It wasn't easy keeping anything from her, though, because Mother was the master of interrogation. She had a way of asking twenty questions, whether fishing for information or not, and was relentless in pursuing every last detail. The deceit and stress involved in keeping Daddy's personal affairs from her was immeasurable, and her grilling to unearth them was worse. Instead of asking him for answers, which he'd made clear were none of her business, Mother manipulated me and my siblings to get the truth.

On one of my visits, Susan and I made plans to share the day with Daddy and Vicky, his girlfriend of two years. She was loving and darling, full of personality and style. Unlike Mother, she and I had many common interests, including clothing, makeup, interior design, shopping, and girl talk. Daddy enjoyed her company and their laughter, and when they were together, it was evident how much they loved one another. I dreamed she'd replace Mother and we'd all live happily ever after.

Daddy, Vicky, Susan, and I drove a couple of hours to Louisiana Downs that day and spent the afternoon watching the horse races. It reminded me of good times in Hot Springs with Jeff, who happened to be joining us for dinner later that evening. When he arrived to the house, Susan and I were coordinating our stories with Amanda to protect Daddy and ourselves from Mother's wrath if she were to have discovered the day's festivities. Though we'd become accustomed to that conniving behavior in our family, Jeff was appalled by it, which made his visit uncomfortable for both of us.

The following day, Mother learned of our trip to the races and became enraged as we feared. Expecting Susan and me to reject our father and his offer to spend time with another woman, she considered our participation an epic betrayal. Seeking vengeance, Mother blamed Daddy for my sister's involvement and held me accountable separately for mine.

As I sat at the kitchen table, she stood over me and smugly proclaimed, "I know where you were yesterday and who you were with," enunciating each and every syllable with exaggeration.

I looked up just in time to catch her penetrating glare, as she continued without taking a breath, "Did you think I wouldn't find out?"

I explained I hadn't mentioned it because I wanted to share time with Daddy but didn't want to hurt her feelings. Before I could finish, she interjected angrily, "Is that Grandmother's ring I see on your finger?" She knew the answer because I had worn it every day for the last five years as a constant reminder of Grandmom's love.

"Yes," I replied.

"Take it off now!" she demanded, lunging towards me with an outstretched arm. I could see the hatred in every ounce of her being as her eyes twitched, her face turned bright red, and her body shook uncontrollably. With spit spewing from her mouth, she declared, "You don't deserve to wear it and you never did!"

I took the ring off, with tears streaming down my face, and gave it to her, as any obedient child would have. Mother was seeking revenge and inflicting pain on Daddy the only way she knew how, through me. As such, she reported the incident to him immediately afterwards. He apologized but that was all he could do. It's no surprise that neither that night nor the ring has ever been mentioned again.

My family's behavior was dysfunctional and totally unacceptable no matter how I looked at it, but they were my family, the only one I had. While I'd have gladly walked away from Mother, I couldn't stand the thought of leaving Daddy alone in her care. The fear of what might happen to him was unthinkable. Besides, I needed his love and support to survive and was sure he needed mine.

Having come from a healthy, intact family, Jeff didn't want to be involved in my family's shenanigans. His disapproval eventually caused friction between us and convinced me he wasn't an ideal mate. As our friendship waned, he began dating a girl whom he'd met in law school.

Unfortunately, Jeff didn't know her well because their relationship had consisted of long-distance phone conversations between Little Rock and Dallas and occasional weekend sleepovers for a year before marriage. Soon thereafter, he found himself living with a total stranger. Though she was an intelligent, successful woman, Jeff hadn't realized she was manipulative and mentally unbalanced. Once he did, he sought counseling, moved out, and filed for divorce.

By the time Jeff and I caught up with each other years later, he was living with his son, the love of his life, close to extended family in Arkansas, and Rob and I were in Kansas City with Thomas, Rachel, and Johnny. Jeff and I kept in touch a couple of more times over the course of my marriage, though our friendship remained naturally distant.

When I contacted him to share the inconceivable news of my separation, Jeff comforted me as he had many times in the past without a hint of longing or expectation. "So sorry to hear that unfortunate news," he said. "I never imagined I'd be divorced either."

We communicated on an irregular basis for three years afterwards before I invited him to spend a weekend with me in Seattle, for what would have been our first meeting in almost twenty years. Careful and clear with my invitation, I explained I wasn't looking to start a long-distance relationship but was instead seeking a date to a charity dinner auction.

"I'd love for you to come up for an event in October. It'd be great to see you, show you the sights of Seattle, and introduce you to friends," I extended. Clarifying, "I haven't dated since the divorce and am not ready yet, but I'd enjoy your company."

I was delighted when he accepted the offer, but quickly found myself a little nervous by the thought of having a man in the house again after a lengthy dry spell, especially since the kids weren't going to be there. Though I was excited to see Jeff, I feared the togetherness might be awkward at times.

In place of uneasiness, Jeff brought the familiarity and comfort of a long-lost best friend. We spent hours catching up while hanging out at home, walking my dog Daisy around the neighborhood, roaming Pike Place Market, dining at the Pink Door, and attending the event. When he left, I was sad to see him and the peace I felt in his presence go.

After treatment, I could see that Jeff's feelings for me were healthy and genuine. His love was unwavering, patient, and selfless, the love I desperately sought from

Mother and intimate partners throughout my life but never received. He saw the good in me when I couldn't love myself. From the time he tried to save me from Amanda's indiscretion with Derek to the support he gave during the divorce, he truly was my knight in shining armor.

I had never experienced that kind of love and didn't recognize it or know how to respond. Besides, my quest for perfection distracted me and prevented me from seeing Jeff for who he was. He felt more like one of my friends, loyal and true, than a romantic partner, needy and weak.

Although I fantasized about falling head over heels in love with Jeff for almost ten years, it never happened, and I eventually married Rob. While they both have soft-spoken, introverted, intellectual personalities, they're complete opposites emotionally. Jeff is considerate, warm, and loving; Rob, self-centered and detached. He allowed me to remain independent and disconnected, which was familiar given my experiences with Mother. It's the very reason Rob's and my relationship flourished, while Jeff's and mine never got off the ground.

My emotional incompetence caused me and Jeff hurt and frustration, but I'm grateful we managed to stay connected through the ups and downs of our relationship. Had we engaged romantically previously, we would have failed and forever changed the friendship I treasure today.

Besides admiring his qualities, respecting his character, and being attracted to him physically and emotionally, I feel comfortable, safe, and at peace in his presence without reservation or pretense. I trust him completely with my heart. Finally, I understand what healthy intimate love feels like.

It's reassuring to know that I'm capable of having these emotions without feeling my survival is at risk. Instead, I have a secure foundation for whatever comes my way in the future. Regardless, I will continue to love Jeff as I always have but that doesn't mean I can't have feelings for another, quite the opposite. Jeff's love for me and mine for him make me confident I'll experience true love one day.

RETURNING HOME

WHEN I THINK of "home," I think of peace in my heart rather than a particular place. It's something I feel in my own surroundings, with Thomas, Rachel, and Johnny, and in the company of close friends. "Home" is not what I experienced in my childhood, where I lived with continuous pain, frustration, and struggle. Mother rejected me and inflicted emotional abuse, Daddy watched but couldn't prevent my nightmare, and my siblings and I were unable to identify with each other. Peace did not exist there.

I haven't had much desire to return to Dallas since leaving for college, however, I look for opportunities for the children to spend time with extended family. As such, Mother and Daddy visit Seattle annually and we travel to Texas every few years to see them, my sister Amanda, her husband Jason, and their three children.

Before our last vacation, Mother had been nagging me for a couple of years to make the trip. I explained it would be nearly impossible due to the custody schedule and my financial status after divorce, but she was unsympathetic to my hardships and wouldn't take no for an answer. Using free miles I'd accumulated over the last three years, I purchased four plane tickets for the cost of their issuance, made arrangements for Daisy to attend doggy camp, had our favorite sitter Marilyn water the yard and care for our cat, and left my car at the airport for the week. It cost me over $1,000 to satisfy Mother's expectations, money I desperately needed for necessities and food.

Daddy and Amanda's children picked us up on arrival and took us straight to Amanda's house. Though Mother had better accommodations, she didn't have room for us, because Daddy had moved back into the family home after a twenty-five year absence. He had failed to mention it previously but claimed his apartment was overflowing with clutter, leaving him no other choice but to live with Mother.

Besides Daddy, Mother had five cats and three dogs. Several were permanent residents and others had been temporarily rescued for one reason or another. None of them got along with each other, so she confined them to separate rooms and spent most of her free time behind closed doors giving them love and cleaning up after their messes. The house smelled like urine, which made me sick to my stomach, but no one else seemed to mind.

One aggressive dog couldn't be socialized with people or animals, so Mother had a custom child-sized house built with a cedar shake roof, picture windows, and a covered front porch, similar in size to the playhouse Grandmom had designed especially for the grandchildren. Mother worked tirelessly to provide the animals humanlike amenities and the finest living conditions. They were all on different feeding schedules based on their personalities and individual needs. Some were allowed outside and some were not, some could roam the house on occasion and some could not, and several never came out of their rooms. The schedule revolved around the clock, giving Mother little opportunity to leave home for more than a couple of hours at a time.

With a full house, Mothered offered for us to stay with Amanda. Her home was piled with layers and layers of stuff—folded clothing, loose papers, purchases still in boxes and bags, hundreds of toys, and trash—much like a hoarder's haven. The sizeable family room was so overstuffed that there were only two walking paths, one to the back door and one to an open seating area where two 72" projection screen TVs sat side by side, one for viewing programs and movies and the other for video games. Extra tables, chairs, and sofas were arranged haphazardly to hold accumulated possessions, mostly items purchased from E-Bay, Amanda's favorite retailer. (Amanda had never been able to refuse a deal!)

Besides her family, a bunny, dog, cat, and several uninvited guests shared the home. Rats roamed at night, which is why she suggested we zip our suitcases or put them atop beds to prevent our belongings from being ransacked. The bunny hutch sat within feet of the kitchen table, looking as if it hadn't been cleaned in weeks. Feces piled in the corners of the cage where the pet nestled, and the pan for collecting waste spilled over into a make-shift container on the floor. Filled with pools of urine and caramel-colored paper towels, it had a foul stench that permeated the first floor.

The master suite looked much like the rest of the house, filthy and extremely cluttered. Boxes, plastic tubs, and personal belongings formed a five-foot-high, two-foot-deep buffer lining the walls of the hallway and bedroom. Clothes were piled on top of the furniture, bed, bathroom counters, and tub deck, and dirty ones were strewn about the floors. The rim of the toilet was lined with dried vomit from Amanda's bulimia, the bathroom floor was covered with urine, hair, and soiled undergarments, and the only operable shower in the house was filled with twenty-seven shampoo and conditioner bottles, several wet washcloths, and children's toys. Hair covered the soap and drain, and black mold grew on the walls.

I'm not sure whether my children noticed, but the clean sheets on the beds, provided by the nannies, were the only proper accommodations we received. However, no one acknowledged the mess, which left me wondering why they thought it was OK for anyone to live under those conditions.

As we considered plans for a family dinner that first evening, eating at home wasn't an option unless we wanted fast food at Amanda's house or ice cream and frozen cake at Mother's, as neither cooks. Instead, we settled on one of their favorite restaurants, an Italian place just around the corner, where the children settled into one booth and the adults, another.

Awaiting the food and Jason's arrival, the kids played while I caught up with Daddy, Mother, and Amanda. After boasting of her children's most recent accomplishments, they informed me of Amanda's nanny's pregnancy. Much to my surprise, Amanda was not pleased, as I expected, but rather furious her tax dollars would be used for the prenatal care and delivery.

Mother explained the costs were covered by the federal government because the Supreme Court mandates all residents are provided education and health care, irrespective of their citizenship. Thus, the nanny would receive Medicaid as an illegal alien, just as her nonresident sister, another one of Amanda's nannies, had the previous year when having a baby.

Whatever the reason, it was evident Amanda was incensed to be funding the expense. "I don't care. I shouldn't be paying for it!" she exclaimed indignantly.

I immediately found myself in the middle of an uncomfortable political conversation, a subject matter not typically broached in my family. I knew better than to engage, though, as Mother had a habit of belittling me when I didn't agree with her. Usually it involved lecturing or degrading me into submission and then ignoring me for days afterwards if I didn't change my opinion. To avoid having my limited time in Dallas shrouded in conflict, I purposely kept my mouth shut.

I wasn't the least bit interested in arguing about why or why not Medicaid may or may not cover the cost of delivering the baby. Amanda's response was disturbing to me on a different level. She was speaking of a woman who'd cared for her family and three small children since birth, yet she was acting as if the nanny were nothing more than a flaw in our country's social system. As far as I was concerned, Amanda perpetuated her nanny's unlawful stay in this country by employing her. Because she refused to pay competitive wages, provide benefits, and file tax returns, Amanda knowingly hired illegal aliens to satisfy her personal needs. Then, she criticized them for receiving the health care benefits they rightfully deserved.

I don't pretend to have the answer to who's responsible for the nanny and her baby's care, but Amanda's response was unacceptable to me. What was the nanny to do? Endanger her life or that of her child? I don't think so. As I saw it, the problem was her residency, not the pregnancy, and I was pleased Amanda was being held accountable for it, even if indirectly.

Amanda's insensitivity to the situation she created angered me, but the comment that followed really offended me. "I don't mind the Hispanics in our country illegally because they actually work for a living, but the blacks are the ones who sit on their asses and drain our welfare system," she declared. I thought of Lillian in that moment and felt profound sadness, disgust, and utter disbelief. How could my own sister feel that Lillian, our surrogate mother, deserved to be treated that way?

After remembering back twenty-five years to the time when Amanda attempted to steal the love of my life in college, I realized her attitudes shouldn't have astonished me. She'd never mentioned regret for her actions or the irreparable damage done to our relationship, and she wasn't going to offer an apology in this case either. I wondered then, as I had before, how Amanda and I could possibly be related.

Mother, Daddy, and Jason didn't react to her comments, so I could only assume it wasn't the first time she'd expressed that opinion, just the first time I'd heard of it. To think their silence was agreement or support was equally as alarming.

I watched Amanda's prejudice play out the following afternoon at lunch when Daddy's friend, Norm, treated the children to some entertainment and our entire gang, a delicious meal. A jovial, bold, obstinate man from Syria and a longtime client of Daddy's, Norm returns the favor of Daddy's legal expertise with generosity and kindness to our family. He's like an adored uncle, except in Mother's eyes.

Unbeknownst to me, Daddy and Amanda had agreed several days prior to our arrival that Norm would take the kids to Chuck E. Cheese. My children had long outgrown it, and more importantly, Rachel had a traumatic childhood experience that caused her to be terrified of mascots. The mere thought of seeing any character in costume, especially the Easter bunny and Chuck E. Cheese, gave her nightmares and panic attacks, and I wasn't going to subject her to that torment.

When I suggested we find an alternative, something all the children could enjoy, Daddy and Amanda looked at me with disbelief and argued there was only one acceptable choice, theirs. "Well, they really want to go to Chuck E. Cheese. It's their favorite place and they've been looking forward to it for days," Daddy explained. "We don't want to upset them. Why don't you see if you can talk yours into it?"

They treated us as if we were intentionally trying to harm her children. After all, they were indulged in everything they wanted, whenever they wanted it, without discipline or restraint. I wasn't going to humiliate Rachel by exposing her fear, and there was no reason for her to have to defend herself. In my opinion, if Daddy and Amanda had been considerate of her feelings in the first place, we wouldn't have been having the debate.

In an effort to end the standoff, Norm asked why my gang didn't want to go to Chuck E. Cheese, and I discretely shared my concerns. Before I could finish, Norm interrupted and announced enthusiastically, "Dave and Busters it is! It's a better place for all of us." Persuasively, he added, "Come on guys, let's go! The adults can have a nice meal and the kids can entertain themselves in the arcade."

Amanda and Daddy reluctantly agreed. The children had a ball there, compliments of Norm, who'd given them spending money to play games to their heart's content. Afterwards, each gathered their winning tickets and headed for the prize counter to redeem their rewards. I stayed with Rachel as she weighed her options, and we waited patiently while Amanda and her two daughters bartered back and forth with the attendant.

"I want that! How many points is it?" "Never mind, give me the other one." "I said that one, not this one!" "I don't like it. I don't want it anymore."

Several exchanges took place in the few minutes we stood there. In the meantime, Rachel asked for her selections, but the young girl politely explained she'd already started Amanda's transaction and needed to finish it before helping anyone else.

Amanda overheard the conversation and responded with disdain. "Just tell me how many points we have left!" she demanded of the employee.

As the girl calculated the number aloud, Amanda rudely interrupted, in a condescending tone with a smirk on her face, "You're dead wrong!" "We had this many points, we bought these things, and now we have this much left to spend," she said, treating her like an incompetent servant.

The young girl apologized by offering, "I'm sorry ma'am, I guess I got confused. Please let me recalculate that number for you."

Amanda interjected, this time firmer than before, "You don't know what you're talking about! Give me our things now so we can get out of here!"

With an exaggerated sigh of frustration, Amanda proclaimed to her girls, "Pick out what you want and let's go!"

As Rachel and I stood there horrified by Amanda's berating of this poor sweet girl, I could see Rachel's discomfort and she, mine. To the contrary, Amanda and her children seemed perfectly at ease in that situation. Like Mother, Amanda considered herself superior in intelligence and others, incompetent, and she wasn't the least bit remorseful for her indignation.

The personal attack I witnessed her launch on that young African-American teenager made me sick to my stomach and brought tears to my eyes. Maybe if I'd realized the truth of my sister's discriminatory beliefs at dinner the previous night, I wouldn't have been shocked by it. However, at the time, I was rendered speechless.

Amanda and I had grown up together in the same house with Lillian who'd taken care of our every need, and I thought we shared the same feelings for her. I knew Lillian's heart and soul to be exactly the same as mine and it didn't matter that her skin was a different color. That was simply a difference in design, not character.

The following morning, my brother David flew in from Florida to join us on a little family adventure. The kids and I hadn't seen him in several years, though he looked the same as we remembered: tall, dark, athletic, and handsome. When he's not working as a staff photographer at a local newspaper, he enjoys music, mountain biking, snow skiing, and Brazilian jujitsu. Like Daddy, he's a likeable guy who's creative and passionate about his craft and takes great pleasure in the company of children. Unfortunately, he maintains autonomy in relationships, avoiding emotional intimacy, which prevents him from having the family he greatly desires.

We'd made plans to spend a couple of nights at Amanda and Jason's lake house in East Texas. While Mother stayed home to care for her animals and clean house, Daddy, David, Amanda, her family, and mine caravanned to the property, which had recently undergone a year-long renovation project.

Amanda had built the home of her dreams by converting the existing traditional brick colonial structure into a Florida-style stucco palace. It was freshly tiled, painted, and redone throughout, as lovely on the inside as it was beautiful on the outside. Shade trees surrounded the property and provided much-needed shelter from the blistering Texas heat, while French doors allowed fresh air and a slight breeze into the family room and kitchen. A cobblestone walkway and patio, hand-crafted by Jason, adorned the front yard, and the back had a grassy lawn with a sandy path down to the water.

While the setting and scenery of the lake were picturesque, Texas's man-made beauty is quite different from the Pacific Northwest's natural splendor. The murky water bordering the property was four feet deep and fifty yards wide, filled with seaweed. The kids could cross it on foot without going under and when they came out, they were covered with a thick film of black gunk.

With plenty of space to roam both inside and out, the lake house was an ideal setting for family fun. Thomas, Rachel, and Johnny had a ball with their cousins and Daddy, David, and Jason, who took them for rides on the go-cart, four-wheeler, and Jet Ski. Additionally, a pinball machine, movies, games, trampoline, and hours of swimming provided them endless entertainment.

Mother came for lunch and watched the festivities for a bit before returning to her responsibilities at home. Amanda probably would have preferred the same, as she wasn't used to caring for children without the assistance of her three nannies. Furthermore, the commotion that came with my fourteen-, twelve-, and ten-year-old children was foreign to her. In fact, she considered them rowdy hellions compared to her three little angels.

It was obvious from the time we arrived that Mother and Daddy felt Amanda had the model family and lived a superior life. Both continually pointed out qualities they admired in her children and their lifestyle, sometimes telling the same story twice, while treating us like stepfamily, the kind who weren't accepted and didn't belong. They praised her children while ignoring mine. Because I was divorced and Amanda had always been the favored child, the shunning wasn't unexpected, just extremely hurtful. However, I kept my feelings to myself to keep from jeopardizing the trip for Thomas, Rachel, and Johnny's sake.

As our stay at the lake house concluded, we gathered for a large breakfast of bacon, eggs, pancakes, and cinnamon rolls, a Sunday family tradition. Shortly thereafter, Amanda's middle child declared, "Mom, I want a chocolate milkshake!"

"Are you sure, honey? I've already cleaned up the kitchen," Amanda replied.

"Of course I'm sure," her daughter responded.

"OK, give me a minute and I'll make you one," said Amanda.

The trash was out, the laundry dried and folded, dishes washed, thermostats turned up, and cars filled with luggage and coolers. We were packed and ready to leave, except for a few clean dishes Amanda was putting away, when Jason asked, "Mommy, why aren't you making her a chocolate shake?"

"I'm cleaning up the kitchen first and then I'll do it," she said.

"Soon, I hope," he replied in a suggestive tone.

"Yes," she answered.

Amanda immediately stopped what she was doing, got out the blender and ice cream, and made her daughter a milkshake. Afterwards, the ten of us and the dog piled into their two SUVs for the drive back to Dallas. We were barely on the outskirts of town when the child with a milkshake still in hand anticipated her favorite drive-in restaurant and exclaimed, "Mommy, I want bubble gum ice cream!"

"OK, honey, let me call Daddy and tell him to stop," Amanda replied without hesitation.

Jason, who was in the car ahead of us, had already contacted the restaurant, located ten miles from the lake house, to inquire of the day's flavors and was sorry to report that bubble gum was not one of them. After relaying the message to her daughter, Amanda promised to stop at another ice cream shop closer to home. When we arrived, I told Amanda mine would not be partaking. She looked at me puzzled and explained, "It's low-fat," completely missing the point that I considered it an indulgence my children could live without.

On the last night of our visit, Amanda and Jason treated us to the country club for dinner and swimming. She had never mentioned the club previously, but we were thankful for the offer and happy to have an activity outside their home.

At the club, we were seated in the main dining room where they were serving a family-style buffet. Before we sat down, Amanda encouraged Thomas, Rachel, and Johnny to follow her children over to the kids' table and fill their plates with cookies and cupcakes to ensure they didn't miss out on dessert. After stock-piling them, they returned for the main course.

The waitress came by to get our drink orders and asked Amanda for her club membership number. With her head down in the menu, Amanda answered, "L-5697."

"I'm sorry, ma'am, I didn't hear that," the girl replied.

"I said L-5697," Amanda stated resolutely without looking up or offering apology.

"Thank you," she responded. "I'll be right back."

The server returned a short time later with our drinks. Approaching Amanda again, she said, "I'm sorry but I can't seem to find your membership number. Can I get your name to look it up?"

Amanda replied, "I'm certain it's L-5697," dismissing her without further conversation.

The girl offered an explanation for the confusion as Amanda scoffed at her, "Maybe it's one of our temporary memberships. I'm so sorry! I'll try again and check back."

The next time the server returned, she was accompanied by a manager who apologized for the ongoing disruption. "Excuse me, ma'am, we can't seem to locate your membership number. Could you please give us your name and any other information that might help us find it?" she asked graciously.

"The name is Lexington and I spoke with Rebecca earlier today. I don't know what the problem is!" Amanda snapped in an irritated tone.

The manager calmly replied, "I believe we can find Rebecca and have this matter resolved. Thank you for your patience."

A few moments later, Rebecca, the club administrator, appeared. Off work, she was still on the premises when the manager tracked her down and requested she pay us a visit. "Hello, Amanda. I'm Rebecca. We talked earlier this afternoon on the phone," she introduced herself. "We discussed your decision to reinstate your membership after you cancelled it last year, but I haven't had time to get it into the system since our conversation." Excusing herself, she offered, "I apologize for the confusion this evening. Enjoy your dinner!"

"Thank you," Amanda said with a grin and a snicker, as if she were delighted by the staff's groveling.

After dinner, the children swam and jumped off the diving board for the remaining hour and a half the pool was open. On the ride home, one of Amanda's children requested Chick-Fil-A and Amanda happily obliged.

Rachel hadn't heard of it previously and asked the girls, "What's Chick-Fil-A?"

They responded, "Tell her, Mommy. Tell her about the good fast food and the bad kind." "We only eat the good kind," the girls claimed.

Amanda explained there were healthy and unhealthy oils used for cooking fast food. Some people ate the bad kind and it made them fat, while her family ate only the healthy kind. It was a good thing her children were convinced of her illogical thinking because they ate out three meals a day.

Two hours after they had pasta, cookies and cupcakes for dinner, Amanda's girls were eating fried chicken nuggets and ice cream for dessert. Once again, Amanda didn't understand why I wouldn't let Rachel participate, but Rachel knew I didn't agree with the bedtime indulgence and didn't question me.

We left for Seattle the following morning, and I was never so happy to be "home." Though Amanda and Jason had been gracious in extending hospitality and their accommodations, as well as treating us to most of our meals, it was time we returned to the comforts and privacy of our own surroundings.

After seeing all of the family except Susan in Dallas, Rachel and I travelled to Colorado to visit her while Thomas and Johnny stayed home with their dad. Rachel was apprehensive at first, not having remembered much of her Aunt Susan, but I was excited to catch up, as it had been longer than five years since any of us had seen her.

When we arrived, Susan was awaiting a plastic surgery fellowship but had been unable to start due to an unresolved conflict with a Manhattan hospital, where she had just completed a two-year residency program. She hated New York City, its people, and her job so much that she smeared the program's good name to new applicants and reported perceived discrepancies to the national regulatory board. As a result, the hospital had refused to release her credentials, preventing her from practicing medicine until a thorough investigation had been conducted.

While Susan's supervisors may have recognized her aptitude and skill in her field, they felt her righteousness and inability to work with others jeopardized patient care. Susan despised them, considering all surgeons unethical conspirators against women, and they deemed her incompetent, but without proof of injury, the contentious matter was eventually dropped.

It wasn't the first time she'd found herself in the middle of controversy, though, as Susan had a habit of getting into them. Throughout the course of her medical school education and residency, she challenged several authority figures and reported them for what she

278

considered gross incompetence. In reality, it was nothing more than a difference of opinion. She challenged politics, burned bridges, and wasn't on speaking terms with many, including Daddy and David.

"They can all just kiss my ass!" she said.

I'm confident in Susan's ability to provide excellent care, but question her compassion, understanding, and empathy for patients and colleagues. Certain her views and only her views are right, she's stubborn, combative, and incapable of respecting the opinions or feelings of others.

Her infallible character is matched only by her flawless exterior, as evidenced by the six laser procedures she's endured to erase all signs of aging. While she boasts her skin looks "fresher than a baby's bottom," her face has been rendered expressionless and distorted. Nevertheless, she proudly displays the latest technology her industry has to offer. Susan would say she's at the top of her game, professionally and personally.

She has her own code of ethics and considers herself morally superior. While she rationalized having an affair with a married doctor who had young children, she threatened to contact his wife and report him to the hospital for his indiscretions when he ended the relationship unexpectedly. In her mind, her sleeping with a married man was acceptable, but his relationship outside of marriage was not. Like Mother, Susan's love is about control and vengeance rather than connection.

She once dated a man forty years her senior and superior, a celebrity in the state of Texas. Theirs was a forbidden relationship, one they managed to keep private from most. Rob was the first in our family to recognize the union, but I couldn't accept the notion that my thirty-year-old sister was sleeping with a seventy-year-old man. By the time I admitted the truth, I adored him and considered him the perfect mate. As thorny as Susan was, she wasn't going to find anyone else to love and accept her as wholly as he did.

Though Susan disapproved of my divorce and didn't speak to me for several years afterwards, she had been good at maintaining contact while the children were young. She spent at least one week with us every year, and Rob and I relied on her when we needed to get away. Neither of our parents was capable of providing proper supervision for Thomas, Rachel, and Johnny, so she was our saving grace.

While Rachel and I were in Colorado, we met Susan's new puppy, a rambunctious six-month-old chocolate Lab named Jessie, in desperate need of training. Susan scheduled classes for her at the local pet store and Rachel and I tagged along for the first session.

As we pulled into the parking lot, we spotted a mother and daughter making their way to the front door with a black Lab mix and an English bulldog. The women were clearly overwhelmed by the larger dog as he dragged the mother across the lot while the daughter struggled to stop them. Had it been my choice, I'd have waited for them to pass before letting Jessie out of the car, but I'm overly cautious due to a childhood pet whose aggression frequently drew blood.

Susan didn't seem affected by the women or the dogs and headed straight for them with Jessie jumping wildly on her leash. I, on the other hand, took Rachel through the parking lot a roundabout way to stay clear of the precarious situation. Looking back, we could see the larger dog's leash tangled with Jessie's and hear him starting to growl.

As Susan freed her, she looked at the mother and daughter and emphatically stated, "Keep that dog away from mine! I don't like mean dogs!"

Walking into the store, Susan grabbed an employee and pointed blame. "See those women? They cannot control their aggressive dog. Keep them and that mean dog away from me!" she announced loud enough for all to hear.

Needless to say, the confrontation didn't go over very well with the two women and before Susan could finish, the daughter began screaming, "You're a bitch! You don't know what you're talking about. My dog is not mean!" Adding, "You better watch what you say, *B I T C H*!!!"

In that moment, Rachel and I found ourselves in the midst of a fight. I'd never seen two strangers treat each other that way, and I'm not sure Rachel had heard the "*B*-word" outside of a movie in her twelve years, but there was no mistaking it that day.

"I don't know what their problem is," Susan said defensively, "but it's certainly not my fault!"

The instructor separated Susan and Jessie from the ladies and their dogs, also there for the training session. As they glared at one another across the room, Rachel and I kept our distance but could see that Jessie was a handful on a tight rein. Conversely, neither of the other two dogs was unmanageable or aggressive. The daughter worked easily with the Lab mix while the mother tried to engage the darling bulldog who kept spreading his fat belly on the cold tile floor.

Much like the incident at Dave and Busters in Dallas, I found myself wanting to apologize to strangers for my sister's poor behavior. Though Susan wasn't the only one at fault, her condescending tone and rude comments elicited a strong response from the daughter, who was trying to protect her mother and their dogs. Susan didn't see it that way and wouldn't have considered she owed anyone an apology.

That evening, we observed Aunt Susan in rare form again. Determined to fit her mid-sized SUV into a parallel parking spot sized for a Mini, she held up traffic while bouncing bumper to bumper, uncaring that she left her mark with each move. In fact, she was proud of her accomplishment, less than six inches to spare between both cars.

She treated us to a Cirque du Soleil show, but Rachel and I never completely recovered from the calamity earlier that afternoon. While she and I didn't dare discuss it until after we left Colorado, we shared mutual feelings of discomfort. Rachel sensed Susan's inhumanity and indifference towards others and remained leery of her the rest of the trip.

———

Because human beings are imperfect by their very nature, some level of dysfunction within families is commonplace. It defines their character, shapes their mode of operation, and colors individual *Life Scripts*.

However, when disrupted Attachment bonds or mental illness exists, those affected are impaired and the family unit, fragmented. In our case, Mother's personality disorder went undiagnosed, poisoning us all, Daddy's insecurity paralyzed him, and my compromised Attachment prevented me from seeing reality.

My recent visits with Mother, Daddy, Amanda, David, and Susan, confirm our individual personalities and family dynamics remain largely as I remember from childhood, now manifested into adult life. Daddy uses Amanda's children, instead of his own, to fulfill his emotional needs, Mother's superiority and control remain intact, Amanda's elitism has become her family's way of life, David's lack of emotional intimacy has cost him happiness and the gift of children, and Susan has isolated herself from virtually everyone. Daddy's analogy—if our family car was stuck in a ditch, we'd all push in different directions instead of banding together as one—is still true today.

Thanks to treatment, I'm not the same insecure little girl who experienced life through the eyes of a wounded soul. I've healed my emotional scars and that healing has changed me for good. My eyes are wide open to the truths in my life, giving me a clearer understanding of my past and a new appreciation for my future.

A NEW DREAM

FROM OUTSIDE LOOKING in, I had all the makings of a perfect childhood, if not an exceptional life. My dad was a devoted parent and successful businessman and my mom didn't work outside of the home. We had a full-time nanny and housekeeper to care for our needs, and extended family to share holidays and special occasions. Living with my siblings and parents in a nice home in a prominent neighborhood, I received a superior education and was exposed to an affluent lifestyle. I attended an exclusive summer camp, received a new Chevy Camaro for my sixteenth birthday, traveled abroad, and graduated from college without the financial burden of student loans.

As I try to provide a secure and enriched life for my children, I'm more than grateful for the circumstances of my upbringing. However, the one thing I needed most for a healthy development was missing, a secure Attachment with my primary caregiver. The broken bond resulted in a debilitating handicap no one could see or accommodate, yet its crippling effects left me in a fight for survival each and every day of my life.

Regardless, I had to find a way to withstand Mother's rejection and abuse. I did the best I could to obey her wishes, while denying my feelings of hatred for the way she treated me. To reconcile the internal conflict, I convinced myself there must have been something fundamentally wrong, causing me to be undeserving of love. The failed relationship was my fault, and I worked incessantly to change it.

There were obvious signs of my compromised Attachment, but no one was able to get to the root of the problem. Even if my therapist Marilyn recognized the impact of Mother's abandonment, feelings of unworthiness etched on my limbic brain permeated my emotional responses and there was nothing I could have done to change them through rational thought or behavior modification. While she helped me identify and associate unhealthy patterns and feelings, therapy didn't reprogram my brain the way treatment did.

I was conscious of Mother's challenging personality previously, but I didn't recognize signs of mental illness until a recent visit. One evening, Thomas was sleeping with our Boston terrier, Daisy, when I was awakened in the middle of the night by a loud bark and growl. Rushing to the room to see what the matter was, I found her sound asleep at the foot of his bed as if nothing had happened. I tucked her under the covers, where she usually snuggled with the children, and returned to my room.

Minutes later, I heard the noise again and rushed back to Thomas's side where I found him sitting up in bed holding a bloody lip. He and Daisy were both half asleep, but he recalled reaching down to pet her and her biting him in the face. There was no time to figure out what had happened then, so I put her in her crate and took Thomas straight to the emergency room.

We spent three hours getting the wound thoroughly cleaned and stitched before returning home at 5:30 a.m. After getting Thomas back to bed, I began researching dog behavior on the Internet, worried I'd be forced to put our beloved family pet to sleep given the circumstances. Though my children's safety was more important than the dog's life without reservation, it didn't make the predicament I faced any less distressing, as the thought of losing her was heartbreaking.

After reading a plethora of material related to animal behavior, I became convinced that Daisy had been startled in her sleep and was reacting out of instinct, not intent. Furthermore, I believed the negative energy Mother exuded created stress in our home, which caused the disturbance. Whether it was her presence or the change in environment, I was uncertain.

Mother asked me what had happened, expressing more concern for Daisy than Thomas. When I explained the scenario, her eyes lit up with recognition. "No way! That's what happened to Christina," she exclaimed.

I had never heard her mention a friend named Christina and wondered who she was and what had happened to her. With curiosity I asked, "Who's Christina?"

Mother quickly replied, "You know, Christina on *Grey's Anatomy*. She and Owen were sleeping together one night when he was awakened and began choking her. It turns out the ceiling fan in their room reminded him of the blades on the helicopters during the war, and the noise caused him to snap. It was an instinctual reaction just like Daisy's bite."

Mother was serious. She was speaking of Christina as if she were a close friend and linking what she had seen in a fictional show on TV to what had happened between Thomas and our dog. It was apparent then she truly considers her shows, their characters and storylines, part of her world. Nevertheless, I was shocked to see her use them as a basis for reality.

Although I failed to find the same relevance in her association, the kids and I use this incident to remind us that animals are prone to instinctual behavior, even though we consider them family members. I'm grateful Daisy is as playful and docile as she ever was and no further mishaps have occurred.

Mother's fascination with celebrity explained why she was so intrigued by Bill Gates. She wanted to know where he lived, where his children attended school, and which of my friends knew him. Everywhere we went, "Does he eat here? Drive down this street? Shop at these stores?" I never understood why it mattered, because his whereabouts didn't impact the children's and my life, but she was clearly more interested in him than us.

Our reality at the time was the unwanted, impending sale of our family home. Upon hearing of it from Daddy, Mother called to inquire if the house was going to be on the market during her upcoming visit. If so, she'd rather come another time to avoid being disturbed by potential buyers. There was no acknowledgment of loss, no concern for our future, and no words of encouragement.

On the same day, I discussed the possibility of having a hysterectomy with my friend Amy and the difficulties a lengthy recovery would pose. "Come stay with us," she said. "We'll take care of you and the children, get them to school and their activities." Though I'm aware of the tremendous struggle it would have presented her and her husband, who have two children and both work outside the home, I have no doubt they'd be there for us if we needed them.

It's no wonder I'd pick my friends over family given those two situations, but that's all I've ever known. It's the reason I consider my close friends "chosen family." With them by my side, I'm never alone. Besides providing unconditional love, they welcome me into their private lives, share intimate moments, and expose their raw emotions. It allows me to experience healthy interactions, something Mother and Daddy were incapable of giving me.

Mother doesn't understand, as her relationships are disposable based on need. They are rooted in superiority, control, and winning, not connection and reciprocity. While she interacts socially at work, she doesn't value interpersonal relationships. I've never known her to have a close friend, or a friend at all for that matter.

Once, when learning of a favor I did for Cate, Mother looked at me, perplexed, and asked, "How in the world is she ever going to repay you for that?"

"I received it back in spades," I thought to myself, but if I were looking for repayment, I would have completely missed out on the joy of giving and caring for others.

My friends and I talk of our most private thoughts, deepest longings, and greatest fears. We share triumphs and heartaches, respect individual differences, encourage each other to strive for personal bests, unite to provide support in times of need, and forgive each other for being human. There's no competition or jealousy, only humility and love.

While I embrace individuality and accept vulnerabilities, I choose not to associate with those who consider themselves more worthy of acceptance than others, as I believe we were all created equal regardless of our human condition. People don't get to pick their family, the color of their skin, or their sexual orientation, and I didn't sign up for an Attachment disorder or a divorce.

As it was during my childhood, I live in an affluent community where designer labels, big houses, fancy cars, and lavish vacations are commonplace. It's not unheard of for the breadwinner in the home to be retired by the age of forty-five, leaving time for family, new business ventures, and philanthropy. My peers typically visit the health club or beauty salon between family obligations, social engagements, and volunteer commitments, and their disposable monthly income is more than my total net worth.

I once enjoyed some of the same benefits of that lifestyle thanks to Rob, but we never had the money that went along with it. Now divorced, I find myself the poor one in the crowd again. This time, however, I no longer feel like an outsider. It's taken me forty-four years to realize it, but my place in this world is connecting with the humanity in people, not competing with their material possessions or accomplishments. It gives me a sense of purpose and belonging beyond my immediate surroundings.

After treatment, I considered that everything I knew about myself could have been the result of my environment and not my nature, causing me to feel uncertain of my identity. It was a relief to discover that my heart and soul are the same, but my self-respect has been forever changed. I'm now empowered to show the world who I am without regret or apology.

The enlightenment also caused me concern for Thomas, Rachel, and Johnny's welfare, as those who suffer disrupted Attachments typically pass it on to their children. In my case, Daddy selected an incompetent, detached mate, and I repeated the pattern by marrying an antisocial man who ignored our children and me. Thankfully, he wasn't their primary caretaker. I was. Mothering came naturally, so I bonded with my children and they never experienced a lack of love, attention, or connection.

Though my feelings were no different than any other mother's love, the relationship the children and I shared was. By giving them the unconditional love I craved, I catered to their every physical and emotional need while neglecting my own. In return, their love filled the void in my heart and temporarily healed the primal wound.

As the children matured and began establishing their independence, we experienced intense separation anxiety.

I had been overinvested in them and their care, and found myself lonely and broken when I could no longer satisfy all their needs. They hadn't developed the skills to take care of themselves, leaving them overly attached and uncertain of their capabilities.

My oldest two have unrealistic expectations of me. They compete for my affection and demand the undivided attention they received in childhood, which creates tremendous jealousy and conflict between the three, above and beyond typical sibling rivalry. It's heartbreaking to observe and difficult to manage.

The children suffered in other ways as well. Instead of being proactive in behavior, as I wished, I tended to be reactive, which created stress in our environment. Easily frustrated with my own imperfections and self-doubt, I was irritable and rash at times. When it occurred, my anger was directed inward, but my agitation and mood spilled over onto them. Sensitive to repetitive sounds and disruptions in concentration, I could frequently be heard yelling, "Stop the noise!"

I'm not the person Rob thought he married, and not even the same one he divorced. Neither is he. He's found his voice and is reliving his teenage years through the children. By allowing them to dodge responsibilities and do as they please, he leaves them essentially unsupervised in his care. As such, the children disregard authority, including me, and he embraces them for it.

Some things haven't changed, like his participation in their lives. Thomas completed his freshman year in swimming and Rachel, soccer, without their dad attending competitions. While I don't point these things out to the children, if they mention it, I encourage them to communicate their desires and disappointments to their dad. If they want something from him, they need to let him know, because he may not recognize it or act on his own otherwise. It's the only chance either has for repair or change.

Thomas, Rachel, and Johnny are learning to put words to their feelings by asking for what they need, an invaluable skill that will benefit them in future relationships. It's worked remarkably well, so much so that they have a bond with their father, one that didn't exist when we were married. He loves them as he can, not as I want him to, and they accept him for what he's able to give without expectation for more. As long as they feel his love, my prayers will have been answered.

Rob's idea that children require only love to survive could be considered accurate, however, the only thing worse than an absent parent is one who condones unacceptable behavior. He claims it's not his responsibility to offer guidance or consequences, asserting his only job is to love them. He's not a parent: he's a golden retriever.

To the contrary, I believe children need supervision, support, and safe boundaries, in addition to love, to mature into healthy, successful individuals and productive members of society. At my house, we talk of effort, accountability, and integrity. I have guidelines in place for homework and computer time, eating and exercise, hygiene and sleep. I expect Thomas, Rachel, and Johnny to give their best effort in everything they do. Having operated this way my entire life, I don't know how to settle for less. It's no longer a method of survival, rather a mode of operation.

Despite Rob's and my differences, the children help me remember that there is no glory in being right in relationships. It leaves a partner, friend, or loved one hurt and defeated, which alienates instead of uniting. In cases of divorce, it creates ill will and puts the children in compromising situations. Without cooperation and compromise on both sides, turmoil and isolation prevail.

As a single parent, I cherish every moment I spend with my children but miss having adult interaction at home. When I'm not with them, working, or volunteering, I look for opportunities to get together with close friends. My rich single life includes social engagements and fundraising events, celebratory lunches and dinners, as well as summer getaways to Roche Harbor and New Year's Eve in the Cascade Mountains.

Rituals are a comforting and cherished part of my existence, especially morning coffee. My routine typically involves getting ready for work, sending the children off to school, and going directly to my favorite Starbucks. There, I find familiar faces and well wishes to start my day. Whenever I can, I try catching up with Cate and her team of retired businessmen—Bobby, Tom, Richard, and Mike—who hold court regularly at their local coffee shop. The camaraderie has become the fabric of our lives.

In the evenings, I occasionally drop by my friend and co-worker Melissa's house to decompress. She, her husband Jack, and I share similar perspectives and humor, so there's never a shortage of conversation or laughter. When I feel like staying closer to home but prefer not to eat alone, I walk down to Kelly and Andy's for dinner. Sometimes I'm dressed and presentable, and sometimes I show up in my sweats, robe, and house shoes. Whatever the case, I can always count on good company and a divine, multicourse meal prepared to perfection. It's what bonds their family—the art of cooking and the joy of feasting. The gene runs strong on both sides and includes renowned chef, and uncle, Mario Batali.

If I'm lucky someday, I'll have a relationship like theirs. Imperfect and unique as all marriages are, it's based on romantic love, shared values, and mutual commitment to one another and their children. They make room for differences, support individual goals, and face conflict with honesty and respect.

More than a year ago, I met a guy who could have been that special someone, but the timing wasn't right. We developed a genuine, respectful relationship, but he's still recovering from past wounds and is uncertain of the journey ahead or his ability to commit to love again. However, in the time we shared, he taught me how to trust completely. Though I'm sad to say goodbye, I'm ready to take the next step towards finding the romantic love I want and deserve.

Where I was once consumed with obtaining love or resigned to loneliness, I'm now able to balance my personal, professional, and social lives without being overwhelmed by emotion. My feelings are appropriate, my behaviors are manageable, and my mind, calm. Unlike the past, I don't need to accommodate others at my own expense and I'm not clinging to *dumb hope* waiting for things to change. Instead, I'm proactive, looking out for my wellbeing and doing what's best given the circumstances.

To provide Thomas, Rachel, and Johnny a role model for a secure, happy future and fulfill my lifelong prayers for love, I'm looking for a partner willing and able to invest in a healthy intimate relationship. A suitable mate will possess the true qualities I seek. A man of integrity, faith, and social conscience, he will be loyal with a sense of humor, charm, and style. He will value family, friends, and love. Self-assured, he will strive for success at work and in his personal relationships. He will participate in life, make an effort in everything he does, and be willing to meet a partner halfway. He will have zest for living.

While I've learned that reconciling the past with the present and thought with behavior lead to a healthy understanding of a person's character and state of mind, I realize there are no guarantees in selecting a mate. Before I enter a romantic relationship, I'll ask the important question: "What kind of relationship did you have with your mother in childhood?" followed by, "Tell me about your parents' marriage."

Another, more resourceful, way to uncover personality traits is to observe a person's driving styles. Are they aggressive or assertive, entitled or courteous, incompetent or skilled? I want someone who's willing to take control but can sit comfortably in the passenger seat, a driver who approaches the task with confidence, attentiveness, and respect for others. In short, I want someone who's mindful of his surroundings and handles unexpected situations in a timely, appropriate, and thoughtful manner. That's my dream guy.

If someone asks what they should know about me, I'll tell them this: "I am Anna; sensitive and strong, devoted and trustworthy, compassionate and sociable, a Southern girl at heart. I like tradition, chivalry, and adventure. I enjoy the comforts of home, the warmth of a fire, the beauty of falling snow, the sound of the ocean, and the energy of loud music. I want to hold hands and kiss often. I dislike walking barefoot, the texture of peaches or wooden spoons, and repetitive noises. I don't care for people who are arrogant, inconsiderate, or lack awareness of others, and I don't have patience for people who have ulterior motives or self-fulfilling prophecies. Intelligence without empathy means nothing to me. I'm practical when I need to be but I don't want to live a practical life."

Weak, wounded, needy, life-sucking applicants need not apply!

2012

Dear Mother,

By uncovering the truths of my childhood, I discovered that you and I did not bond when I was an infant. The insecure Attachment that resulted stunted my physical and emotional development, colored my feelings and experiences, and prevented healthy intimate relationships.

I understand now that you were incapable of caring for me. It was inherent in you and not personal towards me, but it didn't feel that way to me as a child. I worked tirelessly to earn your love, and when I couldn't attain it, I looked for ways to please you or gain acceptance in its place. Constantly frustrated by your indifference, I became demanding and easily irritated in your company.

Your possessiveness over Daddy caused you to view me as a threat and treat me as the enemy. My mere existence incited hatred in you, and there was nothing I could have ever done to change that.

I forgive you for the way you treated me and I forgive myself for the person I became, but I'm not willing to allow either of those to define who I am anymore. By recognizing we may never understand each other, I'm letting go of the hopes I once had for our relationship and accepting you for who you are: my birth mother and Thomas, Rachel, and Johnny's biological grandmother.

While I appreciate your past visits and generosity at Christmas, I'm seeking a new kind of relationship for all of us in the future. One built on respect, acceptance, and trust. The children and I extend it to those we welcome into our lives and we deserve it in return. If that's not possible, I wish you all the best with no regrets or hard feelings.

In the spirit of new beginnings, I strive to find peace in your presence.

Respectfully,

Anna

Epilogue

ATTACHMENT, THE EARLY bond between child and caregiver, affects the development of every human being. It is the foundation from which all intimate relationships are built. In my case, my insecure Attachment with Mother, manifested in deep-seated unworthiness, distorted my identity of self, fostered unhealthy romantic relationships, and changed the course of my life.

As I began journaling thoughts, I uncovered, expressed, and validated my feelings, something I had been unable to do previously. As I continued to write, my life story unfolded before my eyes, and it appeared crystal clear for the first time. As the truth revealed itself, I explored each and every experience, came to a new understanding of it, and made peace with myself. Whenever possible, I made amends with those I hurt along the way as well.

I shut out the world when I wasn't with the children and relived the past, each and every period in my life. Sometimes I'd sacrifice sleep, food, and showers to write from 6:00 a.m. into the middle of the night. I wouldn't leave the house except to get my morning mocha or grab a meal at Kelly and Andy's. Other days, I'd crawl out of bed, take the kids to school, and come straight back to my computer until I picked them up later that afternoon.

I'd gone from being perfectly styled and dressed each morning to wearing the same clothes for several days in a row, and I planned showers for hygiene purposes, not beauty. Cate loved it, as she thought I'd finally let go of my formal Southern ways in favor of a more casual Northwest style. However, as soon as she caught a glimpse of makeup, scarves, and pearls, she realized things hadn't changed as much as she'd hoped.

While I'm comfortable looking disheveled in the privacy of my own home, I don't feel my best when I neglect my appearance. I consider it a reflection of dignity and self-respect.

Rachel asked recently, "Are you depressed, Mom?"

Curious why that question, I responded, "Why do you ask, honey?"

"Well," she paused while assessing my face, hair, and clothing, "did you shower today?"

Both of us knew the obvious answer to that question. "Of course not!" I replied.

"It doesn't seem like you take care of yourself anymore, and I just want to make sure you're OK," she clarified. I assured her my scraggly façade was not an indication of my mental state but rather a sign of my current priorities—writing, writing, and more writing.

Besides treatment, discovering my truth and making peace with myself have been the foundation of my healing. They've freed me from the tremendous guilt and shame I've carried throughout childhood and adult life and lifted the veil of secrecy I used to protect myself and my family from disgrace. In order to conceal their identities, I've changed the names of people and places in the book, including my own. I'm not interested in blaming or shaming anyone, or dissecting my family's dynamics any more than necessary to share the pathology of my compromised Attachment.

Mother would not agree with or understand my account. In fact, she probably wouldn't recognize it. Never having admitted wrongdoing, she would deny the intentional harm and offer pity for my misinterpretation. She would argue she loved me with the best of intentions, taking credit for the good in me without accepting responsibility for the bad.

When an acquaintance once thanked me profusely for a good deed done, she said to him, "Well, I raised her right!" I looked at her with astonishment, sure the comment was made in jest, but could see the sincerity on her face. Not only was Mother taking credit for my honorable character, she was accepting praise for my behavior. It was absurd and incredibly offensive! The truth is: I am who I am in spite of her, not because of her.

There are some indisputable facts about my childhood and intimate relationships that support my account. Mother was the primary caregiver for the first two years of my life. She was admittedly incapable of responding to my needs and willingly turned that job over to Daddy, who was unavailable on weekdays. I developed unhealthy behaviors to get Mother's attention and earn her love, and I repeated them in intimate relationships. From there, deductive reasoning can be used to corroborate the remainder of my existence.

As I've shared experiences and my feelings surrounding them, I've tried to be as fair as possible but realize I've only presented one side of the story. My explanations are not to be taken as excuses for my behavior, rather reasons why it happened, which doesn't change my accountability. I didn't lack good judgment. I simply disrespected my morals and behaved out of character in my desperate search for life-affirming love.

I wouldn't have survived the reckless behavior and despair, nor been able to have three healthy, beautiful children, without God's grace, guidance, and intervention. At times, my faith was the only thing that gave me the strength to persevere. Even in my darkest moments, I knew there was a greater purpose for my being. Today, I can clearly see there was a purpose for each and every person and experience in my life.

A devoted mom, I consider myself extremely blessed to have been home for fifteen years with Thomas, Rachel, and Johnny. I didn't want to work when they were little because I associated absence with abandonment. Working full time now to support myself and my family, I recognize there are many different ways to be a connected parent. It doesn't require a twenty-four/seven presence, but responsive care and emotional availability.

As the children mature, they're developing a sense of who their grandmother is, without explanation. During Mother's last trip to Seattle, Rachel asked me, "Why does she come? She doesn't like us and treats us like she's better than we are."

Rachel doesn't need evidence of Mother's attitudes to feel them, just as she's experienced Amanda and Susan's. The three share beliefs of superiority, intolerance for others, and detachment from humanity, the exact opposite of who my children know me to be. My feelings of inferiority and longings to connect drove me to please everyone else without considering myself. Though unhealthy, it gave me the ability to empathize with the humanness in us all, one of my most rewarding gifts.

I'll share my story with Thomas, Rachel, and Johnny someday to give them insight into their mom's identity and family history. For now, they know I didn't have a healthy relationship with Mother. They're capable of understanding it in physical terms, not emotional conditions. When they ask how she hurt me, I tell them it's difficult to put into words, as most of Mother's abuse was invisible. It was her neglect or the hateful manner in which she treated me, not the treatment itself, that was harmful. She could serve me dinner with a smile on her face, disgust in her eyes, and loathing in her heart, and I knew how she felt about me without anyone else recognizing it.

Mother showed her colors again recently when I called to update her on my new address, the outcome of a forced downsizing, an exhausting, month-long move. Before I could finish, she interrupted, "Well, you didn't call Amanda on her birthday, did you?" Her tone let me know she considered my struggles fair punishment for this perceived crime.

"I know. I was working and moving that day and didn't get a chance to call until it was too late," I replied.

"She's having a hard time right now. You should check on her and apologize," Mother pressed. "Things are changing at Jason's work and they're not sure what the future holds."

Flabbergasted by her apparent indifference to my circumstances, I explained, "I'm sorry to hear that, but I don't need to ask for forgiveness. She doesn't reach out on my birthday and hasn't checked on me once in the last eight years." Adding, "I'm getting tired of the one way street."

"What about my apology?" I thought to myself. "Has Mother ever encouraged Amanda to be a good sister to me?"

"That's not right!" she declared. "Her children have never had to do without anything and this is really hard on all of them."

"What about me and my children?" I pondered. "Why is it OK for us to live on the brink of poverty but not acceptable for Amanda to do without a few luxuries?" It might mean cutting back on her three nannies, saying no to her angels' daily indulgences, or spending less time at the lake house?

"You have to call!" Mother insisted.

I wasn't in the mood to offer empathy for Amanda's apparent hardships, knowing the courtesy wouldn't be returned. There is no resentment, simply no desire to pursue a relationship with someone who exerts no effort. Consequently, I didn't call as Mother wished.

Two weeks later, she punished me by not calling on my birthday. She left a voicemail afterwards with an ill-conceived excuse blaming Daddy, but I knew it was the calculated retribution for the hurt she imagined I caused her beloved Amanda.

False hope for what should be has given way to acceptance for what is, leaving my expectations in line with reality. Because of Mother's cruelty and self-centeredness, it's difficult for me to see past the intentional harm to find any redeeming qualities in her.

The same is true for Rob. While I understand others view them differently, especially my children, who love their dad just as he is, my opinion of Mother and Rob's character remains firm. However, I can choose what kind of relationship I have with them in the future. Meanwhile, I pray to forgive, the final step in my healing process.

Dissecting my past, honoring my feelings, and living my truth have been my greatest achievements, while expressing myself on paper, the most challenging task. If that's all that comes of it, I'm satisfied. However, if I can bring understanding and healing to others by sharing my experience or promote solidarity through a common bond of humanity, I will have accomplished my life's work. If Thomas, Rachel, and Johnny feel at "home" in my presence, my dreams for our family will be realized.

While focusing on my survival, I lost sight of life. As a mended soul, I'll be mindful of the path chosen, as it will serve as the basis for everything that follows. By living in the light of the present, not the darkness of the past, I look forward to a bright future, a new beginning for a resurrected life. Amen.

This is my story. What is yours?

My Mom Anna

My mom has a box of laughter and smiles
that she shares with the world.
She enters a room,
and everyone can feel her warmth.
She is the only one I know who can
make me laugh when I am sad.
She brings hope to my day and her encouraging words
help me get through my hardest times.
She has patience and kindness
with her children.
She is the best person any person can get.
She is brave and strong
for what life may bring.
But the best part is that she is mine.
All mine. My very own mom.

Every Color of the Rainbow
by Rachel Barrett, eight years old

**Thank you for your love, inspiration, and support!
I could not have survived without you.**

Adam, Alana, Altamae, Andrew, Andy, Ann, Anna, Annette, Annie Lee, Anthea, Becca, Becky, Ben, Bennett, Beth, Betsy, Betty, Beverly, Bill, Bob, Brad, Brandon, Brenda, Brian, Bruce, Bucky, Caitlin, Carl, Catherine, Charles, Cheryl, Chris, Christa, Christine, Cindy, Clarise, Connie, Craig, Curt, Cynthia, Dana, Danna, Delores, Dennis, Diane, Donald, Doug, Elisabeth, Elizabeth, Elmer, Eric, Erin, Gary, Greg, Hege, Heidi, Henry, Hilary, Horacio, Howard, Jacqui, Jamie, Janet, Jaymee, Jed, Jeff, Jennifer, Jimmy, Joan, JoAnn, Joceil, Jodi, Joe, Joel, John, John David, Joyce, Julana, Julie, Jullie, Kameo, Kara, Karen, Karla, Katharine, Katherine, Kathleen, Kathy, Kelly, Kerry, Kevin, Kim, Kris, Krista, Kristi, Kyle, Larissa, Larry, Laura, Laurie, Lee, Leigh, Leslie, Libby, Lillian, Linda, Lisa, Lura, Margaret, Margie, Margo, Maria, Marilyn, Marin, Mark, Marty, Mary, Mary Jo, Matt, Maureen, Megan, Mel, Melissa, Michael, Michelle, Mike, Mitch, Molly, Morella, Nancy, Nathan, Nick, Nicolle, Norbert, Norm, Page, Pam, Patti, Paula, Peggy, Polly, Ralph, Rebecca, Red, Richard, Ron, Russ, Sally, Sandy, Sara, Shannon, Sharon, Shawn, Shelby, Stan, Steve, Sue, Susan, Tammy, Taylor, Teresa, Terry, Thanh, Tom, Tony, Tracey, Tracy, Ty, Vicky, Walt, Wayne, and Xuan

5212806R00180

Made in the USA
San Bernardino, CA
28 October 2013